A Short History of
Christianity

A Short History of
Christianity

Stephen Tomkins

William B. Eerdmans Publishing Company
Grand Rapids, Michigan / Cambridge, U.K.

To Meic,

master storyteller

First published 2005 in the U.K. by
Lion Hudson plc
Mayfield House, 256 Banbury Road,
Oxford OX2 7DH, England
This edition published 2006 in the United States of America by
Wm. B. Eerdmans Publishing Co.
2140 Oak Industrial Drive N.E., Grand Rapids, Michigan 49505 /
P.O. Box 163, Cambridge CB3 9PU U.K.
www.eerdmans.com

Printed in the United States of America

13 12 11 10   8 7 6 5 4

ISBN 978-0-8028-3382-2

Contents

Preface   7

Part 1 As It Was in the Beginning

1 Jerusalem (30–33)   12
2 Paul (33–61)   16
3 The Wrath of Rome (61–100)   21
4 Which Christianity? (100–202)   26
5 The God of the Greeks (202–47)   33
6 Blood and Sand (247–311)   39
7 The Christian Emperor (312–37)   45
8 The Puzzle of Jesus (337–95)   51
9 Augustine (395–430)   58
10 The Great Popes (430–630)   64

Part 2 The Rise of Rome

1 The Nightmare Begins (630–700)   74
2 Icons and Stirrups (700–87)   78
3 Charlemagne (787–846)   83
4 A Light in the Darkness (897–1000)   90
5 The Pope's Revolution (1000–84)   97
6 Onward Christian Soldiers (1084–99)   104
7 Love, War and Heresy (1099–1192)   110
8 Innocent (1192–1292)   115

9 Too Many Popes (1292–1443)   122

10 Protest (1443–1516)   129

Part 3 The Reformation

1 Luther (1517–22)   136

2 Water and the Spirit (1522–29)   141

3 Catholic Recovery (1529–45)   147

4 Trent (1545–58)   154

5 Wars of Religion (1558–98)   160

6 The Ends of the Earth (1492–1600)   166

7 More Wars (1600–60)   172

Part 4 Globalisation

1 The Earth Moves (1609—89)   182

2 The Age of Reason (1689—1730)   187

3 Born Again (1734—69)   193

4 Revolutions (1769—1831)   200

5 Planet of the Apes (1831—70)   209

6 World War and World Church (1870—1933)   217

7 Totalitarians (1933—58)   226

8 The New Catholicism (1958—78)   232

9 John Paul II (1978—2000)   238

10 The Third Millennium   244

Glossary   248

Index   251

Preface

Enormous trousers, almost up to his armpits, is how I remember my history teacher. He rode a moped and smoked a clay pipe. And he would hold forth for hours on the French, American and agricultural revolutions, British parliamentary reform and medieval conspiracies, with special attention to those who were 'mad in the head, I'm afraid, boys, mad in the head', while we scribbled in our little purple exercise books garbled notes which we would never – and probably could never – read, bored out of our burgeoning minds. Our survival tactic was to ask after his dearly beloved landlady, and his even more dearly beloved dog, Jill, on which subjects he would hold forth just as interminably (with slides on occasion); but at least we didn't have to take notes, at least it wasn't history. You just don't get teaching like that any more.

And what did I do with my spare time? All kinds of things, of course, including Space Invaders and embarrassingly ill-advised attempts to impress girls. But I also loved movies: I sat enthralled as Ben Kingsley's Gandhi stood up to British tyranny, or as John Merrick the Elephant Man held his misshapen head high in Victorian England. I wore out styluses as Bob Dylan mourned the lonesome death of Hattie Carroll. I followed the miners' strike and the Falklands war on the news (which is what, if not history in daily instalments?). I wolfed down biographies of Eric Clapton and Billie Holiday, with their struggles with drugs and drink, and novels from *Animal Farm* to *The Great Gatsby*. I watched every episode of *Blackadder*, memorising quotes to swap in school the next day.

These things entertained, enchanted, fascinated, moved me. One way or another, they changed the way I saw the world – and myself. I didn't particularly notice this. I didn't particularly notice that I was learning about the past. I was just hearing great stories, some more reliable than others, some upsetting, some funny, but all great stories. And I loved them, because everyone does. At least I didn't have to take notes. At least it wasn't history.

So, whatever the cover may have led you to believe, this is not a history book. This is a storybook. It is a true story, and it is our story, about our past and our world. It is a great story – however well it has survived my telling of it – with heroes and villains, and passion and betrayal, and big questions and big surprises, funny and sickening and inspiring and chastening.

It is your story whether or not you are a Christian yourself. Christianity infused the western world for over a millennium, shaping landscape, language, music, art, family life, the law, the shape of society, the very way our minds work. Trying to imagine what the world would look like today if Christianity had never taken off is like trying to imagine what life on the other side of the galaxy might be like. This is the story of how we came to be who we are.

I have tried to tell the story in a way that makes complete sense to someone coming to it from scratch; who doesn't know their Martin Luther from their Martin Luther King, or their John Paul from their George and Ringo. This means keeping religious jargon to a minimum, and I don't suppose anyone will feel that loss too keenly. Still, there's no way to avoid talking about Arians and Puritans, predestination and transubstantiation. I try to explain these things as we're going along, but there is also a glossary at the back in case you need to refresh your memory at any point.

I wrote the book for all the people I know who don't know the story and would enjoy it. They tend to have a fair idea how it starts, with Jesus and his disciples, and parables and pharisees. And they tend to have a fair idea how it has ended up (so far), with George Bush and Bono and Benedict XVI, with tele-evangelists and terrorists. They just tend to be a little hazy about that 2,000-year hiatus in the middle. How on earth did we get from there to here? What has been going on round here for the last 2,000 years?

Some readers will perhaps be annoyed to find important and cherished episodes of the story brushed past with a cursory nod or even ignored altogether. My instinct is to say, 'We're covering a decade a page, what did you expect?' But to be fair I have my own prejudices and passions, and what I choose to zoom in on and what I cut out doubtless reflect them. I have not tried to neutralise my prejudices – though I have certainly been persuaded to tone them down here and there.

I think everything that's really important is here; but I have also tried to make room for the small, colourful details that may not be important to historians but matter to the rest of us – the Protestant sausage, the crusading goose, the grass-eating monks and the unlikely escapades of the papal corpse.

The disadvantage of a true story is that I can't simply cut out or rewrite all the dull bits. But that doesn't necessarily mean you have to read them. If, for example, you find that the first half of part 2 drags, you can always jump ahead to the crusades, where things liven up rather.

Fiction has a power that factual stories cannot compete with, but the reverse is also true, and some stories are so important to us that we don't even think of them as stories. Every one of us carries around in his or her head versions of the two stories that bookend, as it were, this book – the first Easter, and 9/11 and its continuing aftermath – and our choice of versions has untold consequences, for ourselves and others. There are many such stories here, and if my telling of them helps anyone to rethink their own, then I'm happy. But don't take notes. It's not history.

Stephen Tomkins

Part 1

As It Was in the Beginning

1

Jerusalem (30–33)

Sleeper awake!
Rise from the dead,
And Christ will shine on you.
First-century hymn

A little less than 2,000 years ago, a man appeared in the Roman province of Judea claiming to be a teacher from God. Many Jews left their homes and jobs and followed him, believing that he was the Messiah, their long-awaited, miracle-working leader. But he was executed by the Roman occupation, and his followers dispersed.

The name of this failed prophet was Theudas. He was not the only alleged messiah in this period – you will of course be aware of another, and in fact there were quite a few. They all caused a local stir, and almost all met grisly ends. Jesus of Nazareth was by no means the most famous at the time. Worshipped today by 2 billion Christians (and revered by 1.3 billion Muslims), he is the most famous human being ever, but no mention of him written during his lifetime survives. Judea was an obscure backwater of the Roman empire, and neither the comings nor goings of its rabbis caught the attention of the non-Jewish world.

The First Church

What set Jesus apart from other executed messiahs was resurrection, and not just in the sense that it would set him apart from anyone. No one expected the Messiah to rise from the dead: his job was to drive out the Romans, restore true religion and rule justly. No human in Jewish or pagan legends had ever returned to their body after death. Many Jews thought that true believers would be raised from the dead when God came to deliver his people; they did not expect anyone to jump the gun.

And yet, soon after Jesus' crucifixion in about AD 30, his followers, instead of disappearing like normal disciples of an executed Messiah, were proclaiming throughout Jerusalem that Jesus had risen bodily from the dead, repeatedly visited them and been elevated to the right hand of God, from where he had sent them the Holy Spirit, miraculous powers and everlasting life. Something new was happening.

These first Christians were Jews; they worshipped in the Jerusalem temple and local synagogues as well as in their own homes, lived by the Law of Moses and offered the traditional prayers and sacrifices. Christians saw their faith as the fulfilment of Judaism, outsiders saw it as yet another version of Judaism, but no one saw it as a separate religion.

Many Christians had followed Jesus from Galilee to Jerusalem, and they now settled there. They were led by the apostles – those disciples who had met the risen Jesus and been commissioned to preach his message. The overall leader was Peter, supported by the brothers James and John, followed by the rest of 'the Twelve', who had been the inner circle of Jesus' companions.

The community grew very quickly, which takes some explaining as, for Jews, the idea of a crucified Messiah should have been a ludicrous blasphemy – as to many it was. Jesus had been killed by the very enemy he was supposed to overthrow, and crucifixion was degrading, disgraceful and a sign of God's condemnation: 'Anyone hung on a tree is under God's curse,' says the Law of Moses.

And yet something about these first Christians convinced a lot of people that Jesus was no longer in the state expected of those who have been killed. What was their appeal? Their passionate conviction for one thing, and their courage in facing beatings and imprisonment from the Jewish authorities. Many liked the idea of Jesus' resurrection being the first fruits of universal resurrection too. Still, this does not seem enough to make up for the scandalous offence of a crucified Messiah, so we need to consider the reason that Christians themselves gave for their appeal: 'Awe came upon everyone, because many wonders and signs were being done by the apostles.' The apostle Paul wrote more than once to his churches reminding them of miracles they had seen him perform. However we might explain such phenomena, it seems that onlookers saw what they understood to be miracles, as they had in Jesus' time, and that this was crucial to the movement's survival.

Some Jews, however, hated anything to do with messiahs. Jerusalem was ruled by aristocratic temple priests and the Jewish royal family, who were both firmly in the Roman pocket. A messianic uprising would overthrow their rule, while smaller religious unrest often got them into trouble with Rome. Neither did the priests warm to the idea that someone whose death they had arranged was now God's right-hand man.

So Christian preachers were harassed, arrested and beaten, but since they showed no signs of insurrection, that was as far as it went. This was the church's biggest problem for now, but not for long.

The first assault

The Jerusalem church, though wholly Jewish, was culturally divided. More Jews lived outside Palestine than in it, being dispersed throughout the Greek-speaking east of the Roman empire. This cut them off from the temple – the heart of Jewish worship – and meant that they reluctantly lived among pagans. Jews of the dispersion often visited Jerusalem for the annual festivals, and some resettled there. And so it was that soon a sizeable minority of the Jerusalem Christians were from abroad. Since they spoke Greek rather than the Aramaic of Palestine, they tended to meet separately.

This division will affect the whole of the rest of our story. It seems (although in this period we are reading between the lines of scant information) that as the church thought very hard about what precisely the crucifixion and resurrection of the Messiah meant, some Greek-speakers were drawn to more radical answers than the Aramaic majority. All agreed that the death of Jesus was not a mere tragedy but an act of power overcoming the forces of evil, and a sacrifice atoning for the sins of the nation, or even the world, reconciling people to God. Jesus' resurrection showed God's approval and was the beginning of the age to come. But the Greek-speakers went further, saying that Jesus had displaced the temple and the Law of Moses as the centre of the Jewish faith. The sacrifice of God's own Son overshadowed temple offerings, just as his intimate presence through the Holy Spirit made his dwelling in the temple's inner sanctum less important. Now that they knew God's Son and lived by his Spirit, the importance of the Law as the key to knowing and pleasing God was diminished.

How highly developed these ideas were, how radically and dogmatically they were presented, and how the other Christians felt about them is hard to say. The church was not split, but it was clear to onlookers that the Greek-speakers did not speak for all Christians.

Non-Christians were appalled by what they were hearing, and not just the city authorities now, but the very believers who had been most ardently praying for the coming of the Messiah. Christians were attacked and arrested. One of the Greek-speakers, Stephen, was brought before the city council on the charge that 'This man never stops saying things against the holy place and the Law,' and then illegally lynched.

Christians fled, scattering throughout Palestine and Syria. Even then they were not safe. One at least of the most ardent anti-Christians took a warrant from the High Priest and toured the land collecting Christians and bringing them bound to Jerusalem to face the punishment for blasphemy. And so, for the second time in one chapter, just like at his arrest, the following of Jesus had to all appearances collapsed.

2

Paul (33–61)

If you let yourselves be circumcised, Christ will be of no benefit to you.
Paul, Galatians

The campaign failed for two reasons. One was that Christians were so devoted to Jesus that wherever they ended up they preached his message, so all its opponents achieved was to spread it from Jerusalem throughout the Middle East. The other reason is that a leading activist met Jesus while travelling to Damascus to round up Christians and arrived a convert. Paul was a tent-making rabbi from Tarsus in Asia Minor (Turkey). As a leading Pharisee, he had been strictly devoted to the Law of Moses and hated Jesus as a blasphemous impostor subverting everything the true Messiah was supposed to defend – as quite literally the Antichrist. But on the road to Damascus, he had some kind of encounter with the risen Christ.

Coming into the city, he sought out the Christians, as he had originally intended to do, and got baptised in the name of Jesus, as he had not. He stayed there for three years and caused such unrest with his Christian preaching that he had to run for his life, being lowered over the city wall one night in a basket. Paul then visited the Jerusalem church to compare notes with Peter, but he only managed a fortnight in town before his preaching provoked attempts on his life, so he returned to Tarsus.

Hostility towards the church continued. Becoming king of Judea in AD 41, Herod Agrippa won popular and priestly favour by having James the brother of John executed. Peter and John, and perhaps most of the Twelve, escaped his fate by becoming foreign missionaries.

From now on, the leadership of the Jerusalem church was in the hands of James, the brother of Jesus. He presents an enigmatic figure. Like Paul, he was not a follower during Jesus' lifetime but was converted by a personal resurrection appearance. He led the church for twenty years and is the only first-century Christian famous enough to be mentioned in a non-Christian writing, but he is a minor figure in the New Testament, none of its writers preserving stories of his conversion, for example. The biblical book that bears his name, apart from the fact that it contains two mentions of Jesus, could easily have been written by a non-Christian Jew. In later years, while Paul was telling his converts, 'I died to the Law, so that I might live to God,' James followed the Law of Moses so devoutly that he was known as James the Righteous.

Twelve years after the first Easter, Christianity is still in every sense a movement within Judaism, though of course some versions of it are pretty unpalatable to fellow Jews. But a tectonic change is coming, starting in the city of Antioch.

Circumcision and the Gentiles

Antioch, the capital of Syria, was a major city in the Roman empire and, since perhaps as many as one in five of its population were Jews, it made a natural second home for Christianity. Greek-speaking Christians fleeing Jerusalem during Paul's rampage settled there, and naturally they told everyone about the resurrected Messiah. This is where they first got the nickname 'Christians', 'Christ' being the Greek translation of 'Messiah'. But the story appealed not only to Jews in Antioch but also to Gentiles (non-Jews), and so Antioch became the home of the first mixed-race church.

This created an enormous problem: should Gentile Christians follow the Law of Moses and be circumcised? One would assume so: they were embracing the Jewish faith. Christ followed the Law, so Christians should follow the Law. But then Judaism had always welcomed converts without necessarily demanding circumcision. Many Gentiles found its monotheistic worldview attractive, although to them genital mutilation seemed not merely eye-watering but barbaric, so synagogues offered a two-tier conversion system: 'proselytes' came under the Law, and the knife, and in effect became Jews, while 'God-fearers' believed, prayed and worshipped with the Jews, but did not follow the more uncomfortable demands of the Law – and therefore could not eat with Jews, being still ritually unclean.

In the Antioch church, these distinctions did not work, not least because eating together was a central part of Christian worship. Another church might have resolved the problem by requiring all converts to obey the Law so that all could share one bread, but these Greek-speakers had long questioned the significance of the Law for Christians anyway. Now that they saw the uncircumcised being baptised into the church, forgiven their sins, given the Holy Spirit and promised salvation, simply because they accepted Jesus the Messiah, there seemed to be little that circumcision and kosher food could add to their relationship with God. So they dispensed with them. Gentiles were accepted as full Christians, without the Law.

As if this was not a sufficiently explosive situation already, one of the ministers at Antioch, Barnabas, decided to recruit Paul onto their team as preacher and theologian. Paul was based in Antioch for several years before the great circumcision dispute broke out, but he spent much of that time travelling. He and Barnabas toured Cyprus and Asia Minor establishing other mixed-race churches, where Paul's preaching so outraged mainstream Jews that he was whipped in synagogues, once survived a stoning and was followed for hundreds of miles by enemy preachers.

In about AD 47, Antioch received a visit from some Jerusalem Christians. They were appalled by this sidelining of the Law, demanding (and offering) mass circumcisions. 'We did not submit to them for a minute,' Paul says. Circumcision had no benefit for the Gentiles, he insisted; in fact it would be positively ruinous. They had come to God through his Son, so if they turned back to the outmoded, pre-Christian Law, they were turning away from Jesus. With an appropriately incisive metaphor he told those who succumbed, 'You... have cut yourselves off from Christ; you have fallen away from grace.'

The only thing for it was a summit meeting in Jerusalem – the Jerusalem council of AD 48. James, Peter and John heard Paul's account of his teaching and Barnabas's stories of their successful mission, and they came to a momentous and surprising decision: they agreed with Paul. Gentiles do not need circumcision.

This – though it was the last thing anyone there had intended – was the beginning of the end for Christianity as a branch of Judaism. The church was throwing its doors wide open to Gentiles, providing a new religion for those who liked monotheism but not the choice between circumcision or being an honorary, second-class Jew. At the same time, it would make it ever harder for Law-abiding Jews to be Christians, heightening the scandal of the gospel (the message of or about Jesus) for non-Christian Jews: they saw the holy things that had cost them such devotion and suffering down the centuries being flogged off on the mass market. But this decision also enshrined in the inner sanctum of Christianity the idea that religion is ultimately concerned with relationship rather than the rules of ritual. By acting on the principle that different people can approach God in different ways, they made Christianity a fundamentally adaptable religion.

However, the conflict within the church was far from over. Many circumcisers continued to oppose Paul, and it seems that James never completely dissociated himself from them. Moreover, even many of the Jewish Christians who accepted Gentiles without circumcision continued to follow the Law scrupulously themselves, and this meant not eating with the uncircumcised. Paul and Barnabas did eat with them of course, and so did Peter. For the more conservative Christians, this was too much, and they complained to James that Christianity was turning into an apostate sect for Jews who did not want to be Jews any more.

This time James took their side and asked Peter to desist. Perhaps reasoning that as the conservatives had made a fundamental concession in allowing Gentiles not to be circumcised, so it was fair now for the radicals to compromise to avoid splitting the church, Peter stopped eating with the Gentiles and Barnabas followed. Paul was enraged, accusing them of hypocrisy.

James issued a decree, calling on Gentile Christians to follow a kind of miniature four-point Law of Moses, so that Jewish Christians could accept them as clean enough to eat with. It is not clear whether Paul agreed to this compromise or not. Neither is it clear whether he was reconciled to Barnabas or Peter – he certainly never travelled with Barnabas again. He left that same year on a never-ending missionary tour that took him throughout Asia Minor and Greece and beyond, with great success, though he repeatedly suffered imprisonment, beatings and shipwrecks. Other missionaries went to Rome (including Peter), into North Africa and probably east into the Persian empire. Paul's conservative opponents took to touring his churches, preaching the benefits of the Law, and so this unhappy struggle became one of the main preoccupations of his life. 'Beware of those who mutilate the flesh!' he warned his first church in Europe. 'For it is we who are the circumcision, who worship in the Spirit of God.' It was in this period that Paul wrote most of his letters, those almost incidental by-products of his teaching work that became his lasting monument.

When Paul finally returned to Jerusalem nine years later, in AD 57, it was with a large financial gift that he had collected from his churches. For one reason or another, the church of James was in poverty, and Paul brought aid as a peace offering. He evidently hoped that it would demonstrate the good fruit borne by his mission and that in accepting it, Jerusalem would be accepting of his gospel and his churches. Whether James did accept it, we have no idea, but Paul was there for less than a week before he was recognised and a riot broke out. The Romans arrested him for his own safety, and to diffuse the situation, they imprisoned him in Caesarea for two years. When the governor agreed to let the Jewish council try him, Paul, being a Roman citizen, saved his life by appealing to Caesar's court, and so was taken to Rome, where he was kept under a relaxed house arrest for another two years.

3

The Wrath of Rome (61-100)

And the wine press was trodden outside the city, and blood flowed from the wine press, as high as a horse's bridle, for a distance of about 200 miles.
Revelation

This rather inconclusive and anticlimactic point is where the story of the early church recorded in the Bible comes to an end, in AD 61, thirty-one years after Jesus' death, with Christianity established throughout the Jewish world. It is a happy place to stop, perhaps, as within a few years, its main leaders had been brutally killed.

James was stoned to death with other Christians in Jerusalem in AD 62, during a hiatus between Roman governors, on the authority of the High Priest. Even his devotion to the Law of Moses could no longer atone for being a Christian. This was the final climax of the period when the church's attackers were principally Jewish, and Christians looked to Rome for protection. Until now, Christianity had enjoyed the toleration that Rome extended to all Judaism. (Jewish 'hatred of the gods' was officially licensed because Jews formed 7 per cent of the Roman empire.) But now that a growing number of Christians were Gentiles, they suffered all the distrust faced by Judaism (with the added stigma of novelty), without the protection. In the eyes of Tacitus, the first Roman writer to notice Christianity, it was 'a deadly superstition', and Christians were 'a class hated for their abominations' and for their 'hatred of the human race'. The cult now appeared in Rome because that was where 'all things hideous and shameful from every part of the world meet and become popular'.

Christians made their first bloody mark on the world map because of the great fire of Rome in AD 64. Emperor Nero had lost the confidence of the ruling class; now, amid economic troubles following the fire, the word on the street was that he had started it himself to make room for a glorious new palace and parks, reciting his poems while he watched. His response was to blame the fire on the most unpopular people available; and so it was that the empire picked a 250-year fight with the church that you would have thought it couldn't lose. The Christians of Rome were rounded up and killed. Nero had them thrown to the dogs wrapped in animal skins, ironically crucified or burnt alive as torches to light his public garden parties. Among the nameless victims were Peter and Paul, according to later Christian tradition. This is questionable, but they were certainly executed in Rome about now. Legend says that Peter insisted on being crucified upside down, but the earliest version of this story also has him resurrecting a smoked fish, so it is perhaps not entirely trustworthy.

Maybe it was the death of these witnesses that prompted Christians to start writing down their stories of Jesus. In a culture with little writing, where papyrus was prohibitively expensive and storytelling skills kept events remarkably intact, there must have seemed little point until now in writing down what one could more effectively say. We have little information about when most of the books of the New Testament were written. The majority scholarly view is that the Gospel of Mark was written about now, in the 60s, with the Gospels of Matthew and Luke (which are based on Mark) coming a decade later, and that they drew on earlier, shorter writings about Jesus that have not survived in their original form.

One result of Nero's attack was a backdraft of sympathy for Christians in Rome, who, whatever their crimes, were clearly being sacrificed for PR reasons. Christians were still outlaws and still died, but the authorities did not go out of their way to ferret them out. And so the church continued, rather more stealthily now, to grow.

The fall of Jerusalem

Back in Jerusalem, tensions between Romans and Jews finally broke into war in AD 66, after tax disputes provoked a string of aristocratic crucifixions. Jerusalem was seized by messianic revolutionaries; Roman legions systematically crushed and massacred Jewish forces throughout Palestine; and in the spring of AD 70, they marched on Jerusalem. They were not alone. In an astonishing and appalling act of faith, Jews from every country under heaven – 3 million according to the contemporary writer Josephus – descended on the city for Passover, to celebrate their deliverance from slavery; and before they could leave the siege had begun. For months, Jerusalem was overwhelmed by starvation, disease, barbaric banditry and internal warfare, until it fell to the Romans in August. The entire city, including the temple, was demolished, and hundreds of thousands were killed or taken to die as entertainment in the circuses of the empire. Josephus reckons that 1.1 million Jews died in Jerusalem: 'Victims dropp[ed] dead in countless numbers and the horrors were unspeakable.'

It is almost certain that Jesus had predicted the fall of Jerusalem and its temple. 'In those days there will be suffering', he says in Mark's Gospel, 'such as has not been from the beginning of the creation that God created until now, no, and never will be.' 'Those in Judea must flee to the mountains; the one on the housetop must not go down or enter the house to take anything away; the one in the field must not turn back to get a coat.' It seems they did as he said. Before the siege began, the Jerusalem Christians, now led by Jesus' cousin Symeon, escaped to the town of Pella in the hills across the river Jordan.

The destruction of the holy city and the holy place inevitably transformed the religion of Judaism, and it had a momentous impact on Christianity too – including the fact that it now starts to make sense to talk like that about two separate religions. For one thing, Christianity was no longer focused on Jerusalem, and whatever leadership the Law-loving Jewish church there had still exercised was lost. Jewish opinion of Christians probably suffered from their neutrality in the apocalyptic war against the beast of Rome. But above all, AD 70 changed Gentile Christians' attitude to Jews. The immediate reaction of Christians everywhere was horror; but on reflection, the idea grew that they had seen God's judgment on the Jewish people for rejecting the Messiah and killing the Son of God. Forty is a number full of significance in the Jewish scriptures, symbolic of waiting and testing, and the siege came exactly forty years, Passover to Passover, after the execution of Jesus; so the great fourth-century historian of the early church, Eusebius, amid nightmarish descriptions of the miseries of the Jews, was able to conclude, 'It was indeed proper.' The more time passed, the easier it became to see the Jews as cast off by God. At the same time, synagogues introduced prayers designed to ensure that no Christian could take part in their worship.

Church life

What was church life like in the first century? In the days of Peter and Paul, Christians attended synagogue worship on Saturdays wherever they were welcome, and so they had their own meetings on Sundays, the day of the Lord's resurrection. By the end of the century, no Christians went to the synagogue, but they kept their Sundays, so an arrangement that was supposed to keep Christians united with mainstream Jews ended up as yet another thing separating them into two conflicting religions.

Christians met in believers' houses, having no resources for building. The houses of wealthier Christians were sizeable business premises with plenty of room for worship, but smaller or poorer churches met in apartment blocks. Sunday being a working day, they came together before and after work, sharing an evening meal, the 'love feast'. Some but not all churches, it seems, incorporated the Lord's supper into this, with one person reciting the story of Jesus' death as embodied in the bread and wine. However, *The Teaching of the Apostles*, a manual for church life written about AD 100, gives copious instructions and liturgy for the meal without ever connecting it to the death or the body and blood of Jesus.

They sang biblical psalms, as in the synagogue, and Christian hymns, and they listened to teaching and prophecy. From the start, they worshipped Jesus, which might seem surprising for Jews who believed that God alone, the one God, is worthy of worship. In fact Paul and other New Testament writers seem to have had little trouble incorporating the divine Christ into the rather sophisticated and complex monotheism of first-century Judaism. They clearly saw the Son of God as Lord of creation in more or less the same way as God himself. Of course, how ordinary Christians understood this subtle paradox is another matter, about which we know nothing.

'Prophecy' could mean ecstatic utterances and visions, but it could equally mean what today we would call 'preaching', either approach bringing a message from God. In the earlier years, services offered the opportunity to anyone with the ability: two or three people were expected to prophesy, and listeners asked questions if necessary. Often, travelling prophets would tour from church to church. It is certain that women both preached and led churches, though less frequently than men, as not only was such work unwomanly in Greco-Roman and Jewish culture but few had the education.

Leaders were generally appointed by the missionaries who established the churches and thereafter chosen by members. Churches were led by a team rather than one person, many of the ministers working to support themselves. A great variety of job titles has come down to us: apostle, elder, bishop (literally 'overseer'), deacon (literally 'servant' – also translated 'minister'), pastor, evangelist, prophet and teacher. In the earlier period, the terms seem to have been loose and interchangeable, varying from place to place. By the end of the century, a more settled structure was spreading, in which each church had one bishop overseeing a group of elders and deacons.

Many from the lowest classes of imperial society joined the church, which accepted slaves independently of their masters and wives without their husbands, and let both become leaders, on the basis that all people are equally made in the image of God. This attack on Roman family values was one source of offence among many. Christians were called 'atheists': they denied the gods, refused to sacrifice to them for the good of the community and shunned the city feasts. They met in private in the hours of darkness, presumably to plot revolution and enjoy foul depravities. Talk of love feasts and sharing the body and blood of Christ with their brothers and sisters made it common knowledge that Christians had cannibalistic, incestuous orgies.

Even their books were a stumbling block. The Gospels could seem to be in surprisingly rough Greek for the word of God, while God himself was something of an embarrassment in the Jewish scriptures – vengeful, repentant, partial and rather too human. Their laws seemed barbarous and many of their stories distinctly unedifying. Christians increasingly read the Bible as Greeks read Homer's more questionable passages, as encoding a deeper message; so the laws about sacrificing lambs to God were really about the cross of Christ.

4

Which Christianity? (100–202)

The church, scattered across the world, preserves its teaching as if all
lived in one house.
Irenaeus

In the early years of the second century, Ignatius, the bishop of Antioch, was
arrested for being a Christian and taken in chains to Rome to face the lion.
Travelling overland through Asia Minor, he wrote seven letters to the churches
he passed, using his authority as a martyr-in-waiting to encourage and
instruct them. The three main themes of his letters were the problems that
would preoccupy the church throughout the century: persecution and
martyrdom, heresy and the authority of bishops.

For now, the killing of Christians tended to be sporadic and local, often
when someone needed to be blamed for economic or military problems.
Emperor Trajan's instruction was: 'These people are not to be sought out; but
if they are accused and convicted, they are to be punished – on this
condition, that if any deny being Christians, and make it plain that they are
not, by worshipping our gods, then even if they were Christians before, they
may be pardoned upon repentance.'

For Ignatius, martyrdom was not simply a risk involved with being a
Christian, but a glorious honour and the one sure road to salvation.

How I look forward to the real lions that have been got ready for
me!… I am going to make overtures to them… And if they are still
reluctant I shall use force… Fire, cross, beast-fighting, hacking and
quartering, splintering of bone and mangling of limb, even the
pulverising of my entire body – let every horrible and diabolical
torment come upon me, provided only that I can win my way to
Jesus Christ.

He considered himself a sacrifice on behalf of the churches, a eucharistic offering, and he implored the church in Rome not to seek his release. 'I am yearning for death with all the passion of a lover.'

In the 150s, one of the churches Ignatius had written to, that in Smyrna, near Ephesus, faced its own spate of executions. A group of Christians handed themselves over for voluntary martyrdom, but their leader ended up sacrificing to Caesar to save his life. 'That is the reason, brothers,' said the church, 'why we do not approve of men offering themselves spontaneously.'

A more impressive example is that of Smyrna's bishop, the 86-year-old Polycarp. Tipped off, he was persuaded to hide from the soldiers in a farmhouse, but when arrested and taken to the stadium, he faced death unflinching:

'Swear by the fortune of Caesar,' the proconsul demanded. 'Repent, and say, "Down with the atheists!"'

Polycarp gestured towards his pagan audience and said, 'Down with the atheists!'

'Swear,' said the proconsul, 'and I will set you free. Revile Christ.'

'Eighty-six years I have served him, and he never did me any wrong. How then can I blaspheme my king and saviour?'

He was burnt and the church buried his bones, meeting at the tomb annually to celebrate what they called the 'birthday' of their saint.

Some of Polycarp's flock fled from Smyrna to Gaul, where they were among the many who were killed in the circus of 177, to save on the costs of gladiators. One was the slave Blandina. Lengthy attempts to torture a repentance out of her only got the reply, 'I am a Christian. We do nothing to be ashamed of,' so in the end, she was thrown to the bull in a basket.

A few years later, an entire church is said to have presented itself for martyrdom before the proconsul of Asia. He selected a token number and said to the rest, 'If you wretches want to die, you have cliffs and nooses.'

Docetists, gnostics, Marcion and the Ebionites

Ignatius fervently promoted the idea of the one-man rule of a bishop over his church, making more extravagant claims for episcopal authority than anyone else in this period. 'We must regard the bishop as the Lord himself.' He maintained that only the bishop should baptise or oversee the eucharist. Time was on Ignatius's side. Not only did the church naturally become more hierarchical as numbers grew, but increasing confusion over what precisely the Christian message was made it ever more necessary to have recognised authorities.

Second-century bishops fought against a number of groups or tendencies they saw as distorting Christianity. Just like the circumcision dispute in the apostles' days, these conflicts arose from the problem that Christianity was a version of Judaism for Gentiles, which left it with one foot in either world. But whereas Paul fought people who wanted to tie Christianity too closely to Jewish rites, the problem now was that Gentile Christians were finding it too hard to accept Jewish ideas.

Ignatius campaigned against Docetism, the idea that Jesus was not real flesh and blood and did not suffer and die: he was pure spirit and his physical appearance an illusion. While Jews believed that God created the material universe and did a very good job of it, thanks to Plato, it was a popular assumption throughout the Greek world that matter and the body are intrinsically bad and unreal, so the idea that in Christ, God became flesh, saving souls through physical suffering, went violently against the grain. Ignatius's letters insist that Jesus was 'truly of the line of David… truly born of a virgin… truly pierced by nails in his human flesh'.

As time passed, Docetism became one tributary stream of thought in a river that threatened to engulf the faith of the bishops: gnosticism. Gnostics drew from Greek philosophy, pagan myths, Judaism and eastern religions as well as Christianity. By no means all gnostics were Christians, but Christians were becoming increasingly gnostic.

Though hugely diverse, the basic gnostic ideas were these: matter being evil, they denied that Almighty God could create it, and so they developed an elaborate hierarchy of spirits emanating from him, the lowest of which blundered into giving birth to the delinquent creator-God of the Jewish scriptures; a superior god smuggled spirits into some of the humans he had created, but because they were still imprisoned in the physical realm, the spirit Christ came to give them a secret divine knowledge (gnosis) of spiritual things, liberating their spirits and saving them for heaven.

Irenaeus, the bishop of Lyons, in exile from Asia Minor, was a great opponent of gnosticism. He argued that the idea of one almighty, good creator-God was so basic to the worldview of the scriptures and apostles that to turn it inside-out, with a panoply of gods and an evil creator, was not to reveal the deeper mysteries of the faith but to invent a whole new one.

Instead of the universe being intrinsically evil, he explained that God allowed
humanity to suffer and sin in order for us to take the hard road to maturity.

A third rival version of Christianity that the bishops opposed was the
creation of Marcion, a wealthy ship-owner from Sinope, who was 'Darker
than fog,' according to his great opponent Tertullian, 'colder than winter,
more brittle than ice, more treacherous than the Danube, more precipitous
than the Caucasus.' Marcion came to Rome in 139 and made a huge
donation to its church, which somewhat eased his acceptance as a preacher.
He loved the teachings of Jesus and Paul, which revealed to him a God of love
and forgiveness, delivering the souls of believers to heaven. What he could
not stand was the Bible (still only the Jewish scriptures), with its God of harsh
judgments, fighting and smiting, who creates matter, changes his mind and
walks around in gardens. Other Christian teachers shared some of Marcion's
discomfort, but their habit of reading it symbolically and allegorically allowed
them to avoid its more unpalatable implications. Marcion insisted on
understanding it literally.

His preaching got him expelled in 144 – with a full refund – but he took
enough followers with him to start a successful rival church, which spread
throughout the empire. 'Marcionites build churches like wasps build nests,'
lamented Tertullian.

Marcion also produced a rival Bible compiled from Christian writings,
choosing the Gospel of Luke and ten letters of Paul. His problem was that –
predictably enough, one might think – even these included Jewish ideas such
as creation, and quotations from Jewish scriptures. So he had to edit these
passages out as forgeries, clearly untrue to the spirit of the original – a
remarkably similar approach to that of some more recent biblical scholars.

Tertullian ridiculed the softness of Marcion's designer God: 'A better God
has been found! He never takes offence, never gets angry, never punishes…
He forbids all crime, but only with words.' Tertullian also had a laugh at the
idea that Jesus' fantastically radical denial of the Jewish creator-God should
have been completely dropped by all his followers, leaving no trace of
confirmation or denial, and then be rediscovered a century later: 'O Christ,
most patient Lord, who suffered this interference with your revelation for so
many years, until Marcion came to your rescue!'

The fourth rival that the bishops set themselves up against could not have
been more different. The Ebionites were largely Jewish Christians and, as
Irenaeus put it, they understood the scriptures 'in a peculiar way: they

practise circumcision, continue to observe the customs commanded by the Law, and in their Jewish way of life even venerate Jerusalem as the house of God'. In other words, they were so misguided as to maintain the faith of the first Christians. In fact they were probably direct descendants of the exiled Jerusalem church, their name simply translating as 'The Poor'.

Some mainstream Christians granted that 'such people will be saved unless they strenuously do all they can to persuade others', but others disagreed and even refused to eat with them – much, presumably, as the centurion Cornelius in the biblical book of Acts should have refused to eat with Peter.

Understandably, perhaps, Ebionites did not venerate the memory of Paul or use his writings in church, and their only Gospel was Matthew, which told them that not one letter of the Law would be repealed before the heavens and earth passed away. Over many years they produced their own writings in which Paul – the apostolic stick used by the Gentile bishops to beat them – became an antichrist figure. They were also uneasy about the exaltation of Jesus as God.

Theirs was the last attempt to keep Christianity and Judaism together, but the party lines were too deep. The Ebionites kept going for centuries, but the church did not accept them and neither did the Jews.

Making the New Testament

How did the bishops and apologists of the mainstream church counter these rival versions of Christianity, apart from simply trying to show them to be inconsistent and laughable?

First of all, they argued from the Jewish scriptures, but this did not get them very far. Marcion rejected their authority, while the Ebionites had more obvious support from them than the bishops. So the bishops emphasised their mystical, symbolic interpretation of the scriptures, but this played into the hands of the gnostics: Irenaeus said the four faces of the cherubim proved there must be four Gospels; the gnostics said the fact that Christ was twelve when he went to the temple confirms that there are twelve emanations of God.

So secondly, the mainstream preachers explained how these rivals contradicted the teaching passed down from Jesus and the apostles. But the gnostics replied that theirs was the secret teaching that Jesus delivered after his resurrection for those with the spiritual capacity to accept it, while

Marcion and the Ebionites said that the bishops had corrupted Jesus' teaching, either by adding or subtracting Judaism.

So now the Gospels and letters of the apostles came into their own as documentary evidence of what they had taught. But which Gospels and which letters? The Ebionites rejected the works of Paul and perhaps Luke too as unapostolic, while the Marcionites accepted nothing else. Moreover, the gnostics, soon followed by the Ebionites, had a rapidly expanding collection of writings that also claimed to be by apostles. Many allegedly apostolic writings were emerging that seemed to support mainstream Christianity too, but were of dubious origin.

And so it was that the bishops had to follow Marcion's example and draw a line between those writings that embodied the teachings of Christ and the apostles with all the authority of holy scripture, and those that did not, in other words, to create the New Testament. It was not an easy task.

The core texts were obvious: four Gospels, Acts and thirteen letters of Paul. But there was a bewildering range of other letters and visions said to be from Peter, John, James, Thomas, Barnabas and so on. With no central authority or forum for debate and decision, churches decided for themselves, and so for the foreseeable future, different churches would have different Bibles.

A list of books accepted by the church of Rome in the second century has (mostly) survived. As well as the Gospels, Acts and Paul's letters, it includes 1 and 2 John, Jude and Revelation, omitting up to five books that were eventually included in the New Testament, and adding to them the Wisdom of Solomon and the Apocalypse of Peter. It was a gradual process over centuries by which the churches reached final agreement – European ones being reluctant to accept Hebrews, and the east long retaining suspicions about Revelation – but most local variations had been ironed out by the sixth century.

If the disputes of the second century were the making of the New Testament canon, they were also the making of the bishops. Ignatius had argued that avoiding heresy required obedience to the bishop, and the hubbub of competing gospels throughout the century affirmed his point. If conflicting versions of Christianity were on offer, there had to be someone whom Christians could trust to tell them which was true and original, and the bishop – custodian of the message publicly taught by church leaders since Christ – was clearly the best bet. As Irenaeus told gnostic opponents,

'If the apostles had known hidden mysteries which they taught the perfect in private and in secret, they would have committed them to those to whom they entrusted the churches.' He drew up historical lists of the bishops of various churches, showing that they could trace their succession in unbroken lines back to the apostles.

Irenaeus also saw that should bishops ever disagree, there needed to be one with final authority, 'the greatest and oldest church, a church known to all men, which was founded and established at Rome by the most renowned apostles Peter and Paul... Every church – the faithful everywhere – must agree with the church at Rome.'

5

The God of the Greeks
(202-47)

**Do you see the Greeks and Latins outstripped by the work of one man?
Who could ever read all that he wrote?**
Jerome on Origen

In 202, Emperor Septimius Severus issued a decree forbidding any subject to become a Christian or a Jew, and anti-Christian assaults broke out in many cities. Among those killed in the circus of Carthage (modern Tunis), were the celebrated Perpetua and Felicitas, one a young noblewoman happily leaving parents, husband and breastfeeding baby, the other a slave who gave birth in the cells. They were whipped, sent to the beast together naked in nets and finally put to the sword, Perpetua having to put the reluctant soldier's sword to her neck.

It was about now that Tertullian's magnificent *Defence* was published:

We are but of yesterday, yet we have filled all that is yours: cities, islands, fortresses, towns, meeting places, even camps, tribes, companies, the palace, the senate, the forum. We have left you only your temples...

If the Tiber rises to the walls, if the Nile does not rise to the fields, if the sky does not rain, if there is an earthquake, a famine, a plague, immediately the cry arises, 'The Christians to the lion!' What? So many to one lion?...

You say, we are vanquished. Yes, when we have obtained our wishes. Therefore we conquer in dying; we seize the victory at the very moment we are overcome. Bound to a stake, we are burnt on a

heap of wood: this is the attitude in which we conquer, it is our
victory robe, our triumphal entry.

This attitude does not please those whom we overcome…

Your cruelty, however great, is a better advertisement for us than
for you. The more you mow us down, the more we grow. The blood
of Christians is seed.

Such second-century writers are known as the apologists, being remembered
for their defence of the faith rather than as its early architects. Different
apologists took very different attitudes to the beliefs of their opponents,
however. Justin Martyr was a professional thinker who had worked his way
through several current Greek philosophies, before being converted to
Christianity by the Jewish scriptures. He believed that Jesus was the
culmination of all philosophies, God's Word of truth (in which every
philosophy has an imperfect share) come in the flesh. Those, like Socrates,
'who live according to reason, are Christians, even though they are
considered atheists'. He tried to persuade readers that they did not have to
abandon the wisdom of the Greeks to become Christians. Ironically, he
earned his surname thanks to the anti-Christian policies of his fellow
philosopher, the emperor Marcus Aurelius.

Tertullian, on the other hand, despised Greek philosophy as pagan lies.
Philosophy came from humans, Christianity from God. Those who tried to
learn from both merely corrupted Christianity. 'Wretched Aristotle!… What
does Athens have in common with Jerusalem?'

As well as defending their church from heretics and pagans, the apologists
made major contributions to developing Christian thought. According to
their arguments, the world and humankind, body and soul, are God's good
creation, but corrupted by human rebellion. God's answer to this problem
was to send Christ, fully God and fully human, to live and die for us: 'This is
why the Word of God was made man, and the Son of God became son of
man,' said Irenaeus, 'so that man having been taken into the Word, and being
adopted, might become the son of God.'

It was Tertullian who first used the word 'Trinity' to describe God. Father,
Son and Holy Spirit are all God, and yet there is one God. He denied the
'modalist' idea that they were simply three roles played by the one God (that

'the Father himself was born and suffered and died'). He used the illustration of Christ being the rays of God's sun, coming from him yet inseparable from him, 'light from light'. He also invented the terminology of three 'persons' sharing one 'substance', the same 'godness'.

Montanus the prophet

One more dispute rocked the churches in the second century, but it was rather different from the others we have met, concerning the teachers more than the teaching, its condemnation more controversial.

Montanus had been a priest of the mystery cult of Cybele, and as a Christian convert he became a prophet, alongside two women, Priscilla and Maximilla, based in Phrygia. They did not just preach, but spoke in trances and tongues, bringing God's message in the first person: 'I am the Lord God Almighty, living in man.' They lived by strict moral and ascetic standards, longed for martyrdom and insisted that Christ would return (to Phrygia, naturally) to start his 1,000-year rule in their lifetime. Coming to a place of savage anti-Christian attacks – and recent earthquakes – recapturing some of the raw excitement of earlier Christianity and promising an imminent end of all, Montanism (or 'the New Prophecy' as adherents preferred to call it) caught many Christian imaginations.

There was nothing about Montanist teaching that clearly contradicted accepted doctrine, but it still posed a problem for the bishops. For a start, they were uneasy about the idea of wild, babbling visionaries, especially when they had been working so hard to gain the respect of the empire. The fact that two of the prophets were women did not help either. But the real problem was that the prophets claimed divine authority for their proclamations, on a par with the scriptures and apostolic teaching. This threatened to undermine all the defences against heresy that the bishops had been building. The only way to counter false teaching was to have a final court of appeal – the traditions and writings of the apostles, as interpreted by the bishops. If they let prophets claim equal authority, however sound their beliefs now appeared, they would be relinquishing their power to decide the faith of the church.

And so the first of many centuries of episcopal councils was called, and the bishops of Asia Minor condemned Montanism. The bishop of Rome was more cautious, but he eventually declared that the prophecy was not from God. What happened next is debated. The traditional story is that after its condemnation, Tertullian left the church in disgust and joined the Montanists. It seems more likely that Montanists remained part of the mainstream church outside Asia Minor, or at least in Tertullian's North Africa, so that he did not need to leave anything in order to be a Montanist or to be disgusted. At the same time, he attacked Rome for allowing modalist teaching about Christ being a manifestation of God the Father: the heretics 'put to flight the Paraclete, and crucified the Father'. However, the time had not yet come when it was impossible for churches to disagree without excommunicating each other.

Clement and Origen

Alexandria in Egypt was the intellectual capital of the Roman world. Schools of every major philosophy taught there, drawing on its incomparable library of 70,000 scrolls. The philosophical Alexandrians had little interest in Christianity – for all Justin's efforts – apart from the gnostic variety, which thrived. Alexandrian Christians therefore were a defensive enclave, holding tightly to inherited doctrines rather than engaging with contemporary culture.

The mission of Clement, head of the Christian school in Alexandria for pre-baptismal training, was to demonstrate that Christianity was not just for an uneducated underclass but could hold its own with the philosophers and gnostics. Writing in the popular philosophical style, sprinkling his books with quotations from an impressive array of pagan writers, he argued that Christianity was the culmination of all that was good in Greek thought, especially Plato's. 'Philosophy may even have been given to the Greeks directly by God,' he suggested. 'It was a schoolteacher to bring Greek culture to Christ, as the Law was for the Hebrews.'

The problem was that the Law of Moses did not have a great deal in common with Platonism, with its transcendent, emotionless, abstract God and immortal human souls. So to reconcile them, Clement took Christian allegorising of the Bible further than ever. Arguing that full knowledge is hidden symbolically in its odder passages, to protect those not mature enough to accept or understand it, Clement was able to decode the scriptures to reveal the truths that his Platonist mind knew must be in there somewhere.

He was similarly friendly to the gnostics. While he successfully argued against them, he loved their idea that salvation and knowledge of God are the same thing. For him, Christianity was about being gradually made like God and becoming one with him through knowledge, so advanced Christians are in fact the 'true gnostics'.

Being a pastoral teacher, Clement also wrote a guide to Christian behaviour throughout the day, covering everything from sex being only for procreation to talking with your mouth full. Concerning sex (and other earthly pleasures), Clement was actually the most liberal Christian writer of his age – probably of the whole coming millennium in fact, but the idea that the Christian life was fundamentally about denying physical desire was becoming generally accepted.

His pupil and successor, Origen, was a case in point. He had few possessions, and got by on the minimum food, drink and sleep. For the sake of his spiritual life, he is said to have castrated himself. In the anti-Christian campaign of 202, Clement fled Alexandria, while Origen, aged seventeen, was so desperate to join his father in being tortured and beheaded that he only stayed because his mother hid his clothes. Just a year later, he took over the school.

A brilliant thinker, Origen has been called the most prolific writer ever, though most of his work is lost. He developed Clement's allegorical Bible-reading into a three-tiered system: every text has its plain meaning (which is sometimes erroneous or immoral), then works as a moral parable, then most importantly encodes mystical symbolism. He wrote many vast biblical commentaries unpacking these meanings, the most celebrated being *Song of Songs*: he found in its shockingly erotic verse a wealth of meditation on the union between Christ and the church.

This allowed him to import the God of Plato, 'ever unmoved and untroubled in his own summit of bliss', more successfully into the Bible than ever. It told him that souls existed before birth, and that they are saved by mystical experience of God in Christ. He apparently reinterpreted the resurrection of the dead as reincarnation in new universes, a repeated process of sin and suffering until the soul is purified. This means that no one is eternally damned: God's punishment purifies us, so that all humans and even demons may ultimately become one with God.

Origen also put a lot of thought into the Trinity. If the three are one God, then what is the difference between them? What makes them three? Origen's answer is that some are more God than others. Only the Father is God in his own right, so the Son and Spirit receive their divinity from him: great, greater, greatest; a three-storey hierarchy. Where he really broke new ground is in rejecting the assumption that the Father gave birth to the Son at some point in time. God (Platonism says) is timeless, so the Son is fathered timelessly, 'eternally begotten of the Father', as the Nicene creed agreed a century later.

Origen was a formidably original thinker, by no means orthodox in the common sense – or in the religious sense, according to the sixth-century church, which burnt his writings as heretical. He kicked up controversy in his own time too, the redemption of the devil especially raising eyebrows. He clashed with Demetrius, the bishop of Alexandria, who seemed to find having a theological celebrity in his church somewhat trying, and of whom Origen was probably rather critical. On a teaching visit to Caesarea in 230, Origen was ordained as an elder so that he could preach. This snub was the last straw, and together with the rest of Egypt's bishops, Demetrius excommunicated him as a heretic and a eunuch, though his attempt to have him condemned at Rome failed, and he retained his huge following. Origen spent the rest of his life in Caesarea, until, clothed or otherwise, he finally achieved his martyrdom.

6

Blood and Sand (247-311)

Let us compete to win not only outward martyrdom, but that which is secret.
Origen

Origen's career spanned a half-century of relative peace and tolerance for the church – the first half of the third century. Christianity was becoming fairly respectable – not least thanks to Origen's writings, but also simply because it had been around for 200 years. The church had gone everywhere the Roman empire had, even Britain. There were hundreds of churches in Italy and across North Africa, and it had probably reached beyond the empire as far as India. Emperor Alexander Severus incorporated Christ into his pantheon, employed Christians and allowed them to hold property. Emperor Philip the Arab was said to be almost a Christian.

Decius's assault

Philip's death, however, ushered in the greatest assault on the church yet. There were several reasons for the backlash. The empire was in desperate crisis, overrun by Gothic invaders in Europe, while fighting the Persians in the east, and suffering roaring inflation. Also, the government was in chaos, with a giddying succession of emperors, at least eighteen in fifty years. In the midst of this, in 247, Rome celebrated its rather sorry millennium under Philip. The refusal of Christians to take part in these religious festivities (or in the army for that matter) brought into focus the obvious moral: Rome had tolerated Christian disloyalty and hatred of its gods for too long and this had brought its present nightmares upon it. Murderous riots broke out, and when Decius overthrew Philip in 249, one of his first acts as emperor was to order the arrests of church leaders. The bishops of Rome, Antioch and Jerusalem were killed; those of Alexandria and Carthage went into hiding. Decius decreed that every person, on pain of death, must obtain a certificate saying, 'I have always sacrificed regularly to the gods, and now, in your presence, in accordance with the edict, I have done sacrifice, poured the drink offering, and tasted the sacrifices.'

This was the first attempt to eradicate Christianity across the whole empire, and the carnage was terrible. 'Such blood flowed as might... subdue the flames of hell with its glorious gore,' rejoiced Cyprian, the undercover bishop of Carthage. And yet as it was toleration that had encouraged people to join the church these last fifty years, many Christians had a more ambivalent attitude to being tortured to death than the likes of Cyprian and Origen. In fact, so many rushed to sacrifice that Roman officials had to turn away the crowds. Thousands sacrificed – or at least bought certificates, which the church considered almost as bad – including a number of bishops. 'Why bring a sacrifice, you wretch?' cried Cyprian. 'Why offer a victim? You yourself are the offering on the altar, you the victim. You have slaughtered there your salvation and your hope; in that burnt offering your faith goes up in flames.'

Origen himself faced death unshakeably, though his martyrdom was never officially recognised because he died of his wounds at home. This was not only a personal disappointment, but perhaps what would have made the difference between his acceptance or rejection by the later church.

Cyprian and the apostates

The campaign did not last, Decius being killed by the Goths in 251, but it left the church with a problem – not that torture and execution are not problems, but this was a real theological problem. Many fallen Christians wanted to rejoin the church. Some bishops said this was impossible, such serious sins being unforgivable; others were prepared to readmit the certificate-buyers at least, after suitable penance. What no one was prepared for was that many in prison for their faith – 'confessors' – took it upon themselves to start issuing certificates of forgiveness for those whose courage had failed, claiming greater moral authority than bishops directing their church from rural hideouts.

Bishops saw in this yet another assault on their authority, as well as polluting churches and offering false consolation to the fallen. Cyprian achieved an agreement with the confessors: apostates would be readmitted, at the discretion of the bishop, but after a long course of penance and re-education for the certificate-buyers, and only at death for genuine sacrificers.

It was not an end to the matter. The church had been shaken by Decius's campaign, the failure of Christian nerve damaging it far more than any martyrdom. Disgusted by the leniency of bishops like Cyprian, one of the clergy at Rome, Novatian, declared the church corrupted and led a breakaway group, the Pure. Conversely, the – confusingly – similarly named Novatus left Cyprian's church to form one which offered free forgiveness to all penitents.

So Cyprian had another fight on his hands, insisting that such splits were spiritual suicide. There was one worldwide church, the body of Christ; those who leave it leave Christ. Separatists cannot split it, only split from it. 'There is no salvation outside the church,' he warned. 'No one can have God for a father who no longer has the church for a mother.' Of course, Novatian claimed that the Pure were that true church. Cyprian answered that 'the bishop is in the church and the church is in the bishop'; they had taken their people away from their bishop and therefore could not be a church. Nevertheless, the Pure survived as another rival church for 200 years.

For all his devotion to the unity of the church, Cyprian then fell out violently with Stephen, the bishop of Rome, over the question of whether to re-baptise converts originally baptised by Novatian's pseudo-bishops, Cyprian saying yes, Stephen no. Stephen also said that Cyprian was a false Christ and excommunicated him. 'Every bishop has the right to his opinion,' responded Cyprian, but Stephen argued that as the heir of St Peter it was the bishop of Rome who had the right to bishops' opinions.

The clash was only soothed by renewed persecution. In 258, Emperor Valerian ordered that all bishops, elders and deacons be executed, and Stephen, Cyprian and Novatian joined the martyrs. When Cyprian was beheaded, his blood was caught in a large cloth, which the Carthaginians hung up in church.

In the long run, Cyprian lost to Stephen, and the church renounced re-baptism. Against the rigorist Novatian, in contrast, he achieved more than he meant to. He was passionately committed to the holiness of the church, inspired by his master Tertullian: the church is holy only if its members are holy, and members are holy only if they do not sin. Cyprian's problem was that the church could not sustain the growth it had enjoyed and also maintain such rigorous standards. Novatian chose rigour, Cyprian compromised. In so doing, he opened the door to a wildly different version of what church is: no longer a selective school for saints but an all-comprehending medieval hospital for sinners.

Antony and monasticism

The third century ended as it had begun, with more than forty years of peace for the church. Churches felt confident enough to raise their own buildings for the first time. Converts were more numerous than ever, but also more cautious. In the wake of the great apostasy crisis, it became quite normal for Christians to postpone baptism until late in life, allowing them to commit all their major sins beforehand and avoid the pains of penance.

Suddenly the most fervent Christians started to find holiness in the desert instead of the church. It seems more than coincidence that during the new relaxation of church life a rich young man called Antony heard the call to give all his possessions to the poor, put his sister in care and eventually live alone in the Sahara, devoting himself to prayer and holy solitude, occasional bread and salt his only food, malicious demons his only companions. According to his biographer, Athanasius, who wrote while he was still alive, Antony faced three Satanic onslaughts: first, sexual temptation, then physical beating and then in the form of wild animals. After twenty years, he emerged from solitary confinement to heal, teach and lead a scattering of fellow desert hermits. So holy had he become, says Athanasius, that he wore a hair shirt and 'was ashamed to be seen eating'.

Antony was probably not the first to take to sacred solitude, but he was the most celebrated father of the movement. Despite his privations, he lived to 105, by which time the monastic non-community numbered thousands across the desert.

With Christianity now seeming to be a flesh-hating religion infused with Platonic philosophy, the transformation from its Jewish roots was complete. You would have to go a long way to find a Jewish Christian, and even God had become Greek. In 300, Spanish churches, in a breathtaking reversal of the story of Peter and Cornelius, agreed to expel anyone who ate with Jews.

Church and empire, meanwhile, seemed not only on friendlier terms but to be converging. Just as Christianity had been incorporating Platonic ideas, Roman religion was becoming almost monotheistic – not denying worship to the gods and emperors, but focussing more on one supreme deity, the

Unconquered Sun. Philosophy likewise: the Alexandrian Plotinus launched an influential new version of Platonism, built around the idea of 'the One', incomprehensible, transcendent, the source of all being. The popularity of Neoplatonism made Christianity seem more mainstream than ever, while also providing another attractive source of ideas for Christian thinkers.

The great persecution

The political troubles of the Roman empire were eased by Diocletian, emperor from 284 to 305. He forced back the Goth and Persian armies and introduced extensive reforms, the most important for our story being to divide the empire in half, delegating the west to a second emperor, each emperor with a deputy or 'caesar' – one government in four persons. As well as making the empire more manageable, this east-west split would have a permanent effect on the shape of the church.

In restoring the glory of Rome, Diocletian rebuilt temples and revived traditional worship. In such an atmosphere, Christians were suspect, but Diocletian was cautious about outlawing such a large minority of his subjects. Finally, in February 303 – after a priest failed to read the future in a liver and the oracle of the sun god blamed the Christians present who had crossed themselves – Diocletian was persuaded by his caesar, Galerius, to act. He banned Christian worship, had sacred writings, vessels and buildings destroyed, and he arrested bishops. After a year, Diocletian retired 'to grow cabbages', and Galerius ordered all Christians to sacrifice or be sacrificed.

This was the last and bloodiest Roman assault on the church. Its severity varied: Britain, Gaul and Spain, under the sympathetic caesar Constantius, suffered only token church demolitions, while Egypt and Palestine faced eleven years of intense attack. The historian Eusebius, living in Caesarea, describes torture, scourging, drowning, burning, starvation, crucifixion and killing by various animals and all manner of ingenious devices:

> Sometimes 100 men – not counting women and small children –
> were killed in a day, condemned to an ever-changing series of
> punishments. I was there and saw many of the executions myself,
> some by beheading, others by fire. So many were killed in one day
> that the axe, blunted and weakened by the slaughter, fell to bits,
> while the executioners were worn out and had to work in shifts.

The response of Christians was as mixed as in Cyprian's day. The bishops of Alexandria and Nicomedia (Diocletian's eastern capital) were killed, along with many other clergy and laypeople. The bishop of Rome, on the other hand, sacrificed (though like all early popes he was eventually canonised regardless). In the African province of Numidia, four out of twelve bishops gave up sacred vessels, while one only avoided it by pretending to be blind. The bishop of Carthage got away with handing over heretical writings to the theologically indifferent soldiers and shutting the church.

It was bowel cancer that changed Galerius's policy. Facing death, he realised that assaulting Christianity had helped neither him nor Rome. 'Most of them persisted in their folly,' he announced, 'and we saw that they were neither worshipping the gods in heaven nor honouring the god of the Christians. So, in view of our benevolence… Christians may again exist, and rebuild their meeting houses.' In return, he urged, it was their duty to pray for his recovery and for Rome. Jesus did not save Galerius, but neither did his death save the church, and violence continued.

Predictably, the empire had descended into one of its periodic civil wars between would-be emperors. What no one could have predicted is that would emerge from it baptised – the most extraordinary conversion since Paul's and the most dramatic change of direction for the church since it stopped circumcising. The lion and the lamb are about to lie down together.

7

The Christian Emperor
(312–37)

The champion of the good went forth… extending the right hand of
salvation to all that were perishing.
Eusebius on Constantine

Constantine was a Roman general hungry for the kingdom, the power and
the glory. The son of Constantius – the one who had refused to kill western
Christians – he was sympathetic to Christianity, though his own devotion was
to the Unconquered Sun.

Killing one rival emperor of the west, beating Frankish attackers and
throwing their kings to the lion, Constantine marched on his surviving rival
at Rome in 312. Before the battle at Milvian Bridge, he had a vision of a cross
in the sun and was told, 'Conquer by this sign.' He instructed his men to
paint it on their shields, and despite their small number, the soldiers of the
cross triumphed. 'The pious emperor,' reports the historian Eusebius, who
knew him personally, 'glorying in the cross of victory, preached the Son of
God to the Romans with great boldness. The whole city, reviving from the
burden of bitter, tyrannical oppression, seemed… to be born again into a
fresh, new life.' The unthinkable had happened: Rome had a Christian
emperor.

Constantine and the eastern emperor announced religious freedom for all,
and paid Christians compensation for all property seized in the persecution.
Constantine granted their clergy the privileges enjoyed by pagan priests, the
authority of judges and a lot of public money. Bishops who had been hiding
on farms had glorious churches built for them, including St Peter's in Rome.
Instead of burning their Bibles, the authorities paid for smart, new ones.

But what kind of Christian was Constantine? He ruled with all the bloody
brutality of pagan emperors – or Old Testament kings for that matter – killing

even his firstborn son to protect his throne. But as well as legalising Christianity, he Christianised the law: he outlawed crucifixion, the killing of unwanted children, the abuse of slaves and peasants, gladiatorial games and facial branding (because 'man is made in God's image'), and he decreed that all prisoners should see the sun every day.

Whether a genuine vision lies behind the Milvian Bridge story or simply inspired PR, there is no doubting the sincerity of Constantine's Christian conversion. Just how Christian it was can be doubted, though. His coins and victory arch bore no mention of Christianity or its symbols, preferring the sun deity and even Mars, god of war. When in 321 he single-handedly invented the concept of Sunday as a day of rest (as opposed to worship), his reason was not especially Christian: 'It seems to us improper that the Day of the Sun, which is kept for its veneration, should be spent in legal disputes.' Having to govern a pagan majority as well as Christians made him cautious, and – in the tradition of Justin and Clement – he saw Christianity not as negating his old faith but completing it. Had he not seen the cross in the sun? The crucified Son *was* the Unconquered Sun. Christian attitudes to this fusion are illustrated by that fact that when churches started about now to celebrate Christmas, they chose 25 December, which happens to be the Roman feast of the birth of the Unconquered Sun.

The Donatist division

The church marked this dawn of peace by starting a new era of theological civil war. The first infighting started in Carthage, where once again, state terrorism had divided Christians into hardliners (under Donatus) and compromisers. When Constantine announced the return of confiscated property to the churches, he was unimpressed to find two groups claiming to be the church of Carthage. How was Christianity supposed to be the religion to unite the empire when it could not even unite the Christians?

Before, the two sides would just have slugged it out, marshalling the support of other bishops; now theological disputes had a referee. Constantine summoned a small council of European bishops. The bishop of Rome, who chaired it, condemned the Donatists; they appealed and were then condemned by a larger council. When they continued to dispute the verdict, Constantine took a leaf out of Diocletian's book and started to confiscate their property.

It was no use. Churches across North Africa lined up with Donatus. Condemnation from Europeans merely spurred African patriotism; Constantine's use of force merely reminded them that they were the church of the martyrs, locked in eternal struggle with the beast of Rome. After four years, Constantine gave up and permitted them to exist. The Donatists became the majority in Africa, though they were seen as heretics almost everywhere else. Donatus even appointed a rival bishop of Rome.

Meanwhile, to win Rome's support, the non-Donatist Africans agreed to accept Rome's understanding of the sacraments instead of Cyprian's and to prohibit re-baptism. Before, all African Christianity had had an uneasy friendship with Rome; now those who were not Donatist enemies of Rome were Roman Catholics.

Arius and Athanasius: the divinity of Christ

Half an empire did not sate Constantine's ambition, and in 324 he defeated his opposite number to seize control of the east, on the grounds that he had been harassing Christians. Since Christ had so emphatically supported Constantine's previous war of conquest, it followed that the Unconquered Son would approve of reuniting the empire under one lord. To make sure, Constantine had a huge cross made and carried into battle by fifty soldiers.

'All things were filled with light,' gushed Eusebius after his victory. 'Those who had been miserable looked at each other with smiling faces and beaming eyes. City and country danced and sang hymns, firstly in honour of God, the King of all, and then to the godly emperor.'

But surveying his new domains, Constantine was appalled to find the eastern church split by its own conflict, this one profound enough to make the Donatist controversy look like a scrap in a sandpit. The question that divided them was to dominate the whole century and beyond: who is Jesus? The church worshipped him as God, the New Testament called him God; and yet if the scriptures were clear about anything it was that there was one God, and that worshipping anyone else was blasphemous idolatry. How does it add up? How are the two one?

The church had largely rejected one explanation, modalism, in which God is Father, Son and Holy Spirit in the same way that one person can be a doctor, a wife and a Christian. Equally, it guarded against the opposite temptation to talk about three Gods. Origen's middle way seemed to have won: God exists in a hierarchy, Son and Spirit receiving their divinity from the Father, equally eternal and perfectly united.

But teaching the Trinity is a tricky balance. Those who stressed God's oneness accused others of having three Gods; those who stressed God's threeness accused their accusers of modalism.

So Arius, the elder of a church in Alexandria, tried to end the confusion, and started a theological world war. Where it had all gone wrong, to his mind, was with the idea that Christ was eternal. If he had no beginning then there were two prime movers, two origins of all things, two uncreated creators. This being absurd, the Father must have brought him into being, and so 'there was a time when he was not'. He is, as Paul says, 'the firstborn of all creation', immeasurably greater, more glorious and more godlike than creation, but created nonetheless. Older than time, he is not as old as God; prior to all creation, he is not uncreated. Arius still calls him God, but it reads like an honorary title.

Dispute seized Alexandria. The bishop, Alexander, vehemently opposed Arius's demotion of Christ, and with a council of 100 Egyptian bishops condemned and sacked him. But Arius's robust monotheism appealed to a lot of Christians, and two important bishops offered him a home and platform: Eusebius of Caesarea, the historian, and another Eusebius, bishop of the eastern capital Nicomedia.

Doctrinal propaganda war spread throughout the east. Arius wrote pop songs with lines like 'The essence of the Father is foreign to the Son.' Their arguments were parodied on the pagan stage.

Arius's arch-enemy, champion of the deity of Christ, was Athanasius, a young deacon of Alexander's in Alexandria, who at twenty-two already had one theological masterpiece to his name, The Incarnation, which explored why the Word of God had had to become flesh. His explanation was that humanity was rotten, corrupted by sin, losing the image of God, knowledge of God and everlasting life. The only way to restore human nature was to unite it with the divine in Christ.

Fighting Arius, Athanasius used the standard philosophical and biblical arguments, but the most compelling came back to the incarnation: Arius's saviour simply wasn't up to the job. Who could recreate humanity but its creator? Who could restore the image of God in us but God? He became what we are that we might become what he is. Arius's Christ could not share the divine nature with humanity because he did not share it himself. Athanasius also used the time-honoured sunlight imagery: rays are produced by the sun, not out of nothing but from its own self, and it is idiotic to say that the sun ever existed without its rays; Christ is not just God's son, but the word and power and wisdom of God – how can God ever have been without these?

The council of Nicea

Constantine told Alexander and Arius that the whole subject was 'improper for discussion' and instructed them to forgive and forget. It was too late for that, though, and so in 325, he summoned a worldwide council of bishops at Nicea, the first ecumenical council, to decide who Jesus was.

It was a spectacular occasion. Over 300 bishops gathered from across the world, from Gaul to Persia (though only a handful came from the west), along with countless lesser clergy and laypeople. Many proudly bore disfigurements and injuries from the great persecution, coming to fight for the faith they had suffered for. The emperor himself presided in all his pomp and glory, and how they loved him. He appeared 'like some heavenly messenger from God,' cried Eusebius the historian, 'in robes glittering with rays of light'.

It was immediately clear that Arius had lost. Most of the bishops were not keen on either extreme, of Arius or Athanasius, staying with Origen's middle way, but it was Arius's relegation of Christ that really offended. Arius was deposed, and to kill off his heresy, the council composed an anti-Arian creed.

Creeds were summaries of the Christian faith for converts to proclaim at baptism, varying from church to church. This one, though, was for the bishops, allowing the council to depose any who would not sign it. It proved surprisingly hard to write, Arius's writings being full of ambiguity and paradox. He was quite happy, for example, to state that the Son is God. They pulled out every stop: 'He is God from God, light from light, true God from true God, begotten not made'; and, to make absolutely sure, the creed curses 'anyone who says, "There was a time when he was not."'

Constantine, urged by his Spanish adviser, even threw in a phrase of his own: the Son is *homoousios* with the Father, 'of the same substance'. What precisely does that mean? Well quite. The moderate majority were uneasy – was this not western modalism, making Father and Son the same thing? However, they decided it was a happily ambiguous term, and Constantine, pressing for unity, agreed. In the end, all but two of the great assembly signed up, including both Eusebiuses.

Nicea is traditionally seen as the point at which the church once and for all agreed its fundamental beliefs. In fact, the conflict raged hotter than ever. Eusebius of Nicomedia still basically agreed with Arius. He shared communion with him, which enraged Constantine into sacking him, but he was a great politician, and by 328, he was back – as Constantine's religious adviser, no less. At the same time, Athanasius became bishop of Alexandria, so Nicomedia and Alexandria became the poles of the Christian world, until Eusebius used his position to get Athanasius and other anti-Arian leaders deposed. Nicea was in retreat.

Constantine devoted his later years to founding Constantinople (or New Rome as he more modestly called it) on the site of old Byzantium, where Europe and Asia meet. The pagan temples of old Rome were replaced with churches, though there was a splendid statue of the sun god (looking uncannily like Constantine) and the mother goddess. Again the move was allegedly commanded in a dream; it also in theory made it easier to rule a united empire, though in the long run, it simply provided a capital for the east to rival Rome.

Arius spent his last years pleading to be reconciled to the church, but he was an outcast scapegoat. To Athanasius and friends he was Satan; to Arians like Eusebius of Nicomedia, he was a liability, the name that threatened to damn their cause. Constantine finally agreed to restore him, but if it happened, no one bothered to record it. Constantine himself died soon afterwards, being baptised during his last illness by Eusebius.

8

The Puzzle of Jesus (337-95)

To conceive God is difficult, to define him impossible.
Gregory of Nazianzus

Constantine's three sons inherited his empire, his Christianity and his willingness to kill foes and family to secure the throne. By the time one of them, Constantius, had united the empire, yet another belief about Jesus was dividing the church: Aetius's hyper-Arianism, teaching that the Son was 'unlike the Father'.

Constantius's idea of unity was to ban people from disagreeing. In 357, the Declaration (or 'Blasphemy' as less even-handed textbooks know it) of Sirmium forbade any discussion of the Son being *homoousios*, 'of the same substance', as the Father. Athanasius was exiled (a third time), the doctrine of Nicea was buried, and Arianism – and hyper-Arianism – were official varieties of Christianity.

This had an unexpected side-effect. The mass of eastern bishops resented being blurred together with hyper-Arians, and so, though still suspicious of Nicea's *homoousios*, they talked increasingly about the Son being *homoiousios*, 'of similar substance' to the Father. This was still one iota too many for Athanasius, but the two sides were getting closer.

In 361, Constantius was succeeded as emperor by Julian, a nephew whose family he had butchered. Julian had, surreptitiously, rejected his uncle's religion, and so now paganism was back from the dead. For maximum ecclesiastical disruption, he recalled all exiles, and sure enough, there were soon three rival bishops of Antioch – though Athanasius lasted only a few months in Alexandria before annoying Julian into banishing him again.

Those whom the gods love die young, and the last pagan emperor died after two years, in 363. The new eastern emperor revived Constantius's lowest-common-denominator Christianity, so once again the ghost of Arius was back in the pulpit. Not only was Athanasius exiled this time but moderate 'homoiousian' leaders too, bringing them still closer together.

This middle-ground majority was finally united with Athanasius's Nicene party through the work of the Cappodocian Fathers, three monastic bishops: Basil of Caesarea, Gregory of Nazianzus and Gregory of Nyssa. They accepted the Nicene creed: Father and Son share one substance; they also accepted the traditionalists' insistence that the three are distinct entities. God is one 'substance' but three 'persons'. (Tertullian had established this in the west two centuries earlier, but in Latin.) This united all but the most die-hard Arians.

The Cappodocians also thought a lot about how the Holy Spirit fits in. ('And the Holy Spirit' is all the creed of Nicea had to say about him.) He is a person of the same substance too, and the difference between the three is not levels of greatness after all, but simply relationship: the Son is born to the Father, the Spirit sent by the Father. 'Everything that God does is done by the Father, through the Son, and fulfilled by the Spirit.' This idea was resisted not only by Arians but by a group called the Macedonians, who accepted that the Son was fully God but not the Spirit.

You would assume that all this intricate theological tussling was a matter for esoteric academics, about which ordinary Christians understood little and cared less. Not a bit of it. 'Clothes-traders, money-changers, food-sellers – everyone's at it,' complained Gregory of Nyssa in Constantinople. 'You ask the attendant, "Is my bath ready?" and he replies, "The Son was made out of nothing."' Dogmatic mobs desecrated opposing churches, and in later years, chariot-racing fans were divided along theological lines, the blues and the greens taking different stances on the nature of Christ.

Through a rather bizarre twist of fate, the Goths and some of the other Germanic tribes who were besieging the western empire (now more dangerously than ever) had converted to Arianism, thanks to a Gothic missionary sent by Eusebius of Nicomedia. At the same time, Rome had been converting them from attackers into employees; the army was so full of them that 'barbarian' had become the normal word for 'soldier'. This way, Arianism made major inroads into Europe.

Apollinaris: the soul of Christ

As if the church did not have enough to discuss about the divinity of Jesus, there now broke out a new argument about his humanity. This one was the work of a friend of Athanasius called Apollinaris, a Syrian bishop who tried to pin down in greater detail than yet achieved just who Christ was. He explained that the Son, in all his deity, inhabited a human body, as our own souls do. But did that mean Jesus had no human mind or soul? Absolutely. The human mind is weak, 'changeable, and enslaved to filthy thoughts'. If Christ had a human mind then either (a) he was changeable and therefore less than God; or (b) he had two minds, human and divine, in one body, like a pantomime horse; or (c) he was merely a human inspired by God, like the prophets. Therefore, 'The Word himself has become flesh without having assumed a human mind.'

Apollinaris was attacked from all sides. Antioch teachers traditionally stressed the humanity of Jesus, our brother and example, the new Adam; without a human mind, they argued, Apollinaris's Christ was not the man we meet in the Gospels. Rome officially condemned him. The Cappodocians insisted (as Athanasius had to Arius) that his saviour could not save, failing to unite human nature fully with the divine. 'What has not been adopted cannot be redeemed,' said Gregory of Nazianzus.

This conflict might merely have added another version of Christianity to the range on offer, were it not for the Germanic invaders. In 378, the eastern emperor was defeated by the Goths and killed, and his replacement was Theodosius, a great soldier and a fervent believer in Nicea, who declared the Nicene faith – 'the single deity of the Father, the Son and the Holy Spirit' – not only the one true Christianity but the official religion of the empire. The 'demented and insane' who disagreed would, he warned, be subject to the wrath of God, meted out by himself.

So in 381, after securing imperial borders, he summoned a new council to Constantinople, which reinstated the Nicene creed as the definition of Christianity, cancelling all others since and outlawing Arians of all shades, Apollinarians and Macedonians. It also proclaimed that Constantinople, 'being the new Rome', was the second greatest bishopric, after Rome. This enraged Alexandria and Antioch, and it did not much impress Rome either – it was coming to think of itself as in a league of its own.

The council of Constantinople may or may not have issued what churches to this day confusingly call the 'Nicene creed'. This creed, recited weekly in the majority of churches, is not the original creed written at Nicea. It is longer, possibly based on it but probably not. In truth, we know nothing about where it came from.

Theologically, the council was a triumph for the Cappodocians, but Gregory of Nazianzus was so upset by its political proceedings that he quit both the council and his new bishopric of Constantinople, returning to his beloved monastic life. 'I am determined to avoid all councils of bishops. I have never seen a single instance where they did any good… I will not sit in synods of squabbling geese and cranes.' His farewell sermon to Constantinople eloquently depicts what bishops had become since Constantine:

> I did not know that we were supposed to rival consuls, governors and illustrious generals, or that our bellies were supposed to hunger for the food of the poor, spending their necessities on luxuries and belching over the altar… Find yourself a leader who will please the masses. Give me my desert, my country life, my God.

Monasticism: whips and pillars

There were now hundreds of thousands of monks and nuns throughout the deserts and countryside of Christendom, and the efforts of many of them to torture themselves into the kingdom of heaven became increasingly extreme. Leaving mere poverty and celibacy at the starting post, they lived in caves so small they were unable to stand, or they tied themselves up with chains and ropes that cut their skin. They tied weights to their necks and groins, lived in trees or tombs and whipped themselves and each other. Starvation rations came as standard: in Gaza, Hilarion reportedly ate nothing but dry lentils for three years; 'grazers' ate only grass. Thalelaeus of Cilicia spent ten years in a hanging barrel, unable to raise his head. One monk walked eight miles a day to water a dry stick as an exercise in fruitless obedience. Mother Sarah lived by an Egyptian river for sixty years without ever looking at it. Macarius the Alexandrian, after swatting a gnat instead of accepting its bite, spent six months in a gnat-infested swamp. (He ate nothing but raw vegetables and a little bread, and he is the patron saint of pastry chefs.) Such abuse, which might be enough to destroy a person in weeks if not self-inflicted, was not always successful even in killing off fleshly passions: 'Though my limbs were frozen,' said Jerome of his desert experiences, 'my mind burnt with desire, and the fires of lust kept bubbling up before me when my flesh was as good as dead.' He, like others, was assaulted by graphic hallucinations.

What was driving this frenzy of sublimation? Once again, Constantine seems partly responsible. The first churches were radical, holy enclaves, turning from immoral pagan society. Now that almost everyone had joined, standards inevitably relaxed. Where then do you go to be 'not of the world' if the whole world is in the church? The desert. As the abbot John Cassian saw it, 'Those who still had the fervour of the apostles, remembering that lost perfection, left those who considered an easy life acceptable for Christians and moved to secluded country areas to follow in private the rules that the apostles had given the whole church.' But their ordeals seem bizarre parodies of what the Bible knows as holiness, so surely we also see here the influence (however mutated) of world-denying Greek thought too. Above all, though, martyrdom had become an essential component of Christianity, faithfulness under torture its greatest achievement, violent death its fast track to paradise, martyrs its superstars. Constantine had taken all that away, so the religious martyred themselves. They were, as Athanasius said of Antony, daily martyrs to their consciences – the beasts now their own demons and desires, the arena their own flesh.

Increasingly, however, monks organised themselves into communes. Around the time of Nicea, Pachomius had been building a community on the Nile that soon numbered thousands, growing to nine separate foundations (including two for women), each a self-sufficient, separatist world of agriculture and industry, prayer and study, and of hard, military discipline. Inmates vowed obedience, renounced family and possessions, and rarely saw the outside world.

Basil of Caesarea organised a similar system (which remains the rule of eastern monasteries to this day), explaining, 'These men must have jobs, both to earn a living and to lead more civilised lives.' His emphasis was on charity, his nuns and monks providing hospitals and hospitality. Life was still austere in these places, but the strict discipline was actually used to curb extremes. 'We should refresh ourselves with food and sleep at the proper time even if we don't want to,' said Pachomius. 'Excessive abstinence is worse for us than overindulgence.' Just how you punish someone whose crime is self-mutilation, however, proved a problem.

For vast numbers of peasants, monastic communes actually offered a more prosperous life and certainly a more secure one. For the sake of Bible study, monasteries also offered an education unavailable to many outside. The constant communal worship could be a delight, and the subjugation and self-deprivation were not simply burdens for their own sake but meant to create a community of love and spiritual growth. It may sound idealistic, but it is clear from their own testimony that for many, monastic life was a joy, and leaving it to take a well-paid public post in the church could be – as it was for Gregory of Nazianzus – heartbreaking.

Meanwhile, the hermit tradition reached its pinnacle in Simeon Stylites. After such monastic achievements that he was expelled from a monastery to save the lives of his imitators, his cave was constantly besieged by fans. So, failing to escape outwardly from the world, he escaped upwardly. He took to living on a ten-foot pillar, but of course (whether you call it stunningly naive or great marketing) this only swelled the crowds. So he extended it, until he was sixty feet in the air, and Syria's major tourist attraction – the first hermit, it has been said, to achieve solitary confinement in public. Every afternoon, he preached, took prayer requests, answered questions and explained the Trinity to bishops and rulers. The rest of the time, he prayed constantly and fed maggots to his self-inflicted wounds with the somewhat inconsistent words, 'Eat what God has given you.' He finally descended after thirty-six years, dead.

Against the Jews

Most church leaders now were ascetics, sometimes dragged reluctantly into public office from their cells. The most influential under Emperor Theodosius was, for the first time, a European, Ambrose of Milan. As a provincial governor, he had fought Arianism, until pressed into becoming a bishop – so unexpectedly that he had not yet been baptised. He made himself indispensable to Theodosius in the campaign to unite the empire in one religion, occupying churches to stop them being handed to Arians. He foiled attempts to restore a pagan altar to the senate and persuaded Theodosius to outlaw sacrifice. But at the same time he fought for his principle that 'the emperor is in the church, not above it', making Theodosius do public penance for his massacre of Thessalonika in 390. About now, another great blow was struck against paganism, and in fact all human culture, when the bishop of Alexandria reportedly burnt the library to the ground.

A second group stood between Theodosius and Ambrose and their monolithic Christian empire: the Jews. Throughout the fourth century, Christian attitudes to Jews changed from disapproval to persecuting hatred.

In 388, a bishop and his flock burnt down a synagogue on the Euphrates. Theodosius demanded the bishop rebuild it, but Ambrose intervened and dissuaded him. Hilary of Poitiers had refused to acknowledge Jews in the street, considering the race possessed by Satan. Jerome, the greatest scholar of the age, greatly indebted to Jews in his translation of the Old Testament, considered the synagogue 'a whorehouse, a den of wickedness, the devil's sanctuary,' adding that this was letting them off lightly.

Most sickening are the sermons of John Chrysostom, bishop of Constantinople and the age's greatest preacher. 'I hate the Jews,' he exclaimed. 'Most miserable of all men – lustful, grasping, greedy, detestable bandits, plague of the universe!... Are they not murderers, wreckers, demoniacs?... Jews worship the devil: their rites are filthy and criminal; their religion a disease.' 'You killed Christ... There is no atonement for you, or excuse.' 'The Jew will live under the yoke of slavery forever. God hates the Jews, and on judgment day, he will tell their sympathisers, "Depart from me, friends of my murderers!"' Frustratingly for our inclination to see things in black and white, Chrysostom was also the greatest voice for just provision for the poor in the early church.

It seems that another thing Constantine had deprived the church of was the enemy. The stand against Rome had been an apocalyptic struggle, darkness versus light, saints versus the beast. Now that church and empire were one, a new adversary was needed. Chrysostom explicitly saw his anti-Semitism in terms of the arena – though with Jews the victims, himself the beast 'rushing thirstily to its bloody banquet'. And Judaism was a threat, its very existence seeming to disprove Christianity: how could Jesus be the fulfilment of the Jewish faith, if that faith continued regardless? How could the Bible be Christian if Jews alone obeyed its Law? For whatever reason, the Jewish sect whose founders had moved heaven and earth to get Gentiles accepted was turning the Jews into pariahs. Chrysostom was a hideous extreme – some Christians still celebrated Passover with the Jews – but he was the voice of the future. Hilary, Jerome, Chrysostom and Ambrose were all canonised. 'You killed Christ,' they said, but the persecuting church would surely turn out to be a greater betrayer of Jesus even than Judas.

9

Augustine (395–430)

> God's providence constantly uses war to correct and chasten the corrupt morals of mankind.
>
> *Augustine, on the barbarian conquest*

Augustine was brought up as a Christian in North Africa by his powerful mother, who told him that God, not her pagan husband, was his true father. He abandoned his faith for two reasons. One was traditional teenage rebellion: after dipping into 'hell's black river of lust', he found Christian morals no match for its currents. The other was the Bible: like so many before him, he was appalled when he explored it and found murderous holy men, countless wives, animal sacrifice and God walking on earth like a man.

Still Augustine thirsted for truth, and at eighteen, he joined the Manichees, gnostic believers who revered Buddha, Zoroaster and Jesus as well as their own Mani. Mani said that God and the devil are both eternal, this world a muddle between heaven and hell, which explained the power of Augustine's dark urges. Advanced Manichees lived like monks in poverty and celibacy; Augustine, being only a 'hearer', was allowed to live with his girlfriend, provided he took precautions to avoid the multiplication of sinful flesh.

He continued to study philosophy and science, growing disillusioned over ten years by the failure of Manichee gurus to answer his questions. Moving on to Neoplatonism, he went to the great city of Milan to teach public speaking. Augustine's mother, whose prayers and entreaties had haunted him for years, turned up, sent his girlfriend of thirteen years back to Africa without their son (no precautions are foolproof) and got him engaged to one of Milan's most eligible ten-year-olds. Augustine, who tortured himself with memories of the most trivial sins of childhood, never repented of abandoning the mother of his son: 'it crushed my heart to bleeding', he confessed, but both were rescued from a relationship of sexual passion, and this was good.

She was the more successfully rescued however: while waiting for his fiancée to reach marriageable age, Augustine got himself another woman.

Meanwhile, he attended Ambrose's celebrated sermons, hoping to learn rhetoric. Instead, he learned Christianity. He learned to read the Bible for its more acceptable, undercover, Neoplatonic truths, and, inspired by a child singing, 'Take, read,' opened it at random and read, 'Put on the Lord Jesus Christ and make no provision for gratifying the desires of the flesh.' 'Light flooded into my soul,' he said. Immediately he told his mother who, he recalled, rejoiced that 'you had converted me to yourself, so that I no longer needed a wife'.

He took to celibacy and seclusion in a commune with his friends and mother. After her death, he returned to Africa where he was ambushed by a church and persuaded, in tears, to accept ordination. In 396, he became the happily named bishop of Hippo.

From this position, he broadcast passionate attacks on Manicheeism as hypocritical, half-baked mumbo-jumbo, answering its objections to Christianity and reporting that he had heard one of their celibate elite 'whinnying' (the Latin equivalent of wolf-whistling) at a woman. He also relentlessly attacked the Donatists, who outnumbered Catholics in Africa, in sermons, books and songs. When this had little impact, other bishops recommended more physical attacks. Augustine was reluctant ('No one should be coerced into the unity of Christ') until they demonstrated that it worked. Then he became an apologist for persecution. Had the king in Christ's parable not said of his wedding guests, 'Compel them to come in' (at least in the Latin translation Augustine used)? Had God not used violence in converting Paul? It is the loving man who beats his sons and slaves; tolerating wickedness is the real abuse. The emperor should use loving violence (though not execution) to save human souls. This is the unfortunate context of his celebrated aphorism, 'Love and do what you will.' He had a noticeable impact on Donatist numbers, but he could never beat down a church that had been founded on persecution.

At the same time, the empire itself was collapsing before the barbarian armies. Vandals crossed the frozen Rhine into Gaul and Spain, while Goths ransacked Greece and Italy, and in 410 invaded Rome. Western emperors continued to be appointed for sixty-six more years, but in effect the western empire was finished. The Roman world reeled in shock at the news. Pagans blamed Christianity, and Augustine responded with *The City of God*, his monumental discussion of the difference between human kingdoms and the kingdom of God.

The grace debate: versus Pelagius

The first Briton in our story is, in true Hollywood style, a villain: the heretic Pelagius. He saw Christianity becoming for many little more than a label, so he preached tough morality and led something of a religious revival in Rome, before fleeing to Africa from the Goths. He might have ended up a saint if he had not taken on Augustine.

Augustine's touching and popular *Confessions* disclosed his long struggles with the flesh, rejoicing that God's Spirit had overcome the sin that proved unconquerable in his own strength: 'You command chastity. Give what you command, and command what you will.' Pelagius heard a public reading of this passage and shouted down the reader. Augustine was encouraging sinners to say, 'God hasn't given what he commands, so I can't help myself.' Obedience must be possible in our own strength, Pelagius insisted – unless the Creator perversely made rules we do not have the ability to follow.

Pelagius's optimism struck at the heart of Augustine's faith. Reacting against the God-versus-devil dualism of the Manichees, Augustine saw God in direct control of every event in the world. His own experience convinced him that humanity is so wrecked by Adam's fall that we cannot turn to God – or even desire to – without his 'secret, wonderful, and ineffable power working within'. Moreover, according to his interpretation of Paul's writings, every person inherits Adam's guilt, so we are born damned; God saves some, with the gift of faith and holiness; others he abandons to hell; the decision is his alone.

For Pelagius, every person is responsible for their own life. Adam gives us a bad example and Christ a good example, but we are neither damned for Adam's sin, nor saved by Christ's righteousness. We choose freely and are judged by our own choices.

Augustine garnered powerful support from Jerome (who said that the Briton was a fat dog stupefied with porridge), the bishop of Rome, and most influentially, the western emperor. Pelagius and his followers were condemned by a series of councils, though debate raged on until 430, when North Africa was engulfed by Vandal armies, and Augustine, refusing to run, died of malaria in the siege of Hippo.

The rise of Rome

Suddenly everything seemed to be conspiring to drive the western and eastern churches apart. Politically, the west was controlled by Germanic tribes, all either pagan or Arian, while in the east, the Christian empire remained untouched. Just as important as the fall of Rome was the rise of Rome in the person of the bishop, who had now started to call himself 'the Father' or Pope: in the east, all major bishops were called popes. (They shall now be called 'patriarchs'.) Although the east had several churches founded by apostles, Rome had started to call itself 'the apostolic see' and was claiming the right to adjudicate all disagreements in the church – a claim no one else took seriously – based on Christ's promise to Peter, 'I will give you the keys of the kingdom of heaven.'

Language also proved a growing barrier between the Latin west and Greek east. In the days of Nicea, discussions about Father and Son being two persons sharing one substance were seriously confused by the fact that the Greek word for 'person' was deceptively like the Latin for 'substance'. Augustine hated and never mastered Greek (rarely has history so turned on one child's school grades), which hampered his reading of both the New Testament and Greek theology. Jerome was commissioned by Rome to produce a reliable Latin Bible, the Vulgate, intended to assert Rome's independence of the east. It was a great achievement but inevitably imperfect. Augustine's teaching on persecution ('Compel them to come in') and original sin (the inheritance of Adam's guilt, 'in whom all men sinned') were both based in part on mistranslations. (Correctly, they read, 'Bring them in,' and 'because all have sinned'.) The thinking and outlook Augustine developed, which dominated the west for over 1,000 years and arguably still do, were alien to the east, who knew nothing of original sin or predestination. 'God wishes all to be saved', said John Chrysostom, 'but forces no one.'

Augustine's most incendiary teaching (when it eventually reached easterners) was his understanding of the Trinity. The east, from Origen through the Cappodocians, tended to ask how Father, Son and Spirit could be one God, whereas Augustine, typical of the west, came from the opposite direction: how can one God be three? The east, you might say, saw God as essentially three, stressing their distinct roles and characters; western tradition stressed God's unity – which is why the term 'of the same substance', introduced to the Nicene creed thanks to Constantine's Spanish adviser, caused no controversy in the west. Augustine reinforced this. He was not even all that comfortable talking about the three being 'persons': 'We say "three persons", not because that expresses quite what we mean, but because we have to say something.' His favourite analogy was with the human mind, where three activities – memory, understanding and will (or love) – make up one mind. To eastern critics, this collapses the three into one; and his talk of the Spirit being the 'friendship' or 'bond of love' between Father and Son makes him less than a person. The most obscure divergence was the one that proved to be the explosive for later conflict. Augustine talked of the Spirit proceeding from both the Father and the Son; to the east that would risk blurring their distinct relationships: 'He proceeds from the Father' as the later 'Nicene creed' said. For now, though, east and west went their different ways, oblivious.

It is not too far-fetched, I think, to call Augustine the architect of the middle ages. As Europe came to terms with the fact that it was no longer part of the Roman empire – that Rome's sun was conquered, the realm divided into barbarian kingdoms – Augustine's thinking not only came to dominate the church but redefined what church was. In the first centuries of our story, the church was a select community, membership requiring enormous personal commitment and holy life. The first relaxation was forced on the church in Cyprian's day, with the decision that no sin need put the fallen outside the church forever. Then the conversion of Rome turned the church into an entire Christian society. Once Theodosius was persecuting the unwilling into church membership, the idea of expelling people for not being good enough Christians was becoming nonsense.

So Augustine explained this as part of his new theological system. The church, properly speaking, consists of those chosen by God before all time, who will spend eternity with him; only those are true Christians. Those who look like true believers may fall away, in which case, they were never among the chosen at all (and, conversely, today's sinners may repent); so the church, properly speaking, is invisible to us. Therefore, we cannot keep the church that we can see here and now to the elect or the elite, but we have to include all (apart from the worst offenders) who are baptised. It is not personal sanctity that makes the church holy, it is bearing the name of Christ. And since babies are born damned, baptism at birth becomes essential, rather than an option. In Christian lands, one is born into the church.

This was a theology for imperial society, so it is ironic that by the time Augustine had finished constructing it, the empire was disintegrating, and the church was rediscovering life as a powerless enclave. However, as Europe was to spend the next millennium doing its best to resurrect the Roman empire, his work was not wasted.

10

The Great Popes (430-630)

The humble, when called to supreme rule, should in their hearts flee from it, but against their wills obey.
Gregory the Great

The east never experienced what Europe calls the middle ages. The Roman empire survived and carried on as normal with creeds, councils and christological controversy.

The mother of God

The next round of debate was sparked off by the adoration of the Virgin Mary. Considering her later veneration as queen of heaven, devotion to her had been slow taking off. Her lifelong virginity had now long been universally assumed and celebrated (however the existence of Jesus' brothers was explained), the only debate now addressing whether she remained gynaecologically intact after his birth. The idea of her being free from sin was a more recent development, accepted in the west but not the east. But actual veneration had been reserved for the martyrs, Christians having treasured their relics and celebrated their 'birthdays' at their graves since the time of Polycarp; from here it had been a small step to passing their prayers on to them and seeking their patronage. Now, for the first time, Mary was starting to receive the same sort of attention, and the bishop of Constantinople, Nestorius, was uneasy about it. Was she turning into a goddess? He particularly disliked the popular term 'mother of God'. 'A creature cannot give birth to the creator,' he insisted, 'only to the man.' 'Mother of Christ' was honour enough.

Thus Nestorius walked into a fight with Alexandria. Alexandrians entirely accepted the phrase 'mother of God': they tended to stress the deity of Christ, just as Antioch (where Nestorius was trained) emphasised his humanity. To Alexandrians, Mary is the mother of Christ, Christ is God, so Mary is the mother of God. Moreover, the Alexandrian church was still smarting from being declared inferior to Constantinople, so their bishop, the hard-nosed and somewhat unprincipled politician Cyril, was happy to attack Nestorius as a heretic.

Cyril ruled Alexandria like a king, with the help of armed confrontations with the civil authorities. Installed by rioters, he closed all Novatian churches and (after an attack on Christians) burnt the synagogues and expelled all Jews from the city. 'Nestorius the Incendiary' was also a notorious persecutor of Arians and Novatians in Constantinople.

A war of words broke out, each passionately defending the understanding of Christ that meant so much to him. Nestorius insisted that Mary bore Jesus the human, not God. Likewise, it was the humanity of Christ that thirsted, suffered and died; God cannot die. Cyril accused Nestorius of separating the humanity and divinity that were perfectly joined together in Christ. Whatever is true of the son of Mary is true of the Son of God. 'We must not split the one Lord Jesus Christ into two sons.'

The emperor called a council to meet in St Mary's in Ephesus in 431, to decide between Alexandria, and Constantinople and Antioch. Unluckily for Nestorius, his Antiochene supporters arrived nineteen days late to find that Cyril had already condemned and deposed him, so they had their own council next door, condemning Cyril. The churches excommunicated each other.

Unimpressed, the emperor put both bishops under arrest. Nestorius spent his time behind bars moping about wanting to be a monk again. Cyril spent his bribing the imperial court. Cyril won – and Nestorius had his wish granted too.

Antioch agreed a compromise statement with Alexandria in 433 and condemned Nestorius. This put the lid on their conflict for now, but underneath, enmity simmered still. When Cyril died, one Antiochene bishop said, 'The living are delighted, but the dead will be sorry. There's good reason to think they'll hate his company so much, they'll send him back.'

Ephesus and Chalcedon

Conflict erupted fifteen years later between a new Antiochene bishop of Constantinople, Flavian, and one of his abbots there, the Alexandrian Eutyches. Eutyches disliked Cyril's compromise and preached an extreme version of his theology. Not only were Christ's humanity and divinity perfectly united, they merged into one thing: 'I worship one nature.' Flavian thought this would make Christ a crossbreed, neither one thing nor the other, and deposed Eutyches.

Both sides appealed to Rome for what they considered support, and Rome considered adjudication. Pope Leo the Great sent back a long letter explaining why Eutyches was 'a complete fool and utter ignoramus', so Alexandria appealed to the emperor instead, and he called another general council at Ephesus in 449. Alexandria having won last time, the emperor assumed they were right again and sent hordes of soldiers and armed monks to ensure the council agreed, which it did. Flavian was sacked, and, it seems, beaten to death by Egyptian clergy.

Pope Leo condemned this 'synod of thieves' and deluged the emperor with demands for another, which he ignored. But a year later, the emperor fell off his horse and died, leaving the empire to his sister Pulcheria and her husband Marcian, who favoured Flavian and called a council in Chalcedon, across the isthmus from Constantinople, which met in 451.

Antioch and Alexandria agreed easily enough that Nestorius and Eutyches both represented unacceptable extremes of their respective outlooks, and that the teachings of Cyril, Flavian and Leo were orthodox. With that they were ready to go home, but Pulcheria insisted they write a watertight definition of exactly who Jesus is, to settle the question forever. So the 'Definition of Chalcedon' explained that Christ is entirely God (against Arius), and entirely man (against Apollinaris), his humanity and divinity neither separate (against Nestorius), nor merged into a hybrid (against Eutyches). 'He is a truly impious and sacrilegious person,' proclaimed Emperor Marcian, 'who, after the sentence of so many bishops, reserves anything to be decided by himself.' The council passed other rules too that offer a glimpse of the present state of the church: bishops must not sell ordinations, and clergy must not form lynch mobs, loot bishops' houses when they die or carry off women.

Chalcedon was a theological triumph for Rome ('Peter has spoken through Leo' cried delegates, with which Leo heartily agreed), but it was a political humiliation. Not only were Rome's requests to host and chair the council denied, but the canons of Chalcedon declared that 'the most holy church of Constantinople, New Rome' had equal authority to 'the elder Rome'. The council also marked the downfall of the church of Alexandria, whose demotion was consolidated by bitter divisions.

Chalcedon is often presented as the 'settlement' of the long debate about Christ, the final establishment of orthodox Christianity, but this is reading history backwards. It did state the doctrines that were eventually accepted by mainstream churches, and these were established as the official Christianity of the empire (for now). But there were huge and powerful bodies of Christians who rejected Chalcedon, and so the battles continued without pause. Vast numbers felt that in ascribing to Christ two natures, human and divine, Chalcedon contradicted not only Eutyches but the great Cyril, so the east split into Chalcedonians and Monophysites ('one-naturites'). This was in addition to Nestorians, Novatians, Arians, Donatists, Montanists and more, to the extent that the 'one holy catholic and apostolic church' of the Nicene creed must have seemed rather idealistic. Arianism thrived among the tribes of Europe, and Monophysites dominated Egypt and Syria, while many Nestorians retreated into the Persian empire, where they proved successful missionaries. (Nestorianism survives in India to this day.) Monophysite theologising repeatedly took the form of riots and even assassinations.

In 482, Emperor Zeno came up with a peace plan, decreeing that, whatever the rights and wrongs of Chalcedon, it was not essential to Christianity, and that anyone who accepted the Nicene creed was a true believer. This proved popular, but not with the Pope, who denounced the eastern churches for abandoning the true Christ and caving into heresy, and when no one took any notice, he excommunicated them en masse.

Mission Europe

Europe had become a mission field again for the church, as it had been 300 years ago. One difference now is that we know the names of the missionaries, the first wave being lost to history and overwritten with the legendary travels of Mary Magdalene and Joseph of Aramithea. The first great name is Patrick, who – ironically, considering his present status in Ireland – was a Briton, kidnapped by Irish pagans. As a slave, he rediscovered his lapsed childhood faith in Jesus. When he escaped back home after six years, his captors came to him in a dream saying, 'We entreat you, boy, come and walk among us again,' so after being ordained bishop, he returned as a missionary and was successful in converting tribal kings and establishing monasteries. 'Those who never knew God, worshipping impure idols,' he reported, 'have become a people of the Lord and are called sons of God. The sons and daughters of Irish kings are now monks and virgins of Christ.'

The most powerful tribe in Europe was the pagan Franks, who under Clovis were conquering their way through Gaul. Clovis married a Burgundian princess, Clotilda, who converted with all her tribe from Arianism to Catholicism and urged him to do the same. He refused, until he found himself losing a battle and took a leaf out of Constantine's book. 'Jesus Christ,' he reportedly prayed, 'whom Clotilda declares to be the son of the living God, who is said to help the oppressed and give victory to those who hope in you, I beseech your glorious aid.' He won, and on Christmas Day 499 was baptised along with 3,000 soldiers, going on – with the help of Catholic natives – to take the whole of Gaul.

One whose influence was second only to Augustine over medieval Christianity was Benedict, an Italian who became a monk at the age of twenty, withdrawing from the world after he visited Rome and saw how immoral life in the holy city had become, and mastering his passions by throwing himself naked into thorn bushes. Lots of monasteries were appearing across Europe, following many different rulebooks, inspired by translations of Pachomius and Basil of Caesarea, and Benedict founded his own in 529. Dividing the monastic day into seven 'hours' of worship, he split the rest of the time between labour and Bible study. As well as being obedient, celibate and owning nothing, monks were forbidden to talk too much or laugh. The genius of Benedict's rule was in its concise comprehensiveness; it was so easily cloned that eventually it would overtake all Europe, single-handedly preserving literacy, learning and perhaps even Christianity.

Justinian: the empire strikes back

Someone else planned to overtake Europe too – Justinian, the eastern emperor. He wanted a reunited empire, which meant conquering the barbarians, reconciling Rome with the east and reuniting the east itself, still divided over Chalcedon.

Unfortunately, the latter two aims proved incompatible, as every attempt to find common ground between the Monophysites and Chalcedonians merely provoked the wrath of Rome. So in the end, Justinian abandoned the Monophysites, who became a separate church (including the Coptic church of Egypt and Ethiopia), the Definition of Chalcedon became the official faith of the empire, and east and west were reconciled.

The war was a success too. Justinian drove the Vandals from Africa and the Goths from Italy, and he reconquered Illyria and southern Spain, fortifying the regions with castles and glorifying them with churches. Constantinople rejoiced: the empire was restored; Rome was liberated. Western celebration was more muted, though. A sense of rivalry was growing between east and west, making the latter unhappy to be ruled from Constantinople. Moreover, much of the land Justinian reconquered was wrecked in the process: famine and plague ravaged Italy; Rome itself was left a ruined wilderness. And most of his gains were short-lived, for once Justinian died, the barbarians started reclaiming Europe.

At home, Justinian's achievements were longer lasting. He reformed the tangled mess of imperial law, redefining the Christian empire in the process. The empire was an earthly manifestation of the kingdom of heaven, the emperor 'God's living icon'. It blended church and state into a single organism. The emperor's task was not just law and order but to defend orthodoxy by calling councils and enforcing their decrees – though not in theory dictating their decisions. The west, in contrast, its church conquered by kings, was for now essentially secular.

With these reforms and the second loss of Rome, what had been the eastern Roman empire became the Byzantine empire. Justinian fulfilled his duties with spectacular church building, including the great Hagia Sophia in Constantinople. As defender of orthodoxy, he brutally victimised Jews, pagans and heretics: he closed down the Athenian Academy established by Plato, forbade Jews to build synagogues, read Hebrew scriptures or testify against Christians, and he drove Nestorian Christianity out of the empire, from where it steadily spread through Asia as far as Tibet, China and India. 'In the monstrousness of his actions one sees the power of a devil,' said the civil servant Procopius. 'No one but God, I believe, could count those he murdered.'

Gregory the Great

After some of the unlovely characters we have met in recent chapters, Gregory comes as fresh air and sunlight. He was a rich, young ruler in Rome who used his massive inheritance to found seven monasteries, gave the rest away to the poor and became a monk. Pressed to become Pope in 590, he fled the city in a basket but was caught and forced to become the first monk on the throne.

Gregory's first priority as Pope was Christian aid. Having been conquered both by Gothic armies and Justinian's, and now facing a third assault from the Lombards, Italy was overrun by poverty and disease. The Roman church had acquired vast estates over the years from pious legacies, but the profits from them were largely syphoned off by local rulers and bishops. Insisting that the wealth of the church belonged to the poor, Gregory reformed the system so that all money came to him and then out into farming projects and other relief. From the same motives, he organised penitential marches to win God's mercy.

In fact, Gregory became the virtual ruler of much of Italy; not like Cyril, because he fought for power, but simply because no one else would take responsibility for it. He raised an army to defend Rome from the Lombards, paid off the attackers and agreed a treaty securing peaceful relations. With politics like this, Gregory not only saved Rome but won the respectful friendship of other Germanic tribes.

His great goal was to convert them, and while he saw no result in Italy in his lifetime, he succeeded in Britain, where Anglo-Saxon invaders had conquered the natives (except in Wales, Scotland and Cornwall). According to legend, Gregory saw some slave boys in the market and, transfixed by their blond hair, asked who they were. 'Angles,' he was told. 'Not Angles', he quipped, 'but angels'. His opportunity to win the English came when Ethelbert, king of Kent, married the Christian Frankish princess Bertha. Gregory sent his terrified and reluctant prior Augustine to 'this barbarous, fierce and unbelieving nation'. He converted Ethelbert, baptising him along with 10,000 subjects at Easter 601, established his see in the capital city of Canterbury, and set about restoring the churches seized 150 years earlier.

In his reform of the church, Gregory cracked down on the sale of bishoprics and clerical marriage, publishing *Pastoral Care*, which remained a manual for clergy throughout the middle ages:

He should be pure in thought, but foremost in action; able to hold his tongue, but also to speak usefully; close to all in sympathy, but above all in meditation; a humble friend to the good, an unbending opponent of the evil; neither worldly nor otherworldly.

He is connected with the birth of western music, Gregorian chant taking its name from him, though what and how much he had to do with it we do not know. He compellingly promoted Benedictine monasticism and wrote a biography of Benedict. His stories of the saints were another labour that moulded medieval Christianity. He is criticised for the absurd miracles that fill these 'histories', and which became the staple diet of Catholicism; perhaps there was something about those bloody and uncertain days that made legends of supernatural power comforting. In the same spirit, he pressed purgatory (unknown in the east) and penance onto all believers, putting at the heart of Catholic spirituality the routine of precisely propitiating God today to save time in heaven's fiery waiting room.

Gregory's most remarkable quality was his humility. Leo, for example, had protested his personal unworthiness of the office of pope, while doing all he could to heighten the glory and power of the papacy. Gregory uniquely refused to pursue world domination. When the bishop of Alexandria wrote calling him 'Worldwide Pope', he was mortified: 'I know who I am, and I know who you are – in position my brother, in character my father… I beg your most sweet holiness to call me this no more, since honours which you wrongly bestow on me are stolen from others.' The title he chose for himself was 'servant of the servants of the Lord', and he was true to it; and it continued to be claimed by all later popes long after they had turned it upside down and emptied it of all meaning.

As the church reaches its 600th year, the Palestinian Jew who died in ignominy, leaving a handful of disillusioned Jewish followers, is worshipped by people from Ireland to India: emperors, slaves, nuns, royal mistresses – almost everyone apart from some of the pagan conquerors of Europe and the Jews themselves. The church has kept the teaching and worship of Jesus alive for six centuries; but is becoming an institution of political machination and bloody persecution the necessary price for its success? Has the age of councils degraded Christianity into a pseudo-science where knowing precisely who Christ supposedly was is more important than doing what he said? Is the church anything Jesus would recognise as his own?

The tumult of different Christianities is confusing, and it embarrasses those who claim to have God's one true revelation. There is the Imperial Church State to proclaim which is the official version, but even that keeps changing. And now a vast, slow continental drift is taking the western and eastern churches ever further apart too, culturally, politically and theologically. The east has recently taken an alarming battering from the great empire of Persia and its allies, but emerges from the long campaign triumphant, if exhausted. Once it has recuperated, it will be stronger than ever – assuming it has the chance. They are different worlds now: the born-again empire of Byzantium and the death-warmed-up backwater of Europe; the church of the emperor and the church of the pope. If anything is sure, it is that the future of the church lies in Asia, its home ground and heartland. But nothing is sure. One thing the future has in store, imminently, is the greatest body blow the church has received since Good Friday. And this time, there is no Sunday coming.

Part 2

The Rise of Rome

1

The Nightmare Begins

(630-700)

> It was not by mere numbers that we have conquered those we have conquered.
>
> *Amr ibn-al-Asi*

A Syrian hermit sits watching a trading caravan from Arabia parade past his cell, and he decides to invite the pagans to stay for dinner. They leave the youngest to guard their goods, but the hermit is captivated by him and insists he join. Bahira, as the monk is known, has holy writings in his cell, passed down from one occupant to the next, and he tells his guests, the youngest in particular, about their teachings. And so Muhammad ibn Abdullah, one of the most influential people ever, gives ear to the message of the church.

What truth there is in this story is debatable (one wonders what a hermit was doing with all that food in his cell), especially the part where Bahira finds a sign on the youth's shoulders that proves him to be a prophet. But certainly, one way or another, Muhammad heard Christian and Jewish teaching on his travels and was drawn to their one Almighty God. Arabia was a peninsula of animism and tribal warfare, extending south from between the empires of Byzantium and Persia, ignored by both. What it needed was a prophet, in the tradition of Moses and Jesus, to reveal God to the Arabs.

Muhammad took to prayer and meditation in the caves near Mecca, where one night in 610 he was overwhelmed by a spiritual encounter and found himself speaking prophecy. For twelve years, he relayed messages to Mecca, in surprisingly beautiful verse: submit to the one God, care for orphans and widows, fear hell. He won loyal converts but also faced violent hostility, so he went to Medina where his leadership was welcomed by the Arabs, though not by the Jewish minority, and with their help, he blockaded Mecca until, in 630, it finally submitted.

More than 1,000 Jews lived in Medina, and Muhammad was devastated by their rejection of his message. They said the age of prophets was over and that his stories of Joseph, Noah and so on contradicted their scriptures. On his victory, he had all the Jewish men killed and the women enslaved. He was equally disillusioned by Christians: they turned out to have abandoned the one God for three, to worship images and to have invented blasphemies like the prophet Jesus being crucified – and being God's son. 'God is one,' he proclaimed; 'he cannot possibly have a son.' So Muhammad was not just the apostle for Arabia but a reformer calling Jews and Christians back to the true path. Islam embraced Jewish rituals such as circumcision and food laws while accepting Jesus as Messiah – not unlike the Ebionites – but it also included popular elements of Arabian religion such as polygamy and venerating the Ka'ba, the black stone of Mecca.

Within two years, Muhammad was dead, but he left a large and well-armed following. Another two bloody years, and all Arabia was Muslim. His followers started compiling and editing his sayings into the Qu'ran. And seeing that God gave them victory, they set off to conquer the world.

Holy Island and the Holy Land

At the same time, Christianity was gaining acceptance in the great empire of China, thanks to the Nestorian missionary A-lo-pen. Emperor T'ai-Tsung granted 'the religion of Syria' official toleration in 638, saying, 'This teaching is helpful to all creatures and beneficial to all people,' and he instructed A-lo-pen to translate the Bible. A carving from 781 commemorates the event, along with a summary of the gospel, which describes the crucifixion: 'He hung, a brilliant sun which scattered the darkness… He rowed mercy's barge up the course of light. The souls of men he has already saved. His mighty task completed, he ascended at noonday into heaven.' Some Chinese Christianity incorporated important Buddhist ideas such as escaping desire, but after two centuries it seems to have declined, along with the T'ang dynasty (though in the thirteenth century, Marco Polo claimed there were 700,000 Christians in his region alone).

At the other end of the earth, Christianity was slowly infiltrating the English, through missionaries and royal marriages. At the same time, native Celtic Christianity, which the English invaders had driven out, started to make major inroads back into the north of England from its mission headquarters on Lindisfarne. And so, Kentish and Celtic Christianity started to run into each other.

They did not get on very well. The English church, founded by the missionary Augustine, was thoroughly European and would have no native archbishop of Canterbury until 653. The Celts, after 150 years of isolation, had a proud and magnificent culture, with – trivial as it sounds – a different date for Easter and a different style of monastic tonsure. English Roman Catholics considered Celtic practices the deviancy of 'an insignificant group of Britons and Irish at the edge of the world, pimples on the face of the earth'; the Celts considered their practices hallowed by their many missionary saints, and they considered the Roman church haughty and imperialistic. Conflict loomed.

It was hardly comparable to the conflict erupting in the east, of course. Byzantium did not know what in Allah's name had hit it. Hardly lacking in confidence, the Muslims assaulted the Byzantine and Persian empires simultaneously. Just ten years after Muhammad's death, before Christians had even grasped what Muslims were, they had taken Persia, Mesopotamia, Palestine, Syria, Armenia, Egypt and Libya.

Alexandria was fallen. Antioch was fallen. Jerusalem was someone else's holy city. The eastern empire had only just lost the west, and now it was losing the east too. How was it so easy? Byzantium and Persia had devastated each other in their recent war, so the timing was perfect. The Qu'ran offered a luxuriously earthly paradise for the fallen, while conquest offered earthly riches. With every conquered city, the Muslims' resources and faith grew, and being the soldiers of God's new revelation gave them an extraordinary passion. And Islam was not entirely alien, but one more new version of the faith of Jesus; for multitudes of Monophysites, Donatists and so on, who had suffered such persecution from Constantinople, there seemed little incentive to fight off new religious masters.

The Muslims pressed on to take what is now Afghanistan. They conquered Carthage, raided Cyprus, sunk the Byzantine navy and headed on, relentlessly and irresistibly, towards Constantinople and the heart of Christendom. The sun was going down on the Christian church.

Whitby

Unlikely as it may seem, monasticism was quite a liberating opportunity for women. Since the disappearance of prophets and apostles, there had been little religious work for them apart from being deacons, and in the seventh century, even that was taken from them. Now, though, monasticism offered women a major role in society, combining worship, leadership, study and manual work. There were even monasteries such as the great one at Whitby, Northumbria, which, having male and female divisions, was ruled by a woman, Hilda.

It was here, in 664, that the Catholic and Celtic churches met, chaired by King Oswy, to decide whose religion would rule Britain: the Celtic Eurosceptics or the Roman Catholics. The Celts argued that their ways had been followed by holy men like Columba, founder of Iona, accredited to them by God through signs and wonders. The Catholics replied (mistakenly) that Roman practices united all other churches on earth, except these few stupid and obstinate islanders. Moreover, added the Catholics, Rome was the see of St Peter, to whom Christ gave the keys of heaven.

Did he really? King Oswy asked the Celts.

Yes, they admitted, he did.

And did he give a set to Columba?

No, he did not.

'Then I shall not contradict him... otherwise when I come to the gates of heaven the keyholder may refuse to open them.' And so Britain became Roman Catholic.

With Islam ravaging the east, the Slav tribe increasingly took over the Balkans. The Christian empire of Byzantium was shrinking at a horrifying rate. However, when the Muslims arrived at Constantinople in 672, they found that the Byzantines had made a well-timed discovery: if you mix petrol, sulphur and pitch in a copper tube, you have a rather effective flame-thrower. Five years of siege followed, after which the Muslims decided to change direction. And so, by the end of the century, almost all of Christian Africa – the whole north coast – was conquered. Next in line was Europe.

2

Icons and Stirrups (700-87)

Now that God has appeared in the flesh and lived among humans, I make an image of the God who can be seen.

John of Damascus

Muslims spent the first twenty years of the eighth century taking Spain, failing to conquer Constantinople and crossing the Caucasus into what is now Russia. Soon, they were entering France.

In 722, Caliph Yazid decreed that all Christian icons in Syria be destroyed. This seems natural enough, as Islam did not allow any pictures or statues, let alone their worship, though they had generally been amazingly tolerant. What was surprising was that the Byzantine emperor, Leo, followed his lead: in 726, Leo sent soldiers onto the gateway of his palace to throw down the huge, golden image of Jesus and watch it smash; then he instructed his bishops to do the same. The patriarch denounced him, Leo's soldiers were killed by devout women, and the city rioted. There had always been a puritan stream to Christianity that hated images as unbiblical idolatry; as devotion to holy paintings, or icons, grew ever more extravagant, opposition to it had become a major movement, and now even the emperor was a convert.

At this point, Leo discovered a new problem with losing his Christian subjects to Islamic rule: he could not attack them himself. John of Damascus, enjoying the ironic protection of the iconoclastic caliph of Syria, wrote in defence of sacred art. Icons are not worshipped, he insisted, but used as powerful aids in worshipping God and as 'texts' for the illiterate. Moreover, to prefer spiritual encounters with Christ to his physical depiction is to deny his full humanity. He wrote, 'I do not worship matter, but the God of matter, who became matter for my sake, deigned to inhabit matter and saved me through matter.' Leo called a council in 730, which he persuaded to ban icons and sack the patriarch. The Pope excommunicated them, so Leo seized churches in southern Italy (which was still ruled by Byzantium, as it had been since Justinian's conquest) and tried to have the Pope assassinated. Thus the seemingly interminable debates that had dragged on over ever more miniscule differences of opinion about Christ dovetailed into a new theological war, again turning east against west and east against east.

Seven hundred years after the death of Jesus, the church seems to be on its last legs. Muslims have seized the greater part of Christendom in one century – most of Asia, except Asia Minor, and North Africa. Christian Europe hardly looks unassailable. Of course, defeating governments is not the same as winning the hearts of believers, but Islam has already been doing well on that score, and time is on its side.

Maleus and Stapes

Halfway across France, however, the Muslims met Charles Martel (literally 'The Hammer'), who had been reuniting the Franks under his own rule. He had decided that, in order to stand against the might of Islam, he had to invest in 'cataphracts', the legendary heavy-armoured cavalry of Byzantium and Persia, rarely seen in the west but one day to become the knights of the middle ages. They were hugely expensive, so to balance the defence budget, Martel commandeered masses of church land. He was vilified as a demonic church-robber, but considering that the land had been originally given to the church in political deals that seriously corrupted it, the moral outrage is not clear-cut.

He is also said to have equipped his cavalry with a new invention, stirrups, meaning they could hit people very hard without falling off their horses. The two armies met at Poitiers in 732, and this was the furthest the Muslims ever got. They retreated into Spain, the rest of Europe saved, at least for now, by horse power.

Pagan attackers from Germany also felt the Hammer's force, and in this he was aided by the British missionary monk Boniface. With papal blessing and more worldly backing from the Franks, Boniface converted several tribes, reportedly making an impression by cutting down Thor's Oak and surviving. Appointed archbishop of Germany by the Pope, Boniface established churches, sees and Benedictine monasteries. Martel's successors made him archbishop of the French church too, to reform it morally and, like Britain, realign it with Rome.

An alliance developed between the Franks and Rome, one of the most important in European history. Byzantium had retained Justinian's Italian conquests, but in 751, the Lombard tribe conquered Ravenna, the capital of Byzantine Italy. Lombards surrounded Rome and laid claim to it. Constantinople was powerless, so Pope Stephen II visited Pepin the Short, the son of Charles Martel, and dressed in penitential garb, he fell at his feet, begging him to save Rome. A deal was struck. Stephen anointed Pepin king of the Franks, and in return, Pepin drove out the Lombards, returning the land not to the Byzantine emperor but to the Pope.

Thus the Pope became the king of a 200-mile band of Italy from Ravenna down to Rome, the 'Papal State'; Byzantium lost the heart of its Italian lands to him; and the Franks gained a king, not by election, heredity or conquest, but by the decree of the bishop of Rome. A new age of papal power was dawning.

It was now that Rome started mentioning the 'Donation of Constantine', a document that it had apparently been keeping safe somewhere for 400 years. In it, Constantine grants the Pope supremacy over all churches and 'imperial power' over not only Italy but all the west. It was of course an impious forgery (though whoever says so, it warns, shall be 'burnt in the nethermost hell'); but it hoodwinked the world for 800 years, the deception that proved the rule. It is called the most successful fraud in history, but one can't help wondering how we can be so sure.

In Constantinople, meanwhile, the campaign against icons saw churches purged, while icon-painters and worshippers were imprisoned and tortured. Most Byzantine Christians were relieved when Irene, the young emperor's mother, seized power and restored icon-worship. Celebrations were muted by the fact that she deposed, blinded and then killed her son to do so.

Irene called a council of 300 bishops to Nicea in 787, which restored icons and the status quo. This proved to be the last of the seven 'ecumenical' or worldwide councils that defined the faith of the church. In theory, these are the councils where the whole church agreed, but the reality is more complicated and paradoxical. Only fifty bishops, mostly Egyptian, attended the third ecumenical council (Ephesus 431), for example, and it was opposed by Constantinople and Antioch, so 'worldwide' is something of an exaggeration; moreover, other councils that had the agreement of many more bishops at the time were not accepted by the later church as ecumenical, because their decisions were wrong.

So the church that defines its faith according to the councils has first to decide which councils are right. They are 'ecumenical' in that the worldwide church agrees they are orthodox – the disagreement of Nestorians, Monophysites, Arians et al. not counting, as they are heretical, a judgment established (in part at least) by their denial of the ecumenical councils. To talk of seven ecumenical councils is to accept Eastern Orthodox reckoning instead of that of Roman Catholics, who recognise twenty-one. The question of which councils the worldwide church agrees were orthodox divides east and west.

The person in the pew

What was Christianity like in the middle ages for the vast majority of anonymous worshippers who did not conquer or build or write? Of course, over 1,000 years and thousands of miles there were enormous variations, but there was also a great deal of common ground.

Central to all Christian experience was the calendar. The annual fasts of Lent and Advent prepared for the great feasts of Easter and Christmas and were imposed by law. Feasts, which did not require so much coercion, were dotted throughout the year, to celebrate saints' days and various occasions in the life of Christ and Mary, and these were marked by holidays and the grateful partying of those who otherwise lived in hunger, as well as by more reverent ceremonies. Traditional pagan rituals retained such appeal, however, that when the church failed to wean Christians off them, it simply stole them. The fertility rite of Robigalia, for example, became the Catholic Rogationtide, a day of prayer for the crops.

Christianity governed the arc of a lifetime. Birth, coming of age, marriage and death – each had its own sacrament. It provided the weekly rhythm of life too, with its day of rest and worship (and sport) and its fast day, both again imposed by law.

The church also dominated life in less obvious ways. It was a centre for business, clerics (from whom we get the word 'clerks') often being the only people who could write contracts. Taxes were paid there, and royal decrees and other news were broadcast from the pulpit. The churches themselves towered over the landscape, even before the Gothic creations of the eleventh century.

Where the church was still vying with paganism, a certain amount of pluralism was inevitable. But where it had triumphed, it increasingly demanded universal membership. The church was the state and the state the church; the church was the soul of the national body. Everyone was baptised into it at birth, and moral and doctrinal deviation were, in theory, punished ruthlessly; though in practice, its power was often limited. The great exception was the Jews, who, as in the days of Rome, were tolerated by the government but often hated and molested by the masses.

People inherited their parents' names because they inherited their jobs, their houses and their places in life. They were members of a community first and individuals second. They had very little concept of personal rights or freedom of religion; everyone was a part of everyone else. They depended on the prayers of the monks as much as the ploughing of the peasants and the courage of the soldiers. Heresy was treachery against the community. Demons were an everyday reality behind disease and drought, and so the remedy was as religious as the problem.

The heart of Christianity was the awesome mass. Amid incense and music, robes and gold, at an altar containing the mighty remains of a martyr, the priest would lift up the body and blood of Christ, in the form of wafer and wine, offered to God the Father as a sacrifice for their sins. The quality of the spectacle of course, like the reverent attention of the spectators, varied. Worshippers received only the wafer – a tradition stemming from the popular fear of spilling Christ's blood. If the liturgy was increasingly incomprehensible as language evolved, that probably only added to the wonder. The amount of preaching people heard declined dramatically; and when it increased again in the eleventh century, it would be largely outside church services. Many Christians may have learned more from the teaching of the artwork than from the words. And yet the stories of the saints and those from the Bible, inside church or out, were a central part of Christian life from one corner of the middle ages to the other.

3

Charlemagne (787-897)

Without peace we cannot please God.
Charlemagne

Having created a king, in the next generation, the Pope created an emperor.
Pepin's son Charles was the Franks' greatest king, so great that it became his
name: Charles the Great, or Charlemagne. A devout Christian of many
achievements, he was above all a conqueror. When he died at seventy-three,
he ruled most of what is now France, Belgium, Holland, Germany and
Austria, and much of Italy, with considerable influence beyond, leaving only
the British Isles, most of Muslim Spain and the Byzantine toe of Italy
untouched. As he imposed Roman Catholicism on his domains, he enjoyed
enthusiastic support from Rome – though his execution of 4,500 Saxons
simply because he could not find his real enemy was controversial.

His empire needed new political structures, one being a single currency of
pounds, shillings and pence, retained in Britain until 1971. (Devotees of the
pound may be interested to know that it is only a hangover from the last
European monetary union.) Another was the regional church structure from
which today's parish system evolved. He ensured that all churches shared the
same liturgy, introducing the Apostles' creed, which was largely unknown
(and unheard of in the east).

He also covered his empire in Benedictine monasteries with large estates,
often in the cities. This aided Catholic uniformity and the conversion of
remaining pagans but completely changed monasticism. Their houses
became rich and powerful, closely involved in government and training
grounds for the nobility. Monks employed peasants to do the farming that
Benedict had set them to, freeing them for more elaborate worship and wider
study. This was sell-out of Benedict's ideals, doubtless, but the advantages
were momentous. Monasteries became devoted not just to Bible study but
collecting, copying and understanding the writings of the ancients, both

Church Fathers and philosophers. Amid the cultural collapse of post-Roman Europe, the monastery became its only school and library. Charlemagne himself, for all his academic convictions, could barely read and wrote his name through a stencil – and that was more than most other kings of this era.

With western Europe now largely united in Catholicism, the church seemed to have recovered surprisingly well from its pagan conquest. But then a new pagan terror erupted from Scandinavia: the Norsemen or Vikings. In 793, they landed at the Holy Island of Lindisfarne, ransacked it and moved on. Finding holy places to be troves of poorly guarded treasures, within fifty years they had overrun most of the British Isles. Churches, monasteries and towns were ransacked. Britain's days as a Bible belt of Europe were over.

An unexpected crowning

Charlemagne and the Pope needed each other. Charlemagne protected the Papal State and broadcast Roman Catholicism; Catholicism legitimised Charlemagne's conquests and unified his realm. A question remained, however, which would plague their descendants for centuries: who rules whom? Charlemagne saw himself as ultimately responsible for all affairs in his kingdom, religion included. The Pope saw himself not only as the final spiritual authority, but as the power behind the throne and above the crown. The question is graphically, if cryptically, illustrated by Charlemagne's coronation.

Pope Leo III was unpopular in Rome, and in 799, accusing him of adultery and perjury, his enemies seized him, tried to cut out his eyes and tongue, deposed him and locked him in a monastery. He escaped and appealed to Charlemagne, who considered it his job not necessarily to restore Leo but to try him in Rome. Leo swore his innocence on the Gospels, so Charlemagne allowed him to continue as Pope. Then, two days later, Christmas Day 800, Charlemagne was praying at St Peter's tomb, when Leo burst in with his followers and crowned him Roman emperor.

What did it mean? Reading history backwards, Leo had created the Holy Roman Emperor, an institution that survived (with some ups and downs) until 1804. At the time it seemed to many that he was simply giving a new (and utterly unrealistic) name to Charlemagne's existing achievements. Looked at one way, Leo, having been humiliated by Charlemagne, was reasserting his authority over him; Charlemagne did not use the title, and his friend Einhard says he was enraged by Leo's stunt. Looked at the other way, it was not just the crowning glory on his life's work, but it allied the Pope with the Franks instead of Constantinople, which was undoubtedly Charlemagne's consistent ambition. Others, therefore, would say it was pure political theatre, a carefully rehearsed ad lib, scripted by Charlemagne.

Byzantium's response was unambiguous outrage at the presumption of Rome and the barbarian west. History nearly took an intriguing turn when Charlemagne proposed to Empress Irene: she planned to accept, until she was deposed by Byzantine officials. Politically, west ended up further from east than ever.

Charlemagne helped their theological divergence too. Neither he nor his bishops had been invited to the 787 council of Nicea that restored icons – it had not occurred to Constantinople that they would have anything intelligent to say. Snubbed, Charlemagne attacked its decrees as idolatrous and heretical, the eastern church as 'a filthy pond of hell'.

This had limited results, as western Christians accepted images more unreservedly than the east. Where he really caused trouble was with the Nicene creed. It declared that the Holy Spirit 'proceeds from the Father'; but Augustine said that the Spirit proceeds from both Father and Son, so Spanish churches had come to add the word *filioque* ('and from the Son') to the Latin creed. Charlemagne accepted this change, and so, therefore, did most of the churches of Europe. He pressed Rome to adopt it, but Leo, while accepting the theology, refused to tamper with the creed. Outside Rome, though, the west now had a different Nicene creed to the east.

Feudalism

Charlemagne's resurrected Roman empire did not last long and started disintegrating soon after his own demise. The empire was divided up between his three legitimate grandchildren. Roughly speaking, one got what would become Germany, another France and the third got the region that, even in the twentieth century, Germany and France were still fighting over.

What European kings needed were armies; what they had was land. So any man who proved a useful warrior was made a royal official – *dux* in Latin – and the king leased land to him. In return, he had to fight on horseback, with his own regiment, and pay rent/taxes in the meantime. So the *dux* leased land in turn to those lower down the pecking order, who farmed it. In return, they paid rent and fought in his regiment. That way, he had money and soldiers for the king and spare time to practise his cavalry skills.

This subletting carried on down the food chain until the whole of society was arranged into the pyramid we know as feudalism. Each man had a lord above him and lesser men below (as you can tell, women did not figure highly), including the king, whose lord was God. In time, the *duces* became dukes, the hereditary nobility of Europe, often with more real power than their king.

Viking raids spread through the west, terrorising France and coming far enough south to confront the Muslims in Spain. They were dreaded enough to grow rich on tribute, the ancient equivalent of the protection racket, and they sold European merchandise onto the Arabs and Byzantines. As Europe had little actual produce, they also kidnapped people and sold them as slaves. Christian opposition to this commerce succeeded in persuading the Vikings to restrict their operations largely to the pagan Slavs of south-east Europe, which is why every language in Europe takes its word for slaves from 'Slavs'.

While Vikings terrorised Europe from the north, the Muslims continued from the south. They took a leaf out of what we might generously call the Vikings' book and started lightning raids. In 846, they attacked Rome. Breaching the great churches of St Peter's and St Paul's, they seized all their holiest ornaments and hit the sea. In those dark days, Christian leaders desperately tried to divine why God had abandoned them, and a new prayer was added to services across Europe: 'From the fury of the Norsemen, O Lord deliver us.'

Cyril and Methodius

Now, history does not repeat itself – every event is unique; but what was happening in Constantinople was as close to a repeat as we get. Thirty-five years after icons were restored by Irene, another Emperor Leo banned them. Once again, the churches were purged, and again an empress standing in for her son restored them, in 843. This time, it was final, and Theodora's achievement is celebrated annually in the east as the Triumph of Orthodoxy.

Theodora then launched an attack on the Paulicians, a sect that had been spreading slowly and quietly from Armenia for 200 years. Keeping Manichee ideas alive, Paulicians saw God and the devil as equal powers, the soul as good and matter evil, the incarnation unthinkable. Reviving Marcion's ideas, they rejected the Old Testament and much of the New, taking their name from their preference for Paul. Theodora sent an army to demand their conversion. Because they refused, 100,000 Paulicians were hanged, drowned or crucified, the rest fleeing to Islamic lands where they joined the Muslims' attack on Byzantium – quite a shot in the foot for the empire.

Soon afterwards, Byzantium met the Vikings, who had colonised the lands of the northern Slavs in Russia, and in 860, led them on a terrifying raid of pillage, destruction and kidnap on Constantinople. The Slav tribes – Russians, Bulgarians and Moravians – had long been a menace, along with the Khazars, and Orthodox attempts to convert any of them had seen little success: the Russians ignored their missionaries, and embarrassingly, the Khazars, after they had left, converted to Judaism. Even worse than these Byzantine failures, the west seemed likely to win the Slavs instead – a bleaker prospect than paganism, these days. Frankish Germany controlled Moravia and now formed an alliance with the Bulgarians, who were planning to embrace western Christianity. But to Constantinople's delight, the Moravians felt hemmed in by Bulgaria and Germany, and so turned to Constantinople, asking for missionaries to convert them to Byzantine Christianity. Constantinople sent the brothers Cyril and Methodius, who had had such an impact on the Khazars. Then in 863, the Byzantines moved in on Bulgaria and, shunning undue evangelistic subtlety, stormed the capital and forcibly baptised Boris.

The year 863 was a memorable one for Byzantium. As well as poaching Bulgaria from under Rome's nose, they routed their Muslim (and Paulician) enemies, launching a campaign of re-conquest, and they founded the University of Constantinople, launching a cultural renaissance. Less happily, the patriarch Photius was excommunicated by Rome: his predecessor Ignatius had been unconstitutionally deposed, and Constantinople had refused to buy Rome's acquiescence. The emperor protested the excommunication, only to be told, 'The first see cannot be judged by anyone... I cannot begin to see how a ruler of human affairs could presume to judge those who are in charge of divine affairs.' So in 867, Photius excommunicated the Pope. The schism only lasted two years, because Photius was himself overthrown, but Rome and Constantinople seemed to be becoming natural enemies.

A cold war was developing over eastern Europe between the churches of east and west, which gave the Slavs all the more chance to play them off against each other. King Boris asked Photius to appoint a patriarch for the Bulgarian church, and when he was refused such an honour, turned to Rome. The Pope seemed amenable, so Boris expelled all Byzantine missionaries and swore allegiance to Rome. When Rome failed to provide a patriarch, he did a deal with Constantinople instead, returning to the fold for the price of a patriarch – the first new one since Constantinople, and the only other outside Muslim territory.

Meanwhile, Cyril and Methodius were getting on well in Moravia. Their first priority was to get the Slavs Bibles and liturgy in their own language. This was a challenge, as Slavonic was not a written language, so they invented what became called Cyrillic script. Cyril adapted the Greek alphabet to fit, and it ended up as what we would recognise today as the Russian alphabet.

But Moravia was still under German rule, and predictably the Germans resented this Byzantine mission. They condemned the religion of Cyril and Methodius on two grounds: it was not in Latin, like Catholicism; and they had omitted the words 'and the Son' from the creed. Cyril and Methodius of course explained that the *filioque* clause was a western addition to the original creed, and that Latin was not the only or even the original language of the liturgy and scriptures; that communicating with people in language they could understand was what mattered, holiness lying in the meaning not the sound of the words.

Cyril's solution to this obstruction seems somehow both naive and shrewd. Oblivious to the political tensions between Rome and Constantinople, he asked the Pope to send the brothers as his own missionaries to do the same job in the same place. The Pope was delighted with their work, and did so. Cyril died during their visit to Rome, but Methodius was made archbishop of Moravia. And yet still the Germans hindered everything he did, and when he died, they expelled his followers, selling some into slavery. The Pope bowed to the Germans and banned all services in Slavonic, so the disciples of Cyril and Methodius left for other Slav regions, taking their Slavonic liturgy, Bibles and alphabet with them. Slavonic is still used in Orthodox services today, though few people now understand a word of it.

Viking settlement

Western Europe was feeling cornered. Alfred the Great ruled south-west England and fought to stop the country being reclaimed by paganism now that the Vikings controlled it. As a result of his victories, they drew a line from London to Anglesey, and the Vikings got the north. Their king also converted to Christianity. Elsewhere, the news was less good for the church. The Arabs conquered Sicily, making them even more threatening to southern Europe, and a new tribe from Asia, the Hungarians, joined in the attacks on Germany.

Having carved up England, the Vikings could now concentrate on assaulting France. In 911, the French king followed Alfred's example and cut the map up with them, the Vikings getting a sizeable chunk of northern France in return for peace, cooperation and conversion. As in England, they proved far less formidable as conquerors than as raiders; they just melted in. They took not only the religion but the language and culture of their new home, and soon they were not Vikings any more. After a century, the Norsemen were the Normans.

4

A Light in the Darkness
(897-1000)

Where is it written that the priests of God throughout the earth should
be subject to monsters who know nothing of God or anything else?
The council of Lyons

In 897, Pope Formosus stood trial for perjury, covetousness and unlawful
promotion. The unusual aspect of the proceedings was not so much his
innocence as the fact that he was nine months dead. Taking to uncommon
lengths the idea that revenge is best served cold, his successor and bitter
enemy Stephen VI had him dug up and enthroned in full regalia, then
screamed at him to answer the charges. When Formosus exercised his right
to silence, he was condemned, stripped, deprived of his fingers of blessing
and thrown into the Tiber.

It was a bizarre new low for the interminable brawls of church politics, but
the decline continued. Stephen was strangled that same year, after Formosus's
corpse resurfaced and started performing miracles. His successor lasted four
months, the next, twenty days. In 904, Sergius III had to kill two rival popes
to secure the throne, from where he ruled his bishops with terror tactics. He
cancelled all ordinations performed by Formosus (and therefore, by those he
had ordained and so on), reducing the church to chaos. His regime was
possible because he had the support of Rome's new warrior lord,
Theophylact, and his even more powerful wife, Theodora. Sergius ruled by
and according to their will, and had a child by their 15-year-old daughter,
Marozia.

The eastern church was divided between followers of Photius and his
predecessor Ignatius for many years after their deaths. As Photius stood for
political pragmatism and Ignatius for principled piety, it is no surprise that the
Photians remained in power. But this changed when Emperor Leo the Wise

needed a new wife, his fourth. Even though the other three had widowed him, the eastern church frowned on remarriage: a second union was tolerable, a fourth unthinkable. The Photian patriarch would probably have allowed it anyway, but he was outmanoeuvred by the astute, extremist leader of the Ignatians, who denounced it.

But Emperor Leo had a delightful candidate lined up for empress and was not about to bow to ecclesiastical scruples, so he devised a rather cunning plan. He offered the Ignatians the improbable prospect of coming into power if they approved his marriage; and knowing they would need an excuse for so radically reinterpreting their principles, he asked Pope Sergius to rule on the question. The Pope was delighted to be dictating to the bishop of Constantinople, and he sanctioned the marriage; and in 907, a new Ignatian patriarch, professing obedience to Rome, conducted it. Leo's dynasty was saved and continued for another 150 years.

The Cluny revival

With the western church hierarchy at its most degenerately wretched so far, an extraordinary spiritual rebirth broke out. Constantly pounded by Vikings and Muslims, Europe was disintegrating, political power largely in the hands of local lords like Theophylact who appointed bishops and abbots as feudal underlings. But not all were like Theophylact. Duke William of Aquitaine founded a new monastery in 910, to recapture the ideals of Benedict's original rule, donating his favourite hunting lodge at Cluny. Seeking expert monastic advice, he concluded that what had most compromised monasteries was political interference and entanglements, so his grand innovation was to give the monks complete freedom to choose their leaders. Electing their holiest and most inspiring men, they returned to the full vigour and rigour of Benedict's rulebook for the first time in many years. Their charter called down on anyone who tried to impose an abbot on them some of the most colourful curses in Christian history, including somehow being both eaten alive by vermin and swallowed bodily into hell. Under a succession of inspirational leaders, Cluny became a beacon: many monasteries were reformed on the same lines and they inspired a religious revival among ordinary people.

Back in the darkness, Rome was still being raided by offshore Muslims, until, in 915, a coalition of Italian rulers finally saw them off. At the head of the Roman army was Pope John X, another appointment of Theodora, of whom he was an extremely close acquaintance. When she died, her daughter Marozia took over the city and had Pope John suffocated with a pillow. Historians have traditionally called the rules of Theodora and Marozia the 'pornocracy', though this horror of sexual licence is not generally extended to male rulers who acted the same way.

The next two popes were old men, appointed by Marozia as stopgaps while her son grew old enough to take the office. (This was the boy that Sergius had fathered when Marozia was fifteen.) In 931, the boy became Pope John XI; but he, along with Marozia and her third husband, was overthrown by a Roman mob led by one of Marozia's other sons, Alberic, a rather more devout warlord. Alberic appointed a series of reforming popes who worked with the abbots of Cluny to restore their ideals into Roman religious life.

The light of Cluny reached England too, catching the imagination of successive kings, who raised its greatest English advocate, Dunstan (a musician, craftsman, artist and theologian as well as a reformer), to abbot of Glastonbury and then archbishop of Canterbury. Dunstan had to fight the nobility for his reforms, but with friends in places as high as the throne, he triumphed.

The root problem that remained for the Christian west was its political disintegration, which left church and people at the mercy of local warlords. Hope came from an unlikely source – being simultaneously attacked by Hungarians, Vikings and Slavs. In response, the Germans elected Henry the Fowler as king for all Germany, reviving Charlemagne's holy reincarnation of the Roman emperor. He, followed by his son Otto, drove off the invaders, and as God's kings, they filled bishoprics and abbacies with their own men. Otto was a devout Catholic and gave the jobs to devout Catholics; but being in a precarious political position, he made sure they were also his loyal agents. So a clash of ideologies was brewing: the Cluny movement was about reformation through complete independence from the state; Otto was trying to achieve the same ends by the opposite means, a holy autocracy.

To consolidate his position, Otto needed to be crowned emperor by the Pope, like Charlemagne. But the Pope was deep under the control of Alberic, who felt that if anyone should be the new Roman emperor it was himself, so Otto's chance did not come until Alberic died in 954. At the last minute, Alberic overturned all his reforms by having his 17-year-old illegitimate son made Pope – John XII, the worst yet. The Cluny movement was making people ever less tolerant of debauchery in holy places, but blissfully unconcerned about what anyone was tolerant of, John opened a brothel in the papal palace and sexually assaulted visitors to his church. He is also reported to have consecrated a bishop in a stable and castrated another who criticised him. He considered the offerings of pilgrims his personal income and paid his lovers with church plate.

In 958, he went on a foray to add some Italian districts to the Papal State, but it was a disaster, and soon the Lombards were invading the state. John appealed to Otto. Otto defeated the Lombards, married their queen and added them to his kingdom, also extending the Papal State to two-thirds of Italy. In return, John crowned him Holy Roman Emperor at Candlemas 962. Otto claimed a veto over papal elections and ultimate rule over the Papal State, requiring each new pope to swear allegiance to him.

When John realised what he had let himself in for, he tried to have Otto overthrown by the Lombards that Otto had just rescued him from. When that failed he found Otto marching on Rome, so, filling his bags with ecclesiastical gold, John fled. Otto called a council and had John replaced. But Rome was not happy about a German emperor interfering with the papacy, and overthrew the new Pope, restoring John. Once again Otto drove John out, who died a month later in bed (not his own) of a stroke, in his mid-twenties. Appropriately enough, it was John (previously known as Octavian) who started the tradition of popes assuming a saintly pseudonym when they are elected, dissociating one's private frailties from the holy office.

Some great Byzantine marriages

The Russian Viking leader Vladimir I was looking into Christianity. His grandmother had converted, but his father rejected the faith on the grounds that everyone would laugh at him if he got baptised. As the story goes, he investigated Roman Christianity, Islam and Judaism, and he turned his nose up at them all. Finally, he sent his comparative religions experts to a service in Constantinople, where they were so overcome by its beauty, they came home saying, 'In that place, God lives among men.'

His eventual decision was somewhat more political. The Byzantine emperor Basil, desperately needed aid against a rebel army on the point of seizing Constantinople; Vladimir offered deliverance if he could marry the emperor's sister. It was an outrageous suggestion, Vladimir being a pagan barbarian with four wives and a good 800 concubines, and no Byzantine royal having ever married a foreigner; but it was do or die. Basil agreed, on the condition that Vladimir got baptised, which he did in 988. Taking his conversion seriously, he dismissed his other women, threw the biggest idol in the country off the top of a hill and filled Russia with churches and monasteries – eastern-style, with Slavonic liturgy and scriptures, which is how Russia got its alphabet. He organised a social-welfare system, and he abolished torture, mutilation and the death penalty.

Otto's grandson, Otto III, became emperor at the age of three but developed big ambitions. He wanted to reunite the western and eastern empires, combining the best of both worlds: the holy grandeur, culture and wealth of Constantinople on the one hand, and on the other, the fact that it would be ruled by him, with the Pope by his side – or more precisely, at his heel. So once he was fifteen, Otto asked to marry a niece of the childless Byzantine emperor Basil, sending one of his archbishops, John Philagathos, to negotiate. Philagathos got on well, and Byzantine envoys returned to Rome with him to continue talks in 997. But young Otto was back in Germany, so a leading lord of Rome took the chance to spoil his plans by seizing the city and throwing the envoys into gaol. The Pope called on Otto to come and deliver them, but Otto replied, surreally, that Rome was too hot for him in the summer. The Romans overthrew the Pope and replaced him with none other than Otto's envoy, Philagathos. That winter, Otto finally descended on Rome, restoring the original Pope and measuring out ample vengeance. Philagathos, on the Pope's orders, lost his hands, ears, eyes, nose and tongue, and he was paraded backwards on a mule to the monastery where he survived for fifteen years. Despite everything, plans for the marriage of east and west went ahead, but they failed because Otto died as his bride was on the way to the wedding.

There was a new theologian in Byzantium. In fact that is what he is called – Simeon the New Theologian. The title recognises not so much the absence of new ideas in the east as his exceptional brilliance: the only other people that the eastern church calls 'theologian' – one qualified to talk about God – are Gregory Nazianzus and the apostle John. Like many of the best theologians, he was condemned as a heretic, but posterity disagrees. He was certainly a dissident, though. He had little time for the dry, rationalistic theology that dominated Byzantium; for Simeon, Christianity was about a personal experience of God – 'to become gods by knowledge, experience and contemplation'. He considered any rational understanding of God impossible, but his writings explore his powerful, profound, mystical experiences of God that offer a knowledge deeper than understanding, knowledge that transforms us into what God is.

For this reason, he was also critical of the state of the church, where people were accepted as Christians on the strength of their baptism and orthodoxy, however sinful their lives. 'Among thousands and tens of thousands you will hardly find one who is a Christian in both word and deed.' To be a Christian, he insisted, means not just belief but being born again, baptism not just in water but in the Holy Spirit.

The millennium

Late on New Year's Eve 999, a large crowd assembles outside the papal palace. For once, they come not to overthrow the Pope but to celebrate the millennium and await the end of the world – assuming that the 1,000-year rule of the saints, talked of in the book of Revelation, has been fulfilled in the church, and that the day of judgment will start here. When midnight comes, and the millennium proves inexplicably unapocalyptic, the Pope blesses them and sends them home to continue waiting.

How do things look at this halfway point in our story? In this volatile, brutish world, the church is the most permanent thing people know. The kings of Europe rule over churches and monasteries that are far older than their very kingdoms. Maybe this is why they are so set on being part of the Roman empire: it is the only way to be as old as the church.

Having been besieged and terrorised for centuries by non-Christian tribes, the church has each time managed to bless its enemies by converting them, Muslims being the one great exception; and so Christian kings increasingly fight each other. Conflict is growing between the Pope and the western emperor about who rules the church, and westerners clash with the east over eastern Europe. The latter brings into focus their religious differences: the west use unleavened bread in the eucharist, east do not; the east let their clergy keep wives, the west try to stop them; the west have changed the Nicene creed, the east have not; the Pope claims to rule the whole church single-handedly, the east disagree.

It takes a certain effort to see much more to the recent story of the church than a nauseating deluge of murder, butchery, robbery and amoral political machination. To be fair, the reality of tenth-century life is brutal, insecure and anarchic in ways hard for us to comprehend, let alone judge. Moreover, the moral decrepitude of the western church is not merely tolerated by its members: kings and emperors have appointed reforming bishops and popes, and the Cluny movement has purged monasteries and churches, popularly reviving the idea that Christianity is about more than washing babies and speaking Latin. The campaign now moves on to tackle two great offences: the decline of clerical celibacy and the rise of simony. (This odd word means the sin of paying money in exchange for the ability to offer the gift of the Holy Spirit; and therefore, more usefully, the buying of bishoprics. When, in the book of Acts, Simon Magus offered Peter silver in return for this power, he unwittingly gave his name to the way most medieval bishops achieved office.) One main spiritual outlet for keen laypeople is pilgrimage to see relics. Consequently, the market in holy bones is starting to become both lucrative and somewhat ludicrous. The number of limbs left by certain saints will eventually become nothing short of nightmarish.

In the midst of this new idealism, the papacy sticks out like a spare thumb. The servant of the servants of the Lord has become the king of much of Italy, and now Rome has slipped back into the pocket of the local warlord. The current Pope paid a fortune for the job, without having been so much as a priest beforehand. When he dies, his nephew will become Pope Benedict IX, reportedly at the age of eleven, and go on to provoke a civil war in Rome due to people's disgust at his violence, drunkenness and sex offences.

The prospects for a decent papacy would seem dim. But then so would prospects for all-out war between pope and emperor, and for Roman Catholicism and Eastern Orthodoxy to become separate religions. You just never know what's around the corner.

5

The Pope's Revolution

(1000–84)

The quarrels of popes and kings, with wars or pestilences, in every page; the men so good for nothing and hardly any women at all.
Jane Austen

The drive for reformation moved up a gear when the famously pious Henry III became the western emperor, with a mission from God to clean up the church. He came to Rome to be crowned in 1046, and he could not believe what he saw: the rebels had replaced Pope Benedict; Benedict had deposed his replacement, and then, for a massive bribe (and an appealing marriage) stepped down in favour of a third contender. Later, his family decided he wanted the job back. Henry deposed the lot of them for simony (not caring that one was a reformer) and appointed a German – a forceful reforming Pope, Leo IX. (Benedict, we are told by a contemporary, was turned into a monster, half-bear, half-donkey, and left to roam the earth until the last judgment.)

First of all, Pope Leo got his own house in order, deposing simoniacal bishops and demanding penance of those knowingly ordained by them. He imported foreign cardinals – the clergy of the churches in Rome who worked as the Pope's staff and elected his successor. Drawing in some of the greatest and most zealous legal minds of the church, he helped to rescue the papacy from local politics, making Rome an international church, full of reformers.

He also took the unprecedented step of taking the papacy on tour, preaching against simony and unchastity in Italy, France and Germany and sacking compromised bishops. To give his message clout, he naturally made great claims for his authority as the mouthpiece of St Peter and supreme ruler of the church on earth. There was nothing new about such ideas in themselves, but Leo was, for once, giving them some substance, acting like a genuine head of the church throughout the nations.

The great divorce

What was good for the western church, however, was catastrophic for the worldwide church. A militant, intolerant pope with international outlook and global pretensions was just what was needed to take the western churches in hand, but hardly ideal for handling disputes with Byzantium. And, unluckily, Leo's reign coincided with that of an equally brash militant in Constantinople. Patriarch Michael Cerularius hated Rome's claim to supremacy and was determined to stamp his own rule on the eastern churches. He started by not writing a letter. For centuries, every patriarch of Constantinople had begun his reign by writing to Rome to assure them of his orthodoxy, but Michael was not the man for such humble pleasantries.

Meanwhile, the Normans still had enough Viking left in them to invade southern Italy; and since both Rome and Byzantium had territory and churches there, the Normans achieved what nothing else could: Rome and Byzantium united to drive them out. Or the Pope and the Byzantine emperor united – Patriarch Michael would have none of it. In fact, when he heard that the Normans – with papal approval – were imposing western Christianity (unleavened bread, the *filioque* and so on) on the Byzantine churches in Italy, he retaliated by telling Roman churches in Constantinople to convert to eastern rites, and when they refused, he closed them down.

The military alliance between Rome and Constantinople went ahead without Michael's blessing. The western emperor was not interested in it either, so in 1053, Pope Leo gathered an army and took it off to join the Byzantine emperor in battle against the Normans. Unfortunately, the battle started before the Byzantines got there, so the Romans were pulverised, and the Normans captured the Pope.

While in chains, Pope Leo got a letter from the patriarch of Bulgaria, obviously on Michael's orders, disdainfully condemning western traditions like unleavened bread as 'Jewish'. Before Leo could reply, however, he received a letter from Michael himself, unexpectedly offering friendship, toleration and prayers for unity – presumably persuaded by those who still wanted to liberate Byzantine Italy. But Pope Leo was bitter, ill, in prison and being advised by one of his new cardinals, the vitriolic, bigoted Humbert of Silva Candida. Leo rejected the truce. Humbert wrote belligerent and libellous letters from Leo to Patriarch Michael and the Byzantine emperor, which he delivered to them by hand. 'What an evil piece of arrogance!' he wrote of Michael's opposition to Roman rites. 'You put your mouth in heaven, while your tongue, running through the world, strives... to subvert the ancient faith.'

Coming to Constantinople in 1054, Humbert and the two other legates with him acted with remarkable offensiveness, until they heard that Pope Leo had died. This was their cue to go home, but instead they toured the city denouncing its heresies until they were the most hated celebrities in Constantinople. When a monk published a respectful riposte to the letter to Patriarch Michael, Humbert replied that he was a Muslim pimp. The patriarch refused even to recognise their presence.

Finally, at three o'clock on Saturday 16 July, the ex-papal representatives went into Hagia Sophia during eucharist, and walked up to the altar. Humbert had an ill-informed decree in his hand, in which Pope Leo listed the supposed evils defended by Patriarch Michael, excommunicating him, his followers and, for good measure, the devil. He threw it on the altar and left for Rome. Michael of course replied by excommunicating them.

And so the tensions between Roman Catholicism and Eastern Orthodoxy passed the breaking point, and they finally fell apart. Or so it would look in retrospect. In fact, there seemed nothing final about it at the time. Only a handful of people on either side had officially been excommunicated – even overlooking the fact that, after Leo's death, Humbert was acting purely on his own authority, which was none at all. Everyone assumed it would all be cleared up one way or another – after all, Rome and Constantinople had excommunicated each other before and been reconciled soon enough. But this time there would be no reconciliation.

The papal revolution

The western emperor, Henry III, just had time to appoint a replacement for Pope Leo before he died, leaving his five-year-old son, Henry IV, on the throne. When this Pope died after two years, replacing him was a contest between the reforming cardinals in Rome, the Italian nobility and the advisers of a child emperor in Germany. It was a reformer who got elected and fortunately one who was liked by all parties. Fine; but, wondered the reformers, what would happen when they disagreed, and when the emperor became stronger? Why should their choice of a holy leader of vision be compromised with German political interests?

So Humbert set his unique diplomatic gifts to sorting out the problem of authority between pope and emperor. With the empire somewhat out of action, he took up his pen and ambushed it. *Three Books Against the Simoniacs* repeated the familiar arguments against simony and in favour of celibacy and papal supremacy; but he ended with something far from familiar. Emperors, kings and nobles, he argued, have no authority to appoint popes or bishops. The priesthood 'excels and commands' royalty, just as the soul does the body. For emperors to choose bishops and for the church to rubber-stamp their decision is exactly upside-down; it is not only a sin but invalid: any 'bishop' so appointed (which included an awful lot of them) is an impostor.

It was a manifesto for revolution. It overturned – on paper – the entire machinery of the church since Constantine. The emperor was expelled from his role as overseer of the church. But in the year of its publication, the Pope died and was replaced in an aristocratic coup, the reformers fleeing Rome for their lives. However, they returned with the army of a French duke, overthrew the impostor and duly elected Pope Nicholas II. He put Humbert's proposed revolution into law, restricting papal elections to cardinals alone and forbidding any layperson to appoint priests, from the pope down.

It was still only a theoretical revolution, though. The reformers had the will, but they needed a way; and it was provided, oddly enough, by the Norman conquerors that Rome had failed to kick out of the foot of Italy. Their ruler, Robert Guiscard, was keen for the Pope to recognise his kingdom, and cannily, Nicholas saw in this a way to turn them from invaders into henchmen. He made Guiscard duke of these lands, as a feudal vassal of the Pope, granting him legitimacy (as well as making himself their king). In return, if anyone tried to overturn the appointment of the cardinals by force, Guiscard would prove his loyalty with superior force. (This partnership between Rome and the Normans is also what persuaded the Pope to lend his backing to the Norman invasion of England in 1066.) The papacy now had the military power to assert its independence.

Turks

The east was now in crisis due to the appearance of the Turks. This was yet another tribe from the vast northern plains that produced all the barbarians in this story, but they had long been kept there by the Arabs of Baghdad. After

400 years, however, the Arab empire was in decline; and so, converting to Islam, the Turks started to take it over.

The Turks had no sights set on Constantinople, but as they made their way across Arab lands, fighting continually broke out against the Christians. They conquered Byzantine Armenia, the world's first Christian kingdom, killing hundreds of thousands according to the chronicler: 'babies [were] smashed mercilessly against the rocks, venerable old men degraded in public squares, noble virgins dishonoured and carried off'. 'I tried to find a street where I would not have to walk over corpses,' says a Muslim writer, 'but it proved impossible.' Finally, the eastern emperor mustered the full might of Byzantium and went to see off the Turks. The result was the greatest defeat in 700 years of Byzantine history: at Manzikert in 1071, the imperial army was destroyed. Hordes of Turks charged into Asia Minor and started turning it into Turkey.

Hildebrand versus Henry IV

Back in the west, Emperor Henry IV came of age and set about reclaiming his empire from the German nobility. At the same time, the last and greatest of Leo IX's reforming cardinals became Pope Gregory VII, though, perhaps uniquely, he is better known by his birth name, Hildebrand.

An epic battle was brewing, and in 1075, Hildebrand staked out his ground, decreeing that if any lay ruler appointed a bishop, abbot or priest, then both parties were automatically excommunicated. Then came his *Papal Dictats*, the most powerful statement of papal authority yet heard: 'the Pope may absolve subjects of obedience to unjust men'; 'he may depose emperors'; 'only the Pope may use the imperial insignia'; 'he alone may call ecumenical councils'; 'the Roman church has never erred nor ever shall to all eternity'; 'every duly ordained Pope undoubtedly becomes a saint'.

Henry's reply was to appoint a new bishop of Milan. Hildebrand protested and threatened, but Henry's bishops were his vital power base against the nobility, and there was simply no way he could rule without choosing them himself. So he and his bishops declared Hildebrand unpoped:

> Henry, king not through usurpation but through the holy ordination
> of God, to Hildebrand, now not pope but false monk:...

You have left no part of the church untouched that you could
bring into confusion... You have trodden [the priesthood] underfoot
like slaves who never know what their lord will do next... You dared
to threaten to take the crown from me – as if I received it from you...
Give up the apostolic see you have usurped... Descend! Descend!

In response, Hildebrand excommunicated and deposed Henry, forbidding his
subjects to obey him. This turned out to be a more substantial gesture than
Henry's: German nobles were delighted to rise against the emperor, and even
bishops felt bound to defect. The nobles invited the Pope to a council in
Germany to judge Henry and restore order, so he set off.

Dangerously beleaguered, Henry did the very thing Hildebrand had
constantly demanded and probably the last thing he expected: he repented.
Henry met him where he was staying, halfway to Germany, standing barefoot
in the snow, pleading repentance. For three days, Hildebrand left him
standing at the castle door, but in fact, Hildebrand was cornered. As a pastor,
his duty to readmit penitents was inescapable – as his companion, the Abbot
of Cluny, urged – and Henry was completely fulfilling his demands.
Hildebrand could perhaps have postponed a decision until the council, but
after all his proclamations of absolute power, why would he need a council to
decide the case? Hildebrand absolved Henry and readmitted him to the
church, his one inclemency being to postpone a decision on reinstating him
as emperor.

It hardly mattered. Henry's bishops returned to the fold, while the nobles
felt betrayed by Hildebrand and chose a new emperor without consulting
him. A horrendous war between the two emperors engulfed Germany, and
when, after three years' deliberation, Hildebrand – who was widely blamed
for the bloodshed – again declared against Henry, it was without any of the
authority he had wielded the first time. Within months, Henry had
triumphed, and his bishops again declared Hildebrand deposed and elected
a replacement Pope. In 1081, Henry marched on Rome, and after a three-year
siege, he took the city and enthroned his Pope, who in turn crowned him
Holy Roman Emperor.

Where was the Pope's Norman protector while this was going on? Being
an Italian duke and papal vassal did not content Robert Guiscard: he also
wanted to be Byzantine emperor and was currently leading a successful
invasion of Byzantine Greece. By the time he made it to Rome in 1084, Henry

had got all he wanted, and left without a fight. Guiscard found Rome now trying to repel him as an invader, and so he somewhat exceeded his papal remit by burning and looting the city.

Rome no longer wanted Hildebrand either, so Guiscard took him away. 'I have loved justice and hated evil – and so I die in exile.' Whether that epitaph tells the whole story is open to question, but the grand irony is that for all Pope Gregory VII's astronomical ambition, his fall came not through imperial hubris but from a pastoral act of forgiveness to a humbled enemy.

The contest between pope and emperor – and between pope and pope – dragged on for many years, but compromise was inescapable. An episcopal power base was essential to imperial rule; so unless the pope was going to be Holy Roman Emperor himself, he had to allow the emperor considerable freedom in appointing bishops. On the other hand, after the political and moral authority grasped by Hildebrand at his height, the papacy could not be expected to return to the squalid, impotent obscurity of recent centuries. The kings of Europe had to face the fact that the popes were finally beginning to wield the authority they had always claimed to have.

In fact, with the shrinking empire of Byzantium fighting for its survival against Turks, Normans and pagans, perhaps the time was ripe for Roman Catholic Europe to come into its own as the mainland of Christendom. And so the stage is set for the most extraordinary outbreak of psychotic hooliganism ever to wear the cross of Christ.

6

Onward Christian Soldiers
(1084–99)

> Let those who were brigands become soldiers of Christ!
> *Pope Urban II*

It was all Hildebrand's idea. With Islamic forces overrunning Asia Minor, he would gather the armies of the west, united under his own command, reconquer the lost territory and reunite Christendom. As it turned out, he was hardly a force for unity; and so the dream slept.

Anselm and the rebirth of learning

There is a new mood abroad in Christian Europe. After 700 years of fighting for survival, it has outlived the barbarian kingdoms and is now even driving back the Muslims. The Pope calls it a holy war. New agricultural methods raise populations out of the grinding poverty of the dark ages. Trade, cities and schools grow.

New religious movements multiply. For those who feel that Cluny has become part of the establishment, the first Carthusian monastery, where monks take vows of silence, is founded in France in 1084. The Cistercians, who have no possessions, minimal food, hard labour and a fire only on Christmas Day, soon follow. Freelance preachers start wandering the land, like Robert of Arbrissel, who wears rags, no shoes and has long hair, calling people to a life of apostolic poverty – reflecting a growing belief that one does not need monastic vows and seclusion to live a life of radical holiness.

Theology seems to be coming back to life. The first controversy in this new age is about the eucharist. Berengar, the head of the university school at Tours, challenges the popular idea that the bread and wine change into the actual body and blood of Jesus. There is only a real change if we can observe the difference with our senses. That is how we know what is true.

Opposing him is Lanfranc of Normandy. Human observation is limited and fallible, he observes, while the truth revealed by God through the church is perfect and infallible. Trusting the authority and tradition of the church is therefore a more reliable way of knowing what is true than trusting one's own senses. Rome agrees with Lanfranc.

The first great theologian of the age was Anselm, monk, teacher and archbishop of Canterbury, who fought successive kings in the tradition of Hildebrand. On the question of independent reason versus Catholic tradition, he took a middle line: he entirely accepted the truth revealed through the church, but he also held that independent reason will come to the same conclusions. His books put God's revelation to one side and attempt to prove Christian beliefs, from the existence of God to the perpetual virginity of Mary, by logic alone.

His proof of God proved extremely influential. Defining God as the greatest thing imaginable, he argued that what exists must be greater than what does not, so God must by definition exist in order to be the greatest thing imaginable. Such condensation may not do Anselm's argument any favours, but the impression of its being a philosophical conjuring trick is not, perhaps, completely unfair.

Just as influential was Anselm's explanation of the cross. The traditional understanding was that Satan held the human race captive and Jesus' blood paid the ransom. Anselm dismissed this: since Satan stole humankind from God, God could justly reclaim us by mere force. Our real problem is not the devil but God. As the ultimate feudal lord, we owe him perfect service and obedience, and we have failed to give it. He cannot overlook this dishonour – that would be to treat good and evil as one and to tarnish his dignity. Reparation must be made. But what? 'If I owed him myself and everything I do before I sinned, then after sinning I have nothing with which to pay.' Only God is in a position to make reparation; 'but only man ought to, or man has not made satisfaction'. Thankfully, Christ is both human and divine, so his self-sacrifice is offered by a human on behalf of humanity, and yet has the divine worth needed to appease God. There have certainly been other theories of the atonement, but Anselm's has proved (with some modifications) by far the most widely accepted. However, the question remains whether it makes as much sense outside feudal society.

The people's crusade

It has been a long time since we heard from Jerusalem. Since AD 70, its influence over the development of the church has been on a par with that of the Isle of Wight. But it was also the greatest pilgrim destination, and pilgrimages reached an unprecedented peak of popularity in the eleventh century, until the Turkish conquest of the city and much of the route. Unlike the respectfully tolerant Arabs, the Turks made pilgrimage impossible.

In 1095, the Byzantine emperor appealed to Pope Urban II, who was trying to mend their fences, for soldiers to help him recover Asia Minor. Urban contemplated driving back Islam, championing the pilgrims and reclaiming the eastern church, and he agreed. The emperor had no idea what he was unleashing; but then neither did the Pope.

Urban announced the crusade in a field in France – it was supposed to be in Clermont cathedral, but the expectant crowds were too great. He painted a deliciously glamorous mission, part heroic liberation, part holy war, part pilgrimage. He called on Christians to stop their wicked wars against one another and unite in one that was not only permissible, but would, if they fell, send them straight to heaven. They would wear a red cross and continue to the legendary city of Jerusalem.

'It is God's will!' cried the ecstatic crowd, and hundreds surged forward to take the vow. Urban then toured France enlisting the nobility. That was how feudal warfare worked, not with individual recruits but by lords mobilising the forces on their lands. But the vision proved more contagious than Urban had bargained for. Peter the Hermit was a permanently muddy wandering preacher who rode a donkey and ate nothing but fish. His electrifying sermons throughout France and Germany sold the crusade to ordinary peasants, who heard that he carried a letter from God promising certain victory and paradise on earth. Jerusalem fever gripped Europe; and while the official crusade was still being organised, 40,000 men, women and children followed Peter eastwards.

Smaller mobs followed, led by less reliable visionaries, including, we are told, a prophetic goose. Some took detours and massacred hundreds of Jews throughout the Holy Roman Empire. 'Why did the heavens not grow dark and the stars not withdraw their brightness...' demanded a Jewish chronicler in Mainz, 'when on one day, on the third of Siwan, a Tuesday, 1,100 souls were killed, including many children and babies who had never sinned?' The bishops who tried to shelter Jews were attacked too. Alas, these holy warriors got no further than Hungary, where the king proved unsympathetic to their methods and had them all killed.

Peter's crusade reached the Byzantine empire, but he had completely lost control. They killed 4,000 by rioting in Hungary, and they ransacked and pillaged Belgrade. Constantinople was bewildered and appalled to see them: they had expected mercenaries, led by a lord, sent by the Pope; instead they got a lawless mob, led by a filthy monk and sent by God. The emperor directed them across to Asia Minor to wait for their betters, but impatient to see God's enemies crushed beneath their feet, they marched into Turkish territory bearing palms and crosses. They raided Nicea and tortured, robbed and killed the locals, roasting their babies on spits. They showed little grasp of ethnographical subtleties here as, despite being ruled by Turks, the Niceans were in fact Christians. The Turks then ambushed the crusaders and killed the lot of them.

The official crusade

The official crusade was less colourful but made up for it by actually achieving something. As each contingent arrived at Constantinople in 1097, the emperor shipped it over to Asia Minor to besiege Nicea. Then, just as the Turkish defenders were giving up, the emperor's own men slipped into the city at night and persuaded them to surrender to Byzantium instead of to the westerners. The first conquest of the crusade had gone to the emperor after all, and he would not even let the crusaders loot it.

It took four months to reach Antioch, through scorching heat, ambushes and land devastated by retreating Turks. Some also took a detour to conquer Edessa – not a strictly legitimate target for the crusade as it already belonged to Byzantium. Antioch was a massive, impregnable city with an excellent water supply; there were not even enough crusaders to surround it. They started the siege heartily, catapulting a shower of 200 Turkish heads over the wall, but they were there for eight months, freezing, famished and repeatedly ambushed. Thousands starved to death. Some took to cannibalism, particularly a group of Flemish survivors from Peter's crusade, who acquired such a taste for roast Turk, they fought on the frontline to get the best joints.

Antioch finally collapsed, just as Turkish reinforcements were arriving. After a refreshing bloodbath in the city, the crusaders discovered they were now themselves besieged in a place they had successfully reduced to starvation. At this point another visionary peasant called Peter came to the rescue. He found the Holy Lance, which pierced the side of Christ when he was on the cross, buried under the cathedral (despite its already being on display in Constantinople.) It was enough. Mad with hunger and apocalyptic despair, they charged the Turks and utterly routed them. For the first time in four-and-a-half centuries, the city that invented the word 'Christian' was back in Christian hands.

The crusade might have stopped there. Many thought that, now they had finally won something, they could put the nightmare of crusading behind them. And Jerusalem had already been recaptured by its previous Arab rulers who opened it up again to pilgrims. There was no one to rescue. The emperor wanted them to forget about Jerusalem, and so did the Christians there. But for many, Jerusalem had become an all-engrossing obsession, so the 60-year-old French count Raymond decided to lead the more zealous contingent to Jerusalem, going ahead barefoot as a pilgrim.

Again, the city was formidably fortified. Its new ruler had poisoned all water supplies outside the walls and cut down all the trees so the crusaders could not make siege towers. But thanks to guidance from yet another visionary called Peter, and a crusader stumbling on the stash of cut-down trees while looking for somewhere to relieve his bowels, they broke into the holy city in July 1099.

When the Muslims had first taken Jerusalem, in 638, their leader had treated the Christians with gentleness and respect, taken a tour to honour their holy sites and protected them in law from persecution. The crusaders worked on a different philosophy. They charged through the streets, hacking to pieces every man, woman and child they saw.

It being Friday, they found the mosque full. So, on the same spot where Jesus had purged the temple 1,000 years before, they stripped the Dome of the Rock of its treasures, promised the worshippers their lives in return for an enormous ransom and killed every one of them. The synagogue crammed with Jews was burnt on the sabbath, 'a just and splendid judgment of God', as Raymond's chaplain declared. In a race to claim the best houses, the crusaders killed their inhabitants and piled them up in the road, not forgetting to slice them open in case they had swallowed their gold. In an orgy of sacrificial butchery, they waded through narrow streets ankle deep, in places knee deep, in blood. For some reason, they let the ruler and his retinue buy their lives; they killed everybody else. (The Jerusalem Christians escaped, purely because the Muslims expelled them when they saw the crusaders coming.)

Before the news reached home, Pope Urban had died, but the rest of Europe rejoiced to hear that in the city where the Son of God gave his life for the healing of the nations, the cross had once again triumphed over the powers of darkness.

7

Love, War and Heresy
(1099–1192)

Jerusalem the golden, with milk and honey blest,
Beneath thy contemplation sink heart and voice oppressed.
Bernard of Cluny

More controversial than this carnage, there was a new theologian in France, the extraordinary Peter Abelard. As a student, disappointed by his famous Parisian teacher, Abelard gave rival lectures nearby to correct him, taking his students and eventually his job. Later, Abelard moved on to study under the greatest biblical scholar alive. 'Useless,' was his verdict. 'He was a master of words, but not their meaning.' This time, his rival lectures got him expelled, and he returned to Paris as head of the school and the greatest philosopher alive – the only one, in fact, by his own reckoning.

A canon of Notre Dame asked Abelard to coach his beautiful young niece Heloise, but she learned more from him than expected. They fell passionately in love, and in lesson time 'our desires left no part of lovemaking untried'. Abelard gave up philosophy in favour of writing love songs, but when the canon caught them in the act, and Heloise was found to be pregnant, he injured Abelard in such a way as to ensure the affair was over. Marriage being a greater bar to advancement in the church than fornication, Abelard wed Heloise on the understanding that it was to be kept secret, but naturally her uncle spilt the beans, so Abelard sent her to a nunnery and became a monk himself.

As a reforming abbot, he made such an impact that his monks tried to kill him, but he also produced the theology that made his lasting reputation. His remarkable *Yes and No* simply compiled conflicting or contrasting passages from the Bible and the writings of the Church Fathers, to encourage readers to grapple with the issues for themselves: 'Doubting leads us to enquire, and enquiry leads us to truth.'

He also offered a new understanding of the cross. Rejecting Anselm's belief that God needs satisfaction before he can forgive, he saw the atonement being achieved through Christ's human life, not just his death: 'He took human nature on himself and taught us by word and example to the point of death.' Such love kindles grateful love within us, reconciling us to him. This interpretation has become popular today as it avoids the overtones of the feudal blood feud in Anselm's theory, though it still leaves the question of why God's gift of inspirational love needed to be so bloody.

Still nursing an unbearable longing for Abelard, Heloise became abbess of a nunnery he founded, and they exchanged letters until he died. They share a grave.

The second crusade

On Christmas Eve 1144, Edessa fell to the Turks, amid carnage sufficient to avenge the conquest of Jerusalem. The west went into shock, but the moment found its hero. Bernard of Clairvaux was a Cistercian abbot, theologian and powerful figure in papal politics who had got one pope deposed for having a Jewish great-grandfather, with the immortal words, 'It would be an insult to Christ if the offspring of a Jew were to occupy the throne of Peter.' Violently opposed to everything Abelard stood for (including, evidently, the use of reason in theology), he got him condemned at Rome as a heretic.

King Louis VII of France wanted to visit Jerusalem to atone for some ghastly recent massacres, and so he planned with the Pope to renew the crusade. Bernard was its publicist. A brilliant preacher (they called him Doctor Honeytongue), he relit the crusading fire with his guarantees of inevitable victory, salvation and fabulous wealth. At his first rally, again in a crowded French field, so many came forward to take the vow that he ran out of sew-on crosses and had to cut up his own clothes. Again Jews were massacred in the warm-up, but Bernard turned protector of the Jews, forbidding attacks and dismissing an agent who encouraged them.

Bernard persuaded the Holy Roman Emperor Conrad to join King Louis, and Conrad reached Byzantium first. After the Germans burnt a town assuming its local juggler was in league with the devil, they were hurried through to Asia Minor. They set off towards Edessa on their own, were decimated by Turks and crawled back to Nicea to wait for the French.

The united crusade suffered debilitating assaults but eventually reached Antioch. There the French queen allegedly had an affair with the ruler of the city, her uncle, so King Louis fell out with him and took the crusade on a pilgrimage to Jerusalem instead.

Louis and Conrad assessed the situation: there was an awesome Turkish force standing against them, and all that held them off were the Muslims of Damascus who sided with the crusaders. Inexplicably, the crusaders decided to attack Damascus. The idiotic siege was a fiasco, and within weeks, the crusaders were cutting their losses and on their way home.

Bernard had a lot of explaining to do. He and Louis agreed it must have been the Byzantines' fault and (encouraged by acquisitive Normans) planned a crusade against Constantinople. For now, though, this betrayal came to nothing.

Cathars and Waldensians

Western Europe was thriving. Its new stability could only be enhanced by its great warriors being in Asia. New engineering produced awesome Gothic cathedrals. Universities appeared in Oxford and Paris. Peter Lombard revived Abelard's enquiry with his inspiringly titled *Book of Sentences*: just like his teacher Abelard, he used reason to judge between contrasting teachings, but with such reverence that even Bernard accepted it. It would become the primary theological textbook of the west.

But the same winds of change that invigorated Catholicism also inspired new movements and thinking that the church could not licence. Reformers and preachers had done a better job of denouncing priestly sins than stopping them, and now in France and Italy 'the Clean' or 'Cathars' started breaking away from the church to keep pure. They were inspired by the Slavic Bogomil missionaries, who in turn took their ideas from the Paulicians, which means their roots probably go all the way back to Augustine's one-time friends, the Manichees. As well as saying that matter and the Old Testament were the work of Satan, they demanded celibacy (with divorce for the married) and were vegans, as all animal products 'are the result of fleshly congress'. (Fish were permitted, being spontaneously created by water.) Even then, they fasted three days a week. They also banned all killing, possessions and oath-taking, and they allowed women priests (on the grounds that bodily differences are irrelevant).

The values and anti-Catholicism of the Cathars were popular enough to give the church a fright, but the lifestyle was too demanding for a mass movement. So, like the Bogomils, they had a two-tier system: the 'perfect' were initiated and lived the so-called life; the 'believers' supported them. Only the perfect were saved, but believers aimed to be initiated into their ranks on their deathbed. Those who did not would be reincarnated.

Catharism was clearly and deliberately a seriously anti-Catholic movement from the start, but the Waldensians were turned into dissidents by the church. In 1175, Valdes, a rich French merchant, heard a wandering minstrel sing a moving song about St Alexis, sold his possessions and gave the money to the poor. This was a similar story to that of many monks, but Valdes had no interest in becoming a monk. He just preached repentance in the streets and lived off donations from supporters. Local clergy opposed him, so he appealed to the Pope, who ruled that he and his followers could preach only with the consent of local clergy, in other words, not at all. They kept at it, and, along with the Cathars, were excommunicated at the 1179 Lateran council. (The growing distance between Rome and Constantinople is exemplified by the fact that in 1123, Rome had revived the tradition of 'ecumenical' councils, which now involved no eastern Christians.)

Once beyond the pale, Waldensian numbers increased and their thinking turned radical. The Bible became their only rule, excluding all Catholic traditions not prescribed there, such as mass and prayers for the dead. Like the Cathars, they condemned killing and oaths; they even let women preach and ordinary people baptise. At their height, they reached from Spain to Moravia.

The third crusade

It was going to take a lot to revive the crusading spirit after the last wash-out. The man who did it was a Kurdish Muslim called Saladin. He conquered his way round the Turk cities until the crusaders were surrounded. Jerusalem sent repeated appeals to Rome for help, but no one responded.

The massed armies of the crusader states came out to meet Saladin and were trounced. In Jerusalem, as a desperate act of divine propitiation, mothers made their daughters take cold baths on the hill of Calvary. It didn't work. Once again, in 1187, the Muslims marched into Jerusalem.

They did not loot a single house or kill a single civilian. Instead, Saladin offered Christians their freedom for ten pence each, with a special offer for anyone who would redeem a batch of peasants who could not afford it. In a spirited demonstration of Christian leadership, the bishop of Jerusalem paid his ten pence, and, once free, went to the church, packed its vast treasures into carts, and ran. Saladin released thousands anyway, and within days, the church of the Holy Sepulchre was reopened for pilgrims.

Again the western church was devastated. The Pope died of shock, and his successor proclaimed another crusade, launching an even more formidable force than last time. Frederick Barbarossa the Holy Roman Emperor, King Philip of France and Richard the Lionheart of England all led their armies.

Frederick left first. Typically, the Germans were not welcome in Constantinople and were hurried through. And typically, they suffered such an ordeal of heat, hunger and thirst in Asia Minor that they were reduced to extracting drinks out of horse manure. What followed was less typical. They finally came upon a great river, and Frederick Barbarossa dived in and drowned. His son preserved the royal corpse in a large barrel of vinegar and took him on to fulfil his vow of reaching Jerusalem. The army, unhappy at being led into battle by a pickle, largely went home.

The English and French took the port of Acre, thus gaining a stepping stone towards Jerusalem. But they could not defeat Saladin, and they had to return in 1192 with little more than a stepping stone to show for the crusade.

8

Innocent (1192-1292)

To me it is said... 'I have set you over nations and kingdoms, to root up
and pull down, to waste and destroy, to build and plant.'
Innocent III

Before his swimming accident, Emperor Frederick Barbarossa had devoted his
life to the power struggle with Rome. After taking him to Jerusalem in his
barrel, his son became emperor, and by a canny marriage, he added southern
Italy and Sicily to the empire. This not only ended Norman rule there but had
the Pope dangerously surrounded. In fact, it was to be the papacy's greatest
hour, depending of course on how one measures greatness.

The new emperor died in 1197 with his sons in infancy, and so two rival
successors went to war, both appealing to the new Pope Innocent III.
Innocent humbly replied that it was the right of German princes to elect their
own emperor, and less humbly that it was his own right to correct their choice
if wrong. He chose Otto of Brunswick because he promised to recognise the
growing Papal State and not to interfere in church appointments. Once
crowned, Otto instantly forgot his promises, so Pope Innocent declared him
deposed. What added force to his deposition was that the king of France,
unhappy to see the empire getting so powerful, joined the fight against Otto,
who was successfully overthrown – the beginning of the end for Germany's
superpower status. The Pope's word ruled.

The Pope, Innocent once told the patriarch of Constantinople, was given
'not only the worldwide church to govern, but the entire world'. Whatever
else his words were, they were not idle. He successfully overruled the divorces
and marriages of kings. When King John of England tried to appoint his own
archbishop, Innocent not only excommunicated and deposed him but called
every English priest out on strike until he submitted, becoming the Pope's
feudal vassal. (Less successfully, Innocent declared the Magna Carta void.) At
his consecration, he declared himself 'the vicar of Jesus Christ, successor of

Peter, the Lord's anointed, Pharaoh's god, set between God and man, lower than God but higher than man'. Previously, the Pope had been the substitute of St Peter; now he was the substitute of Christ.

The most perverse crusade of all

Innocent was the man to work the Jerusalem miracle where others had failed and immediately announced a fourth crusade. As Egypt was the weakest of the Muslim states, it made sense to attack there first. This meant a sea journey, so the crusade leaders ordered warships from Venice to carry 4,500 soldiers. Unfortunately, when word got around that the crusade was not heading straight to Jerusalem, only 1,500 men turned up. The crusade found itself enormously in debt to Venice, whom it was forced to appease by attacking Christian Hungary instead of Egypt. Innocent excommunicated the crusade.

The crusaders then had a visit from Alexius, the exiled heir to the throne of Constantinople. He offered to finance the Egyptian crusade (and submit the Eastern Orthodox church to Rome) if they restored him to his throne, and the crusaders agreed. They toppled the emperor and enthroned Alexius in his place in 1203. But Alexius's side of the deal now seemed rather hard, so an impoverished Constantinople saw their new emperor introduce scorching taxes and melt down church plate, all to pay their barbarian invaders. Talk of submission to Rome did not help either. After a drunken Frenchman set fire to Constantinople, Alexius was deposed.

So the crusades hit Constantinople. Crusaders ransacked the city in a three-day carnival of rape and murder, not sparing nuns in their convents. They pillaged and desecrated Justinian's Cathedral of Hagia Sophia, and stood a prostitute on the patriarch's throne to dance and regale them with bawdy songs. They burnt whole districts of the city and filled their ships with an unimaginable wealth of treasure and holy relics.

Innocent raged when he heard the crusade had taken such a wrong turning, but when he saw the dream of a reunited church coming true at last, he changed his mind. When the crusaders failed to hand the conquered Byzantium over to him, and instead the Venetians appointed the new emperor and patriarch, he returned to raging.

Francis and Dominic

Innocent's reign saw the birth of the two great, new monastic orders of the later middle ages. Around 1206, a fun-loving Italian soldier called Giovanni Bernardone was told by a crucifix to 'Go, repair my falling house.' Rather missing the spirit of the calling, he rebuilt the local ruined church with money stolen from his father. Two years later, he heard a Bible-reading in which Jesus sends out the disciples to preach the gospel, telling them to do good, work wonders and take no possessions. He followed this literally too, and under the strangely inappropriate name of Brother Frenchy – or 'Francis' – he devoted himself to preaching, helping people, begging and singing. Rejecting the monastic ideal of holiness in seclusion, Francis and his followers found God in his world and honoured him by respecting the lowliest of his people. They worked alongside peasants and cared for lepers, and they quickly grew fantastically popular. Francis was also the first known person to get stigmata – bleeding from the five points where Jesus was pierced on the cross.

Pope Innocent was loath to recognise the ragged order, so similar to the Waldensians, but perhaps learning from their heavy-handed treatment (and guided by a dream of Francis holding up a crumbling church) he eventually did. They took the name Lesser Brothers or Friars Minor, a traditional term for the lowest orders of society. And so the Franciscans become the saints of the middle ages, while the Waldensians, for most of the same reasons, were the heretics.

The Dominicans arose at the same time and became the secret police of the middle ages. This was not what they were created for. Dominic's passion was for mission, especially to win the Cathars back to the church. Innocent had sent missionaries, but failing to match the self-denying passion of the Cathar preachers, they had had little impact. So Dominic came as a Catharesque preaching pauper and started to get a better response.

But then Innocent got crusade-happy. Realising that crusades need have nothing to do with Palestine or Muslims, he directed one at the Cathars. Twenty years of war followed, against the Cathar hotspots of southern France, where typically the crusaders, having trouble telling the sheep from the goats, killed everyone. It was a great success, and we will not be hearing about the Cathars again. The blood of martyrs is not always seed; sometimes it's just blood. Dominic and his friends split up and went throughout Europe, especially to university towns, to rescue from heresy and to teach the truth – often joining the university staff.

Innocent's last achievement was the fourth Roman Catholic 'ecumenical' council of 1215, which lay down the law for the Christian world. It established the doctrine of transubstantiation – where the bread and wine turn really and wholly into the body and blood of Christ – and the requirement to confess to a priest and take mass annually. It summoned a fifth crusade against Egypt. It condemned the Cathars and Waldensians, and it forbade the founding of new monastic orders. Jews and Muslims were required to wear a badge so that one knew whom to persecute. (Similar distinctions were imposed on Christians and Jews in Muslim countries.) And, obscurely, clergy were banned from wearing green. The fifth crusade did not achieve much, though it did give Francis the opportunity to have long evangelistic talks with the sultan of Egypt, which did not achieve much either.

One year after the ban on new orders, the new Pope recognised the Dominicans, and soon Rome had a new job for them. Innocent had been sending men to hunt out and arrest heretics, and the Dominicans, with their learning and connections, seemed ideal to continue the work. When another pope founded the Inquisition in 1231, to find and try heretics then hand them over to the state to be executed, he put it in Dominican hands. Rome sanctioned torture – a standard medieval tool of law and order – to encourage confessions and accusations, in 1252.

Wherever they went, inquisitors encouraged people to make confidential accusations against heretics. They took accusations as proof of guilt but gave heretics the benefit of a secret trial, without counsel. If they confessed, they were let off with a penance, which often included confiscation of all property. If they did not, they were tortured until they did. If they still did not confess (and sometimes if they did), they were burnt. Confiscating property made the war on error a useful way of financing the work of the church.

With the papacy at its height, eastern Christians were in desperate straits. Russia was conquered by the pagan Mongols in 1237, though the church survived as a force for national identity among the conquered. The Byzantines regained Constantinople from the crusaders in 1261, but after sixty years of the basest misrule and the politics of looting, they found the empire broken and unruleable, a ruin of its former glory; and they faced repeated western attempts to recover it. For now, the Turks and Mongols were too busy fighting each other to have eyes for Constantinople, but, to be realistic, the empire of

Byzantium was sitting at the top of the rubbish chute of history, hoping not to be pushed. Its only hope was in military aid from the west, and even that unappealing prospect depended on a difficult reconciliation.

Since the Mongols had also invaded Poland, Austria and Hungary, the Pope sent a Franciscan missionary who was welcomed into the Mongol court. Here, the Khan staged a debate between the Catholics, Nestorians, Muslims and Zoroastrians, which did nothing to dissuade him from animism. But when the Polo brothers visited Kublai Khan in 1266, he sent a message to the Pope asking him 'to send 100 men skilled in your religion... so that I might be baptised, followed by my nobles, and then their subjects'. The Pope sent two Dominicans nine years later, who got halfway and turned back. Nevertheless, by the end of the century, a Franciscan missionary in Mongol China could claim 6,000 converts, and he was made archbishop of Beijing.

Thomas Aquinas

The next character is our story is, unlikely as it seems, Aristotle. While his tutor, Plato, had had more influence over the church than most Christians, Aristotle's work was largely lost when Europe fell apart after the collapse of Rome and persecuted pagan philosophers took refuge in Islamic lands. But now that Christians were constantly mingling with Muslims, for the first time they came across silk, sugar and Aristotle, whom the Muslims had kept in circulation. He was a bit of a shock.

For Plato, the spiritual realm is infinitely more real than the physical, matter but a shadow of the eternal. So we understand life and God by reason, by contemplating eternal truths. Aristotle, in contrast, accepted the physical realm as real. So matter matters, and we understand by observing with our senses. Truth comes not through divine revelation, then, but human investigation. Aristotle studied physics, biology and cosmology. His research established that there must be a God to have set the universe in motion, but he had little room for the God personally encountered in Christian Platonism. He also concluded that souls are mortal and the universe immortal, the opposite of Plato. It was a serious challenge to traditional Christianity. The Pope and Paris University banned Aristotle. The man who brought him in from the cold was Thomas Aquinas.

When Thomas's family decided he would become a monk, what they had in mind was a rich, powerful Benedictine abbot. Instead, at university, he fell in with the Dominicans and became a beggar for Jesus. Outraged, his family had him kidnapped and locked up in the family castle with a prostitute to demonstrate the kind of monastic respectability he should aspire to. Thomas spent his time there writing an essay on logic. Rejoining the Dominicans, who called him 'the dumb ox' for less than flattering reasons, he taught throughout France, Germany and Italy, becoming the west's greatest thinker since Augustine.

Thomas amalgamated Aristotle and Christian tradition, creating a new Christian worldview. Reality now had two storeys: 'nature', the realm of the five senses, and 'grace' (what we might call 'supernature'), the realm of God. This means there are two kinds of knowledge: natural – what humans can work out for themselves (the movements of planets, the speed of falling objects, the existence of God), where Aristotle reigns supreme; and supernatural – what we only know because God tells us (the Trinity, transubstantiation). Thomas encapsulated this double-decker truth in two vast books: *Manual Against the Heathen*, which proved as much Christian doctrine as possible 'naturally' before completing it with divine revelation; and the overwhelming *Manual of Theology*, which brings together a millennium of Catholic dogma in one average-sized bookcase, showing how Christian revelation perfects human understanding of truth.

The universe, you might say, came into its own, no longer just a distraction for the soul, but God's basic means of communication with humanity. Thomas stirred up furious controversy. Soon after his death, his bishop would condemn him for heresy, while Oxford and Paris Universities banned him. A friar who appealed to the Pope on his behalf was forbidden to speak again for the rest of his life. Fifty years later, Thomas was a saint. (He also invented the limerick, though his own were not especially funny.)

In 1273, aged forty-nine, Thomas had been writing *Manual of Theology* for eight years, with no end in sight. He celebrated mass on St Nicholas's Day, and something, who knows what, happened. He emerged from the chapel saying, 'I can write no more. After what I have seen, everything I ever wrote seems like straw.' He never wrote another word of the book.

A short reunion

In 1274, the Pope had word from the eastern emperor, offering to submit to Rome in order to reunite the church – a desperate measure but the only way he could see to hold off the next generation of crusaders intent on retaking Constantinople. So Orthodox representatives came to that year's council of Lyons, ready to capitulate totally. The Pope summoned Thomas Aquinas as an expert on the errors of the east, but he was killed on the way in a low-speed donkey-riding accident. The easterners accepted papal supremacy and the western version of the creed; they had to sing it there and then, repeating the *filioque* line three times to make triple sure. Two hundred and twenty years after the great divorce, east and west were reunited. When news reached Constantinople however, the church was appalled. Rome had been a bitter rival for centuries, but since the crusade, it had become the devil. Almost no one would use the Catholic creed, not even the emperor's 1277 council of Constantinople. The Pope angrily condemned them and the reconciliation broke down.

Francis of Assisi had spent his unhappy later years trying to keep his movement faithful to the spirit of free and simple brotherhood. After his death, it was increasingly embraced by the institutional church, increasingly led by bishops and academics, its more stringent demands increasingly compromised. A series of papal bulls culminating in 1283 knocked howling loopholes into Franciscan poverty, decreeing that any possessions the friars needed could be owned by the papacy, while they 'used' them. This sleight of canon law was more popular with some than others, and the Franciscans split into the Conventuals and the Spirituals.

9

Too Many Popes (1292–1443)

Out of the thick Gothic night,
our eyes are opened by the glorious torch of the sun.
Rabelais

Those who, not unreasonably, felt that the papacy had entirely discredited itself over the last 100 years, using the whole machinery of pastoral care to wage war for material gain, were delighted by the papal election of 1294. For two years, there had been no pope because the cardinals could not agree. Then a letter came from the famous Spiritual Franciscan hermit Peter Morone, threatening divine vengeance if they dragged their heels any longer. So they chose him. This burst of spiritual idealism lasted six months, until the embarrassingly incompetent Peter became the first pope to quit voluntarily.

Still, he was popular enough for his successor, Boniface VIII, to keep him in gaol until he died – according to rumour (and his relics) with a nail through his head. Boniface revived the more hard-headed politics of Pope Innocent III and others, but they were getting more difficult to put into practice. Europe was changing, not least through the birth of nationalism. Before, there had been little to be nationalistic about: one had a village, a family, a language, a squire and a religion, but no nation to speak of. Now, however, feudal economy was starting to weaken, with kings gaining power over their aristocracy. The Pope's rights as feudal lord of Christendom started to seem less obvious.

In 1295, France and England went to war, and so their kings needed money. In England, Edward I had to create the House of Commons, and both kings taxed their clergy. An outraged Pope Boniface threatened excommunication, but then Philip IV of France cut off exports of gold to Rome. Boniface was forced to decide that kings could tax clergy after all. The times they were a-changing.

Then in 1301, Philip put one of his top bishops on trial for treason. Once again Boniface was all threats and judgments, but Philip created the French parliament, which gladly supported their king against the Roman. Boniface issued one of the most extreme proclamations of papal power ever. 'It is absolutely impossible for anyone to be saved without being subject to the Roman pontiff.' It did not stop him being arrested by Philip.

In 1305, the papacy passed to a French puppet of Philip, Clement V. As if to underline the point, he quit Rome and set up the holy see in the town of Avignon. (Avignon was not part of the French kingdom but was French enough for people to feel that the papacy had moved to France.) The papacy also became the enemy of the most popular spiritual movement of the age when Pope John XXII took on the Franciscans. He not only outlawed the Spirituals, burning four of their leaders for persisting, but refused to 'own' the Conventuals' possessions for them, declaring it heresy to say that Jesus had no possessions.

Divine light and Black Death

In 1347, Mongols besieging a Genoan trading colony in the Crimea catapulted diseased bodies over the wall. The survivors of the siege came home, and within forty years, a third of Europeans were dead, most of them in the first few years. England lost half its population and 1,000 whole villages to the Black Death. Those that were left faced hunger and poverty because there were so few people to work the land – which also meant that peasants could start charging wages for their work for the first time. Another crack spread across the power of feudal landowners.

The tendency to turn to religion in the face of death seized all Europe. Preachers flooded the towns, and evangelists danced about dressed as skeletons. Parades of peasants whipped themselves and each other to appease God. The rich increasingly left money to monks to sing masses for them, to cut down on their cooking time in purgatory. For Byzantium, plague came in the wake of civil war, and was followed by a new onslaught from the Turks, who took most of Byzantine Greece and Macedonia. From this foothold, the Turks started to conquer eastern Europe, starting with Serbia. The Byzantine emperor became a vassal of the sultan, and repeatedly tried to make deals for Catholic aid, none of which came to anything. Further east, the Nestorian church was largely destroyed by the vicious ravages of the conqueror Tamerlane, except in south-west India and northern Persia.

The Renaissance

Christian civilisation had a wealth of artistic achievement to its name, from the icons of Constantinople to the cathedrals of France, from the melodies of Roman plainsong to the illuminations of Celtic manuscripts. But all this of course was religion. There was also romantic and heroic verse, folk songs and the like, but the greater part of serious art was not a mirror to the world but a window out of it. File art under worship. Once again, we can sense in this the ghost of Plato, who disapproved of art. If the world is only a shadow of the eternal, then depicting it is making a shadow of a shadow; vanity of vanities.

But in 1320, Francesco Petrarch enrolled at Avignon University. He learned theology and philosophy, and for the sake of grammar and rhetoric, he studied the great writers of ancient Rome. He was bitten and smitten; it seemed that nothing so glorious had been written for 1,000 years. He chain read his way through every ancient writing he could get his hands on, and to expand his range, he did what few westerners had done in a millennium: he tried to learn Greek. (He failed, however, and had to employ the only Greek-speaking monk he could find to translate Homer – until he was inauspiciously struck by lightning.) He and his friends wrote poetry in the classical style and in classical Latin rather than the 'corrupted' Latin of medieval Europe; and it was about the things Latin poets wrote about – not the glory of God and the mystery of the sacraments, but life and love and people behaving badly. Artists started to depict the saints looking like real people in actual landscapes, rather than two-dimensional gods standing on gold foil. Petrarch is said to be the first person ever to have climbed a mountain because it was there, rather than because it was between him and where he wanted to go.

This is the start of the spectacular movement we call the 'Renaissance', the rebirth of ancient art and learning in the west, or 'humanism', the restoration of human life to the focus of study and the arts. It was by no means anti-Christian (though humanists generally despised university-style theology from Anselm onwards), but it was devoted not only to God but to his creation. Counting the last millennium as a cultural drought, the humanists started calling it the 'middle age' between the Romans writers and (eschewing false modesty) themselves. Medieval cathedrals were so vulgar compared with classical simplicity; they were clearly the work of barbarians and so were dismissed as 'Gothic'.

Wyclif, Hus and the embarrassment of Popes

The bishop of Rome had been in France for seventy years now. The relocation had been a profound shock for many Christians, underlining the woeful state of the institutional church – worldly, corrupt, luxurious, cynical and immoral. In 1377, the Pope finally returned to Rome to find it in ruins. In 1378, he died. The cardinals, being largely French, wanted to go home, but the Romans forced them to stay and choose an Italian pope. Unfortunately, the one they elected annoyed them intensely, so they sacked him, picked a French one and took him back to Avignon. So there were two popes at once. It was hardly the first time, but each had his own court and city, and half the European churches on his side. It looked set to run and run. The papacy's esteem sunk from ground level right through the floor.

The most radical attack came from the Oxford don John Wyclif. He argued that whatever political or religious authority church leaders had was based on their moral authority, so the decrees of an immoral pope had no weight at all. In fact, even a righteous pope was only the bishop of the city of Rome: the head of the worldwide church was Christ alone. He ended up concluding that the papacy – good pope or bad – was the Antichrist.

Wyclif challenged the universal idea that the church was the final authority over Christian life and belief, preferring to see the Bible as God's only revelation. Rome held the Bible in equally high esteem but insisted that only the church could interpret it reliably. Wyclif had no faith in Catholic hierarchy, and so his followers translated the scriptures into English to let ordinary people hear God's truth for themselves. This was anarchy, said the bishops; translation unauthorised by the church was bound to be twisted and heretical. 'Condemn the word of God in any language as heresy and you call God a heretic,' replied Wyclif.

Delighted by this excuse to encroach on the power and wealth of the English church, the nobility protected Wyclif. But in 1379, he started denouncing the idea that the church could turn bread into the flesh of Christ – 'That ear you reap today shall be God tomorrow!' – which lost him influential support. He was blamed for the peasants' revolt of 1381 and condemned, living his last years in busy seclusion. His followers became another illegal movement of penniless preachers.

What was to be done about the embarrassing duplication of the papacy? Repeatedly, papal candidates promised to bring peace and reconciliation, by resigning if need be, but once elected, they started to see the issue differently. The two heads of the body of Christ came face to face in 1407, but failed to find a compromise, so in the end, the only way out seemed to be an ecumenical council. Finally, the two sets of cardinals met with the leading bishops, abbots and academics at Pisa in 1409 – without the decree, consent or presence of either pope – declaring them both deposed and appointing a new pope. Predictably, as you might have thought, neither pope accepted his dismissal, so now there were three.

Wyclif's ideas were given an unexpected new lease of life when a princess from Bohemia married the English king and Bohemian students came to Oxford, taking Wyclif's anti-papal thought back home. Bohemia belonged to the Holy Roman Empire, divided between the German elite and Czech natives. Czechs rallied to these radical ideas, led by Jan Hus, the principal of Prague University and a thrilling preacher. One of the popes excommunicated Hus, but attempts to silence him merely started a riot. In 1411, one pope declared a crusade against another, offering forgiveness of sins to those who supported the crusade financially. Hus condemned him and Czechs burnt the crusading decree in the street. Three Hussites were executed, Prague as a whole was excommunicated, and Hus was persuaded to leave.

The council revolution: Constance and Basle, Ferrara and Florence

Despite the failure of Pisa, it was clear that only another council could reduce the number of popes. Learning a lesson from last time, the cardinals got the western emperor to summon it, with the consent of the third Pope and almost all the supporters of the popes. The council met in 1414 in Constance, lasted four years, drew 50,000 members and had revolution on the agenda.

After an undignified struggle, the newest Pope was persuaded to accept his deposition, on the grounds that he was an unpopular, dishonest, sexually voracious, avaricious murderer, and become the bishop of Tusculum. The Roman Pope also agreed to step down on the conditions that (a) he should be said to have called the council; and (b) after it, he would be second in command to the new Pope. At ninety, he was not expected to survive the council anyway. The Avignon Pope did not accept his deposition and moved to an obscure, well-armed castle in Spain, which he declared to be the one true church.

Having got rid of their popes, the council brought the whole papacy down a peg. The council, not the pope, was to be the final authority in the church, so regular councils were to be called every few years. After all these centuries, the pope had a master.

The council wanted to deal with the corruptions of the wider church, but with so many contending political interests, nothing was agreed, and they left reform to the new Pope. They acted resolutely enough against the new heresy: Wyclif was dug up, burnt and thrown in a river; they invited Hus to come and talk about the problems of Bohemia, promised him safe conduct and burnt him at the stake. They also discussed the beleaguered, demoralised and bankrupt empire of Byzantium, whose emperor had been reduced to touring Europe, appealing for help against the Turks, but once again, they did nothing.

The new Pope did not accept his demoted status, nor was he interested in reform. He called a council in 1423, as he was supposed to, but an outbreak of plague gave him the excuse to dissolve it before it achieved anything. His successor tried the same trick with the 1431 council of Basle, but with the German emperor's help, they forced him to leave them be and enacted radical reforms of the church and papacy.

The Byzantines appealed once again for reunion talks so that they could get help against imminent Turkish invasion. The Pope announced that he was transferring the Basle council to Ferrara in Italy to meet the Byzantines under his oversight; but most of the council refused to move, so now there were two councils. Ferrara was closer and the Pope was there, so the Byzantines chose that one. The Basle council had lost most of its credibility; when it declared the Pope deposed, threatening to revive the two popes nightmare, it lost the rest of it. It dissolved itself. The Pope was back at the wheel.

The emperor and patriarch came from Constantinople to Ferrara with 700 Orthodox authorities. To assert his pre-eminence, the Pope had a hole knocked in the palace wall so that he could ride his horse up to his throne and not be seen with his feet on the ground. The impression of pomp was diminished when he had to move the council to Florence to save money. After tortuous debate, the east again largely capitulated to Roman Catholicism. They were allowed to keep some traditions, and the clause about papal supremacy was happily vague (the western church being somewhat vague about it themselves now); but the great concession was that although the east accepted the truth of the *filioque*, they did not have to use it in church. The decree of reunion was signed in 1439, and across the west, church bells rang in celebration.

But in Constantinople, the rejoicing was rather more muted. According to one chronicler, as the returning bishops disembarked, 'the citizens greeted them as was customary, asking, "What of our business? What of the council? Did we prevail?" And they answered, "We have sold our faith."' The truth was that most Byzantines would rather have gone down to the sultan than the Pope. And this was just as well, because when, after all these years of negotiation, the Pope finally launched the crusade to save Constantinople in 1443, it got as far as Bulgaria before being mown down by Muslims.

10

Protest (1443-1516)

If elephants can be taught to dance… surely preachers can be taught to preach.
Erasmus

The Byzantines' visit to Florence, the hub of the Renaissance, was a boon for humanists, who had little difficulty persuading some to stay and teach Greek. Finally, westerners read the New Testament in the original language, and it was, so to speak, a revelation. Lorenzo Valla condemned the Vulgate of Jerome, which had been read in every Catholic service for a millennium, as inaccurate and inelegant. He also proved that the Donation of Constantine was a forgery (along with other vital texts of theology and canon law) and that the Apostles' creed was not by the apostles. He was investigated by the Inquisition, but he enjoyed the surprising rescue of becoming apostolic secretary to the Pope Nicholas V. The church had been predictably hostile to humanism, but it offered good career prospects to people who spoke Greek, which is how the humanist Nicholas gained the papacy in 1447. He used its wealth to draw new art and architecture to Rome, and he collected 1,200 manuscripts, the start of the Vatican library. The papacy became the patron of the Renaissance: for the arts, it was a jackpot; for church finances, it was a money bonfire.

While Nicholas's clerics were busy copying out the writings of the Church Fathers and philosophers, the Gutenberg family in Germany unveiled the revolutionary invention that would make such copiers redundant and transform the western mind: printing. Suddenly, limitless copies could be made of every book, cheaper than ever and infinitely quicker. Humanist ideas spread around the reading public at unprecedented speed – and the reading public grew almost as quickly.

Just as this brave new world was being born, a brave old world passed away. On 28 May 1453, Orthodox and Catholic Christians in Constantinople met in the church of Hagia Sophia for an unprecedented joint service. For seven weeks, the Turks had besieged the city, outnumbering them twenty to one. The Byzantine defence had been heroic, resourceful and utterly hopeless. The emperor took wine and leavened bread, and went out to die. That afternoon, the city fell, and the Byzantine empire was at long last finished.

Islamic law allowed three days of looting. The fact that the sultan called an end after one day may reflect the poverty of the half-empty city; it certainly reflects the ferocity of the day's pillage. One witness talks of mountains of corpses, nuns and girls dragged by the hair from churches, 'men groaning and women screaming, amid looting, enslaving, separation and rape'. As the sun set, the 21-year-old sultan entered Constantinople and went straight to the church, declaring it would be the chief mosque of Istanbul. The imam mounted the pulpit and proclaimed, 'There is no god but God and Muhammad is his messenger.'

In the long term, the sultan tolerated the Christians of Istanbul, but he made them pay heavier taxes and wear special clothes, and he forbade them to evangelise or marry Muslims. He appointed the patriarch of Constantinople and resold the job every few years to the highest bidder.

Rome was horrified by the defeat, and Pope Nicholas's successor declared another crusade. Cutting off funds to the Renaissance masters, he created wild new taxes and sold off art and books to finance it, but European rulers were too embroiled in nationalist conflicts to take much interest, and now that the Byzantine empire was buried, papal first aid was of limited value.

Russia had at last gained complete independence from its Mongol rulers, and when Constantinople had temporarily become Roman Catholic in 1439, the Russian church had become permanently independent from Byzantium. Now Russia became the new heart of Orthodoxy, calling itself 'Third Rome', its king, 'caesar' or 'czar'. Almost immediately, Orthodoxy was split by violent conflict between those who thought monasteries should continue owning a third of Russia in order to fund its hospitals and schools, and those who insisted they should live in simple poverty and let the world look after its own. The 'non-possessors' also opposed the killing of heretics, and their movement was ruthlessly crushed by the czar, although ultimately, the church canonised the leaders of both sides.

Erasmus

The first book to come off the printing press was the Bible, and so were most of the others. Ninety-two different editions of the Latin Bible appeared within fifty years, and in the 1460s and 1470s, new translations appeared in German, Italian, Dutch, French and Spanish. (Illegal Wyclifite handwritten scriptures were the only ones in English.) Ordinary Christians increasingly read for themselves and were puzzled to find no papacy, purgatory or pilgrimages in the Bible.

At the same time, Spain was finally driving out its last Muslim rulers and becoming a united monarchy for the first time under Ferdinand and Isabella. In fewer than forty years, it changed from the weak, anarchic backyard of western Europe to a burgeoning superpower, dominating Italy and ruling Austria, the Netherlands and the Holy Roman Empire. Ferdinand and Isabella achieved this largely by religious crusade. The reconquest of Spain united the Spanish in fervour against Islam, and they followed it up by expelling all Muslims and Jews – hundreds of thousands – who would not convert. This proved a major contribution to the corsairs, Muslim pirates who terrorised the coasts of western Europe for centuries, taking hundreds of thousands of slaves. England and France had expelled their Jews 200 years previously. The Pope gave Ferdinand and Isabella authority to enforce an impressive reformation of their church, rooting out corruption and immorality, reforming the monasteries and educating priests. He also allowed them their own Spanish inquisition, under Tomás de Torquemada, who burnt Christians of Jewish or Moorish descent suspected of backsliding and various other heretics, as well as all Bibles in Spanish. Something like 2,000 people died at his hands.

The popes had largely given up their hope of ruling Europe and their claim to be its spiritual leaders. Their area of pre-eminence was splendour. They lived lives of ostentation and luxury, filled Rome with new churches and showered fortunes on their families. ('Look at all his children,' it was said of Innocent VIII. 'Well may Rome call him father.') It was all a massive drain on the tithe-payer. Taxation went through the church roof and sales of indulgences (the absolution of sin without penance) rocketed. Innocent started the trend of creating meaningless ecclesiastical jobs and selling them off – but then of course the salaries had to be found from somewhere.

The Pope who took Christendom into the century of reformation was

Alexander VI, the infamous Rodrigo Borgia. On gaining office in 1492, through huge bribes, the 61-year-old celibate had a 19-year-old girlfriend, and he divided the best posts available among his eight children. He had the Florentine reformer Savanarola tortured and killed for political reasons, as well as to silence his criticisms. He made assassination a standard fund-raising activity. He commissioned work from such Renaissance illuminati as Michelangelo and staged vast sex shows at the Vatican. He died aged seventy-two, allegedly in a botched attempt to poison one of his cardinals – 'The most evil and most lucky Pope in many years,' a contemporary judged.

As humanism penetrated northern Europe, it became something of a protest movement, led by the great scholar and satirist Erasmus. Targets included the traditional ones of ecclesiastical corruption and immorality, but with unprecedented irreverence: Erasmus's outrageous tract *Julius Barred* portrays the late warrior Pope being turned away from the pearly gates by St Peter, whose suggestion for reforming his see is that the people should arise with stones and bash this vermin out of the world. Humanists also lampooned the ignorance of local clergy and the depravity of the friars.

But they went beyond all this to assault the fundamentals of medieval spirituality. They despised the superstition of relics, indulgences, pilgrimages and the idea of priests conjuring up a mass-produced messiah by mumbling muddled Latin they did not understand. They rejected the asceticism that had been at the heart of Christianity for 1,000 years, preferring classical and biblical moderation to either world-hating austerity or episcopal carnality. They scorned medieval theology as sterile, pedantic navel-gazing.

Their motto was 'Back to the sources': strip off the excrescences of the middle ages and recover the faith of the apostles and the Fathers. The German Reuchlin pioneered Hebrew studies. Erasmus published the west's first Greek New Testament, making a popular translation from that instead of from Jerome's Latin Vulgate, which other recent translations had used. One of several shocks in it was that John the Baptist says, 'Repent,' instead of Jerome's tendentious 'Do penance.' Penance had vanished from the Bible. It was all part of Erasmus's campaign to educate – to make priests competent, people aware and religion sensible again. He dreamed of getting Bibles read by 'the farmer, the tailor, the mason, the prostitute, the pimp, the traveller and the Turk'. 'Do you think that the scriptures are only fit for the perfumed?'

The eve of the Reformation

Protestant historians used to say that religion on the eve of the Reformation was an intolerable burden – confession and penance, guilt and good works. There is very little evidence for this. Humanists may have ridiculed Catholic superstition, but those who took it seriously seem to have been perfectly happy with the religion of the seven sacraments.

What almost no one was happy with was the condition of the church. The years spent trying to reform it had achieved nothing at all. It clawed in appalling amounts of money, for which local worshippers often saw nothing but a poor, ignorant priest and a corrupt monastery; it all went abroad so that a decadent criminal in Rome could live like a prince. In an age of increasing nationalism, it was more intolerable than ever. And if anyone had been under the impression that this was more or less what Jesus had had in mind for the church, a deluge of Bibles was fast disabusing them.

On 18 April 1506, Pope Julius II laid a foundation stone for the rebuilt St Peter's church in Rome, the glorious new abode of St Peter's ancient corpse and the most impressive basilica the Renaissance had to offer. It was going to cost.

Part 3

The Reformation

1

Luther (1517–22)

> A Christian is free. He has no master except Christ. A Christian is greater than the whole world.
>
> *Martin Luther*

It is autumn in a German mining town. A Dominican friar is street-preaching, a papal bull stamped with the Pope's coat of arms borne beside him on a velvet cushion. He has indulgences for sale, offering forgiveness of all sin for any who contribute to the St Peter's building fund. This redemption is means tested, from twenty-five guilders for princes down to half a guilder for paupers. The wages of sin is death, but the gift of life costs no more than 1 per cent of annual income.

More generous still, these get-out-of-purgatory-free cards are available at the same rate for one's dear departed. 'Listen!' cries the friar. 'The wailing voices of your dead relatives and friends implore you, "Have mercy, have mercy! We are in wretched agonies, and you can redeem us for a pittance, but you don't want to."' Even if you have violated the Blessed Virgin, according to one hearer, you are promised salvation. The jingle declares, 'When a coin in the coffer rings, a soul from purgatory springs.'

Martin Luther, an Augustinian friar teaching nearby at the undistinguished Wittenberg University, was disgusted and furious when he heard of this scam and found his own parishioners being taken in by the papal bull. His response could hardly have been less practical: he wrote ninety-five theses on the subject in Latin for a university debate, nailing them as custom dictated to the church door. As well as condemning the salesman's more outrageous claims, he denied that the Pope could release anyone from purgatory – if he could, then why did he not empty it, out of charity, instead of plucking out individuals for cash? He questioned the whole institution of indulgences: certainly, the Pope could remit penance, but was it not better for Christian souls to face God's discipline and spend the money on bread for their families, or give it to the poor?

Compared with Luther's later Protestant writings, it sounds tame, but someone printed a translation, and it provoked uproar throughout Germany. Luther was dismayed to find himself the hero of a movement against the dominion of Rome.

Pope Leo X summoned Luther to Rome for questioning. If he had gone, we would probably never have heard of him today, but he was protected by his ruler, Elector Frederick the Wise of Saxony – an unlikely ally, being an ardent Catholic and the proud owner of relics sufficient to shorten purgatory by 1,902,202 years and 270 days for paying visitors, including hay from Christ's manger, Christ's nappy, bread from the last supper, a branch of the burning bush from which God spoke to Moses (no longer alight), one of the children killed by King Herod and milk from the Blessed Virgin. Nevertheless, Frederick was delighted that Luther was putting his university on the map and feared that indulgence trafficking would hurt his own revenues.

The controversy allowed Luther to broadcast the more radical ideas dearer to his heart. He had always been a fervent and holy monk, but he was oppressed by a sense of sinfulness, which no amount of mass, penance and good deeds could expunge because they left his inner imperfections unhealed. God in his righteousness would have to damn him, he knew, and he could not understand why the apostle Paul talks of 'the righteousness of God' as good news. Luther realised he hated God, which did nothing to ease his conscience.

As he studied, it dawned on Luther that Paul was not talking about righteousness as a part of God's nature but as what God gives to Christians: 'All have sinned and fall short of the glory of God, and are now made righteous by his grace as a gift.' He was delighted to find that Augustine agreed with this; but he went further than Augustine or anyone else ever had, with the possible exception of Paul himself. How does God make us righteous? By enabling us to keep his laws, according to Augustine; but that underestimates the perfection demanded by God's laws, said Luther. Rather, when Christ died, the righteous for the unrighteous, his righteousness was spent in our favour and is transferred to our account, as it were, when we believe. In Paul's words, 'We are justified by faith', 'at once a sinner and righteous'; in Luther's, 'I felt myself reborn. I had looked through the gates of paradise.' Away with the futile struggle to appease God, faith alone is all he asks.

This is why the indulgence racket so enraged Luther. To humanists, it was superstition and swindle; to Luther it was an assault on the grace of God and the souls of Christians, who thought they had bought with money what can only be got by faith.

The break with Rome

Unable to arrest Luther, papal envoys publicly debated with him, arguing that his ninety-five theses contradicted official papal teaching on indulgences and agreed with the heretic Hus against the council of Constance. Luther realised they were right. Pope and council had denied the gospel that he read in scripture. The Bible had to overrule the church. The Reformation had begun.

In 1520, aged thirty-seven, Luther was excommunicated and his writings were burnt; in return, he burnt the bull of excommunication, along with books of canon law and medieval theology. That year, he published three great books presenting his vision of true Christianity. *The Babylonian Captivity of the Church* went for the jugular of Catholic spirituality: the sacraments. He reduced them from seven to two or so, excluding confirmation, marriage, ordination, extreme unction and (up to a point) penance, the elaborate priestly machinery that had stopped people coming directly to God in faith. He also denied that the mass re-sacrifices Christ, that it works irrespective of the recipient's faith and that laypeople should receive only the bread.

The Freedom of a Christian Man explained the life of faith: we are free from any moral law, free from subjection to any human authority and yet bound, from love of God, to live in perfect love and dutifulness. *To the Christian Nobility of the German Nation* was a war cry. Since the church would not reform itself, Luther called on rulers to root out its corruptions themselves. Rulers should reform the papacy by a council, stripping it of its riches and pomp, its Papal State and international jurisdiction. Clergy should marry and monastic vows should not be irrevocable. 'It is time for the glorious Teutonic people to stop being the puppet of the Roman pontiff!'

Luther was now the greatest celebrity in Germany, but his assault on the sacraments cost him much of his support and sympathy. Still, his proposals appealed to a number of the rulers of German states, so when they met together with their new emperor, Charles V, the 19-year-old heir to the Spanish empire, at the city of Worms in 1521, Luther was at the top of the agenda. He was summoned with a promise of safe conduct – little comfort for 'the Saxon Hus' – and rode there through adoring crowds.

At the Diet of Worms (not a monastic culinary regime, but the meeting of the imperial princes), Luther's interrogator asked whether he recanted the heresies condemned by Rome. But he could not deny the gospel. 'How will the Jews and Turks rejoice to hear Christians discuss whether they have been wrong all these years!' cried the interrogator. 'Martin, how can you assume you are the only one who understands the meaning of scripture? Do you prefer your judgment above that of so many famous men?'

'Unless I am convinced by scripture and plain reason – I cannot accept the authority of popes and councils because they have contradicted each other – my conscience is captive to the word of God. I cannot and will not recant anything, for to go against conscience is neither right nor safe. God help me.' He may or may not also have said, 'Here I stand. I can do no other.' And so, shortly after six in the evening on 17 April 1521, the modern age began.

Luther himself saw it more modestly: 'I had expected that his majesty the emperor would have collected fifty doctors of divinity to confute the monk in argument. But all they said was: "Are these books yours?" "Yes." "Do you recant them?" "No" "Then get out!"'

The diet waited until sympathetic members had gone and then, led by the appalled emperor, condemned Luther. To save his life, Frederick the Wise kidnapped him and hid him for a year in his castle under the name of George, where he suffered from insomnia, constipation and depression but wrote twelve books and translated the New Testament from Erasmus's Greek all the same. Luther's earthy yet majestic Bible was to shape German language and culture every bit as much as the Authorised Version did English. He set a pattern for all Protestant Bibles by removing the 'Apocryphal' books, such as Maccabees and the Wisdom of Solomon, from the Old Testament. Less influentially, he relegated Hebrews, James, Jude and Revelation to a kind of second division of the New Testament, denying they were by apostles – James because its 'gospel of straw' denied justification by faith and Revelation because it was incomprehensible. Everything that the Church Fathers had been undecided about was up for grabs again. Copies poured off the presses, and within months, one Catholic scholar lamented that 'tailors and shoemakers, even women and other simple idiots' were debating texts with priests and monks.

While he was away, his friends reformed Wittenberg church. The priests recited the mass in plain clothes, in German and without music, and they gave wine as well as bread to the people. Priests married and monasticism was largely scrapped, there being, as Luther said, no higher calling than to be a Christian in the world. Fast days and masses for the dead were abandoned. Images were smashed. Luther approved, until things got violent. Then he came back to Wittenberg, took control and suspended all the changes. Many of them he gradually reintroduced, but Luther's churches always retained more traditional rituals, ornaments and vestments than those of other Protestants. Hymn-singing (largely using Luther's own compositions) became a central part of Lutheranism, as it both involved and educated the people.

After the diet, Emperor Charles spent nine years in Italy fighting the French, so despite the imperial sentence, Luther was, if not safe exactly, free to lead the Wittenberg church and tour Germany encouraging and advising other reforming churches. Reform was spreading throughout Germany and Switzerland, largely in the new cities, where Protestantism appealed to the rising middle classes. Luther had no interest in running a franchise or designing a template for reformers, so there was plenty of variety. The essentials that they shared were an emphasis on the Bible and preaching; a belief in justification by faith; the abandonment of Latin, the saints and some traditional rituals; and the end of allegiance to Rome.

Earlier dissidents like the Waldensians and Hussites threw their lot in with Protestantism. In Denmark, the ruling classes seized upon Lutheranism as an excuse to throw off the control of unpopular foreign churchmen, while paradoxically it took root in Sweden as part of the movement to throw off Danish control.

No Protestants had any thoughts at all of leaving the Catholic Church and setting up a rival. They were reforming the Catholic Church, purging its corruptions and popish errors. There was one worldwide church, and eventually, by the grace of God, it would all be repaired and renewed. Historically, you could say, the great failure of the Protestant churches is that they exist at all.

2

Water and the Spirit (1522-29)

Grace is grace despite of all controversy.
Shakespeare

On 12 March 1522, a printer ate sausage and egg in the Swiss city-state of Zürich. This being Ash Wednesday, he had broken Lent, and the city council investigated. He explained that, as their great preacher Ulrich Zwingli told them, there is no law over Christians but the Bible, which places no restrictions on food, because true religion is spiritual not fleshly; also, he had been overworked and hungry.

Zwingli defended the printer (he had watched him eat the sausage), so the council arranged a public debate in 1523 between Zwingli and the bishop's deputy. Zwingli argued that 'God does not desire our decrees or doctrines if they do not originate with him.' The council found in his favour, which meant both that he could continue preaching Protestantism unchallenged, and that the council had effectively wrested control of Zürich from the bishop. This is how reformation was seizing the towns of the empire.

More radical even than Luther, Zwingli gradually persuaded the council to strip their churches of all images and ornamentation and to brick up the minster organ. Services became short and simple, with no hymns. Instead of a priest in robes at the altar offering mass with his back to the congregation, a plainclothes minister would hand round bread and wine from a table in the midst of the people. The monasteries were dissolved, the buildings used for teaching and relief of the poor.

The basic difference between Zwingli and Luther was in their attitudes to the Bible. Zwingli saw it as a precise blueprint for church life. For Luther, what is not forbidden is permitted; for Zwingli, what is not permitted is forbidden. The robes and rituals that for Luther were harmless, venerable traditions were for Zwingli the invention of the Antichrist.

Also, for Luther, the New Testament replaced law with grace, freeing

Christians from restrictive rules. For Zwingli, the New Testament replaced ceremonial religion with spiritual, obliging us to strip away outward ritual. He, like many Protestants, had first been a devotee of Erasmus, and so he was suspicious of superstition, driven to restore Christianity to its original simplicity and sensibleness.

On the whole, Luther and Zwingli let sleeping dogmas lie; but the issue that drove them apart was their understanding of the eucharist. Luther believed something similar to traditional Catholicism: the bread and wine contain the actual flesh and blood of Christ. To Zwingli, this was unreconstructed popish hokum. He saw the sacrament of the Lord's supper merely as a reminder of the death of Christ, a thanksgiving. 'Sacrament', after all, originally meant an oath, so the sacrament is our pledge, an act of faith in and commitment to Christ, spiritual not magical. Luther felt that human reason was robbing the mystery of God and denying Christians the power and comfort of God's gift.

Anabaptists

Before long – in a pattern to be repeated throughout the Reformation – Zwingli himself was horrified to see some of his followers taking his own ideas too far. Conrad Grebel, a Zürich scholar, argued that if the sacraments were not mystical channels for the power of God but our own expression of faith, then baptism should be for adult believers only. There were, after all, no infant baptisms in the Bible, but rather the instruction, 'Believe and be baptised.' For Zwingli and almost everyone else, this seemed not only misguided but violently antisocial. All Europeans (except Jews and Muslims) were baptised into the church at birth, and leaving it was generally either the direct result or direct cause of death. Christianity was what held society together; and Grebel wanted to make it optional.

But it was the perfect logical conclusion of Zwingli's thought. It was, it has been said, the worst shot in the foot in theological history. There was no way Zwingli could agree with Grebel: for all Protestants and Catholics alike, the church was society and society was the church. To make it a voluntary sect was not only to abdicate control but to unleash utter anarchy. They felt like we would feel about letting people decide whether or not to be under the law of the land.

It became clear that Grebel and his friends were not having their children baptised, so in January 1525, the council gave them eight days to catch up or be expelled from Zürich. On 21 January, Grebel baptised fifteen adult dissenters. They repudiated their infant baptism as false, concluding that there had been no true baptism, and therefore no true church (baptism being entry to the church), for 1,000 years. For them, church became a strict community of committed believers, and their separation from the state went so far as refusing to work for the authorities and being pacifists. They were also the first Protestants to deny predestination. This was no longer reforming the Christian church but recreating it from scratch.

Zürich outlawed these Anabaptists ('re-baptisers'), and in 1527, it made one of their first martyrs, Felix Mantz, through the droll method of drowning in the river Limmat. Just seven years after Luther had staked his life on the right of Christians to interpret the Bible against the will of popes, the Protestants were killing those who read it differently from themselves. But they had not learned as much from the apostle Paul as they liked to think, for their persecution, like his, merely spread the heretics from their home city throughout the empire, and those that were scattered abroad went everywhere preaching the word.

At the same time, Luther was facing another misappropriation of his beliefs, this time by armies of German peasants. From 1524 to 1525, thousands of peasants revolted against their lords, looting episcopal palaces and monasteries. It was the greatest rebellion in European history before the French Revolution of 1789, and many of the rebels arose in the name of Martin Luther and Christian liberty. Luther deplored insurrection, but at first, he also blamed the 'wild dictatorial tyrants' for driving the peasants to despair. But when the violence got excessive, he became less ambivalent. His tract, *Against the Robbing Murdering Hordes of Peasants*, burning with guilt and anger, called on readers to 'stab, smite or slay, secretly or openly'. The Christian nobility of the German nation needed little encouragement in that direction, and 10,000 peasants were killed.

Divorce

The war left divisions between Catholic and Protestant more entrenched. Those who had been cool towards reform now saw it as a danger to society; reforming rulers and councils increasingly felt the need to use force against opponents. The Catholic states of the empire formed military alliances, which persuaded the Protestants to do so too, led by Philip the Landgrave of Hesse.

The Protestant forces were outnumbered, but at this point, the Turks came to their aid. From Constantinople, they had been conquering westwards across Europe, and they invaded Hungary in 1526, destroying its army at Mohács. With Islam on the border of the Holy Roman Empire, this was no time to be fighting over the authority of the Pope, so Protestants and Catholics there agreed to leave each other alone for a while. Less fortunate for the reformers was that Emperor Charles V had made peace with France, allowing the two to join forces against Protestantism; but happily, the Pope – blissfully unaware that Protestantism had any significance at all – sabotaged the alliance in the hope of diminishing the emperor's control of Italy. In 1527, Charles V took the Pope prisoner until he became more compliant.

It is this of all improbable points in the history of the Reformation that drew England in. King Henry VIII was an ardent Catholic who had countered Luther's *Babylonian Captivity* with *The Assertion of the Seven Sacraments* and was rewarded by the Pope with the title 'Defender of the Faith' (kept with increasing irony by succeeding monarchs and inscribed 'FD' on British coins to this day). But he needed a son for the sake of the Tudor dynasty and the peace of the realm, and his Spanish wife, Catherine of Aragon, seemed to have stalled after one girl. Catherine had been his brother's widow, and Henry noticed that Leviticus 20:21 curses with childlessness him who takes his brother's wife; Henry was convinced he had to be rid of Catherine. Only the Pope could cancel the marriage, and normally, for a consideration, he would have done so; but Catherine was Emperor Charles V's aunt, and Charles would not let the Pope disgrace her. Henry had to find another way out of his marriage. He had enough closet Protestants around him to convince him that if he broke with Rome, he would be the head of the English church and a canon law unto himself. So he set them to work creating the English Reformation.

It was a pretty minimalistic one. New laws dismantled papal control of the church and made the king 'supreme head in earth of the Church of England'; the monasteries were commandeered by the crown and sold off; English Bibles were allowed and eventually appeared in church, as did some English prayers. Overall, however, little changed in parish worship.

Emperor Charles V finally defeated the French and the Pope in Italy, leaving him free to purge his empire of heresy. He called a diet of German rulers in 1529, which decreed in effect that Protestant states must re-establish Catholicism. The Lutheran minority of six princes and fourteen cities delivered an official protest, the *Protestation* from which Protestants take their name. Philip of Hesse wanted to unite all Protestants in a military alliance, but they were divided into followers of Luther and Zwingli. So Philip arranged a meeting of both sides at his Marburg castle in September 1529 to attempt some kind of agreement on the eucharist. Everyone apart from Luther wanted a compromise, but he managed to wreck it. When told that Christ's human body could not be on earth and in heaven at the same time, he insisted, 'I do not want to hear reason... God is above all mathematics.' 'If he ordered me to eat manure, I would do it.' He started the discussion by writing, 'This is my body,' on the table – the words of Christ that proved the bread was his real flesh. The Zwinglians had their own proof text too – 'It is the spirit that gives life, the flesh is useless' – and they batted them back and forth fruitlessly.

They were up against the fundamental problem of Protestantism: they agreed that the Bible had the final say over their beliefs, but they could not agree about what the Bible did say. The church had, for better or worse, always placed ultimate authority in living judges, whether apostles, bishops, councils or popes. The Protestants, for the first time, were placing all authority in the written word – the sixty-six infallible books of their Bible (and, on a lower level, the Church Fathers). But of course the living had to interpret the text, which in effect made every Bible-reader his own pope or her own ecumenical council. Ancient writings, from Hebrew erotic poetry to Greek apocalyptic visions, had to be applied to sixteenth-century European church life, so countless differences of opinion were inevitable, each claiming the unique authority of God's written decree. The fragmentation of Christendom had begun.

State-church Protestantism was now divided into two great parties, Lutheran and Reformed: the Reformed accepted the Lutherans as misled brothers, but Luther wrote off the Reformed as unbelievers and blasphemers with whom no discussion was possible or desirable: 'Your spirit and our spirit do not go together.'

Martin Bucer, the reformer of Strasbourg, looked for a middle way between their two positions, uniting the insights of both. He accepted, like Luther, that we receive a gift of Christ's humanity when we share his supper, but like Zwingli, he denied that any real change comes over the bread and wine: we receive spiritually, if we eat with faith. Luther shunned Bucer ignorantly and ungraciously, but this interpretation was to become the standard Protestant view, thanks to Bucer's future deputy at Strasbourg, John Calvin.

3

Catholic Recovery (1529-45)

The best way to beat the heretics is not to deserve their criticisms.
Cardinal Bonomi

In 1529, the Turks entered the Holy Roman Empire and laid siege to Vienna.
It was a short and somewhat unconvincing siege, Turkish forces being at the
limit of their supply lines, but enough to alarm Charles V, who became
desperate to reunite his divided empire. The obvious answer was an
ecumenical council reforming the church well enough to win back the
Protestants, but the Pope refused, fearing an assault on his power. So instead,
Charles called an imperial diet at Augsburg in 1530 to discuss reunion.

Luther, still officially banished, was represented by his right-hand man,
Philip Melanchthon, a far milder character than Luther, who prepared a
statement of Lutheran beliefs for the occasion, the Augsburg Confession. The
confession, which was to become the central document of Lutheranism, put
the most Catholic spin possible on their faith, skirting over issues like the
papacy and purgatory. Melanchthon explained the positive distinctives of
Protestantism, such as justification by faith and the importance of preaching,
without apology or aggression, but also presented Lutherans not as anti-
Catholics so much as the true, reformed Catholics.

It was to little avail. Many Catholics had considerable sympathy for
Melanchthon's ideas, but there was enough intransigence on both sides to
prevent agreement. Instead, all German powers that could agree with the
Augsburg Confession – including Bucer's Strasbourg – joined together in the
powerful Schmalkaldic League, and more authorities than ever joined the
Reformation.

Zwingli, whose own statement of faith was virtually ignored by the diet,
formed an alliance of Swiss Reformed cities, fighting a successful war to gain
the freedom of Swiss villages to choose their own religion. They then imposed
trade sanctions on Catholic Switzerland, which drove the Catholics to invade

Zürich in 1531. Zwingli was killed in battle, axe in hand. His body was burnt and mixed with manure to stop his followers venerating the relics; perhaps Zwingli would have approved. In fact, alleged pieces of his heart circulated, miraculously preserved amid the flames, but presumably without the power to remit sins.

Anabaptist martyrs and revolutionaries

Zwingli's unwanted children, the Anabaptists, had gained a vast following throughout the lower classes of the empire, despite the most savage persecution and abuse of every kind. The authorities attacked them for the same reason that a less holy Roman empire attacked the first Christians: their religion was a threat to imperial rule and social order; they feared that if the movement survived, its values would overthrow the sacred structure of society, and in both cases they were right.

The greatest surviving Anabaptist leader, Michael Sattler, a former monk married (like Luther) to a former nun, was arrested by imperial forces in the Black Forest in 1527 and tried for denying transubstantiation, infant baptism and last rites, as well as for despising the Blessed Virgin and saying that it was wrong to fight the Turks. (He said it made more sense – if fighting were permitted – to fight the 'spiritual Turks' who called themselves Christians.) After a spirited and reasoned defence of Anabaptism, he had his tongue cut out, his flesh torn with hot irons and his body burnt. His wife was drowned.

Jakob Hutter led a large Anabaptist community in the Tyrol, which banned private property, not to live in monastic poverty, but to share everything in common, as the first church did in Jerusalem. When caught in 1535, Hutter was thrown bound and gagged into icy water, then pulled out and scourged, with flaming brandy poured into his wounds, and finally burnt.

In extraordinary counterpoint to these pacifist sacrifices, Anabaptists led by the baker Jan Matthijs overthrew the government of the German city of Münster and, in a bizarre inversion of Anabaptist ideals, forced the whole population to undergo baptism. Thousands of Anabaptists flocked there from across Europe. The leaders took all property into common ownership (out of which they did rather nicely) and burnt all books but the Bible. They started by introducing the death penalty for adultery (among much else), and they ended up allowing polygamy and quickie divorces; Matthijs led the way with fifteen wives at once. Besieged by the bishop of Münster, Matthijs was convinced by his lieutenant, Jan Beuckels, that God would give him victory if he marched on the enemy with a tiny band of soldiers. Matthijs was butchered, and Beuckels took command of Münster, having himself crowned king of New Jerusalem. He presided over the starving city wearing sumptuous robes and a golden globe driven through by swords. When the bishop finally reconquered Münster in 1535, the surviving population was killed, Beuckels himself being tortured to death, then hung from St Lambert's in a cage you can see to this day.

Münster was of course a perversion of everything Anabaptism set out – and generally continued – to be. On the other hand, since many were drawn to its radicalism who had previously espoused the rather different radicalism of the Peasant's Revolt, there had long been that more dangerous strain to it as well, though it largely died along with Beuckels. But however unjustly, Münster and Anabaptism were now synonymous, and Anabaptists became the bogeymen of Europe.

After Münster, Menno Simons emerged as the leader of original, pacifist Anabaptism. He had preached Anabaptism for years, despite being a Catholic priest, but seeing his converts fall into the clutches of the state or of fiends like Jan Matthijs, while he lived in safe comfort, meant he finally quit to become a travelling preacher. He planted Mennonite churches in the Netherlands and Germany, and he survived twenty-five years as one of the most wanted men in Europe.

Calvin in Geneva

Mainstream French Protestants went to much less trouble to blacken their name. On 18 October 1534, the French king woke to find a poster on his bedroom door violently attacking the mass. These posters were all over Paris. The king led a procession with torches and relics to purify the city and repent of French toleration of heresy. Perhaps as many as thirty-five Protestants were burnt in the purge.

Among those who fled the fires was the 25-year-old John Calvin, a lawyer by training and a recent convert from humanist Catholicism. He took refuge in the Reformed city of Basle, where he wrote a primer in true Christianity, known as *Institutes of the Christian Religion*, though *Instruction in the Christian Religion* would be a better translation. Officially addressed to the king, one of its aims was to bring Protestantism out from the shadows of its disgrace in

Paris and Münster into its true light, not just exposing the errors of Catholicism but dissociating Protestants from Anabaptists and other such dangerous anarchists. After twenty years of fleshing out 'my little book', it was fourteen times the length and the primary text of Protestantism, after the Bible.

Calvin planned to settle in Bucer's Strasbourg, but his journey was disrupted by a new Franco-German war, forcing him to take a detour and stay one night in Geneva. The city government had been Protestant for just a matter of weeks, thanks to the French preacher William Farrel, who, feeling inadequate as an architect of reform, implored Calvin to stay and help. When Calvin declined, explaining that he was a timid scholar with no inclination at all to leadership, Farrel called down the curse of God on his studies and tranquillity if he deserted them. 'I felt as if God had laid his mighty hand on me from heaven to stop me,' said Calvin. 'I was so terrified by this curse that I gave up my journey.'

Despite Calvin's lack of ambition and his abhorrence of Anabaptism, Münster was the only place that had tried more far-reaching reformation than Calvin in Geneva. His first proposals centred around communion: it should be monthly instead of annual; district overseers would report those whose lives showed 'they do not belong to Jesus', who would be excluded from communion and ostracised, and if this did not bring them to heel, Calvin suggested the council should think about whether such contempt for God should go unpunished; those who would not sign a Reformed creed would also be excommunicated. The council largely accepted the proposals, but they were unpopular. Calvin was accused of Arianism and spying for France; his opponents rioted and fired shots under his window. He saw himself as the prophet Jonah, reluctantly preaching repentance to a godless city; the council took a leaf out of the same book and threw him overboard. Calvin and Farrel were expelled from Geneva in 1538. Their work completely collapsed, and Calvin was able to settle in Strasbourg after all: 'I was not sustained by such greatness of mind that I did not rejoice excessively.'

Catholic reformation: Valdés and Loyola

The Roman Catholic Church was haemorrhaging souls – and, for that matter, territory and revenue. It seemed to be do or die for the church, and Rome decided, slowly and not altogether surely, to do. Its response was the

'Counter-Reformation', a campaign both to counter the Protestant schism and to reform the church on its own terms. Catholics were no more unanimous about what reform might entail than Protestants: there were those who wished to clean up corruption and crush dissent, and then those who wanted to learn from the Protestants and win them back.

It is no coincidence that two major reform movements were led by Spaniards, Spain having been through vigorous Catholic reformation before Luther's time – nor that both left Spain after conversations with the Inquisition. The first was a humanist, Juan de Valdés, who settled in Italy and gathered a circle of enthusiasts for theology and the arts. They liked Protestant ideas on justification by faith, the focus on the Bible and the lack of interest in ritual. They were a potentially powerful force for reconciliation in the church, if only the Pope would take an interest.

The other exiled Spaniard was Ignatius Loyola. He had been a courtier, until, wounded in military action, he was converted to the religious life by the spiritual reading he was stuck with during his convalescence. Giving up his knightly apparel and weapons, he vowed to become a spiritual soldier and spent a year in reading, penance and ecstatic visions before going to Jerusalem as a missionary. In that year, he wrote the first draft of *Spiritual Exercises*, a practical four-week programme using vivid imaginings of hell and the cross to help followers to subject their will perfectly to Christ and his church. It is often said – and no less true for it – that this is the fundamental difference between Loyola and Luther: Luther emerged from his spiritual struggles with a vision of God that forced him to rebel against the church; Loyola's forged an iron obedience in him.

Nevertheless, he was not wanted by the Franciscans in Jerusalem, so he turned to education instead, spending twelve years at several universities, gathering a circle of friends, following the *Exercises* with them and dodging the Inquisition. In 1534, they vowed to visit Jerusalem, but after three years of trying, they decided to offer themselves instead to the Pope in utter submission to whatever he might ask. In 1539, they founded the Society of Jesus (the Jesuits), adding papal obedience to the usual monastic vows.

So when in Paul III Rome finally got a pope who saw that the church would not survive without far-reaching reform, he had no shortage of human resources – including many traditionalists who loathed both Valdés and Loyola. Paul was rapidly persuaded that the Jesuits were a force for spiritual renewal, and he officially recognised them. He encouraged the founding of other new orders, such as the Theatines and Ursulines whose members lived very strictly but in local parishes rather than monasteries, working for the spiritual revival of ordinary people.

Paul appointed reformers as his cardinals, notably Giovanni Carafa, a leading traditionalist, and Gasparo Contarini, one of Valdés's humanist circle. But he had no intention of letting reform cramp his personal lifestyle, and his earliest acts included giving the most lucrative posts available to his 14- and 16-year-old nephews. He found his own illegitimate children more secular preferment.

From the start, Paul laboured to arrange an ecumenical council, but the French king and German emperor prevented it. In the meantime, he set up a commission, including Carafa and Contarini, to report on the state of the church. When they delivered the report in 1537, its unsparing analysis of institutional decline and corruption was leaked to the presses, providing an invaluable arsenal for gleeful Protestant propagandists.

Protestants scored a less honourable own goal when Philip of Hesse, whose commitment to reform had never restrained his sex life, decided to make a somewhat more honest woman of his latest lover, Margaret, and commit bigamy (which bore the imperial death penalty). He asked Luther, Melanchthon and Bucer for their consent in 1539, suggesting he might turn to the Pope if they failed. The defection of the most powerful and ardent Protestant ruler would threaten the shipwreck of the Reformation, so like the Münster Anabaptists, they revived Old Testament marriage practice, 'for the sake of his conscience', as a lesser evil than adultery, so long as it was kept secret. When rumours leaked, Luther proposed 'a good, strong lie', but Melanchthon confessed and fell seriously ill with the stress. The crushing irony was that the scandal destroyed Philip's political leadership: with Protestant princes distancing themselves from his infamy, the emperor offered him pardon on the condition that he form no further alliances.

In 1538, the Franco-German war ended, and the Pope demanded that the powers unite against Protestant England. This helped Henry VIII rediscover his Catholic ardour, and the following year, he passed the Six Articles, which reasserted all Roman beliefs short of the papacy, imposing death by fire for denying transubstantiation (though this never stopped him executing overzealous Papists as traitors) and insisting that monks, whatever land they may have lost, keep their vows. Partly thanks to this display of orthodoxy, no attack was forthcoming.

Cardinal Contarini, who was close to Protestant thinking in many ways, arranged conciliation talks with Melanchthon and Bucer in Regensburg in 1541. They managed a number of impressive agreements, including justification by faith, but it was not nearly enough. By the time they realised that they would never agree about the mass, both Luther and the Pope had repudiated their earlier agreements. In two decades, Protestantism and Catholicism had drifted apart beyond the reach of peacemakers. Their differences had set too hard, become too profound and too important to be compromised. As Aquinas said, 'Unity is the agreement not of minds but of wills,' and their churches no longer had the will to reunite. Even if Contarini and Melanchthon had agreed joint statements on every issue, the agreement of moderates on either side does nothing to reconcile zealots.

Contarini returned to Rome facing accusations of heresy and died under house arrest. Now the gung-ho, anti-Protestant Carafa had his day, selling Pope Paul a new policy: 'If you can't join 'em, beat 'em.' The Pope established a Roman Inquisition with Carafa at its head, primarily to crush Italian Protestantism, in which, it succeeded admirably, while seriously injuring humanism too. Carafa had already built a new house with dungeons at his own expense.

There was no longer a breach to be mended, only a war to win. It was in this spirit that the Roman Catholic Church finally managed to come together at the ecumenical council of Trent in 1545. Within weeks of its start, Luther was dead, and Henry VIII died a year later; meanwhile, Charles V destroyed the Schmalkaldic League of Protestant states in a war of 1545–47. The first generation of the Reformation – the generation of Protestants that had wanted to reform the Roman Catholic Church, and the generation of Catholics who had wanted to win them back – was dead.

Copernicus

While the Catholic Church was trying to keep a lid on the religious revolution in Europe, the Renaissance of learning was quietly turning into an even greater revolution: science. In 1543, the Polish Catholic Copernicus died, leaving behind a book that suggested the extraordinary theory that the earth is not the centre of the universe but revolves around the sun. Counter to all common sense and received wisdom, and without much in the way of evidence, very few people took it seriously.

4

Trent (1545–58)

If the Church proclaims that what seems to be white is black, we ought to believe it to be black.
Ignatius Loyola

When the council of Trent met in 1545, on the closest thing possible to neutral ground between Germany and Italy, there were about 600 Catholic bishops in Europe, twenty-eight of whom attended. They started with the fundamental question between Catholics and Protestants: authority. For Protestants, it was a blasphemous tyranny for human ecclesiastical authorities to override what they read in the Bible; while for Catholics, to let every Bible-reader overturn the doctrines and practices of Christ's church was blasphemous anarchy. So Trent denied that the Bible is the only source of Christian truth: the apostles did not write down everything that Christ and the Holy Spirit had taught them, and so the church is a custodian of unwritten traditions every bit as God-breathed as the scriptures. Church authorities have a veto over the interpretation of scripture, forbidding anyone 'to interpret it in any way that disagrees with the understanding of holy mother Church, the only judge of its true meaning'.

They reaffirmed the seven sacraments and condemned the idea of justification by faith alone: it is impossible to be saved by one's own efforts – we need God's grace; but in those who have faith, grace and free will work together to enable them to keep God's law. We are saved by faith and by works. They affirmed original sin, against Anabaptist denial, while condemning the opposite extreme of the state reformers, that original sin annihilates free will so that we cannot even choose to accept God's call without his help.

Charles V was not happy with the uncompromising direction the council was taking. Having broken the forces of Protestantism in his empire, he could see reunion in his grasp, but only if Trent made concessions instead of erecting barriers. To avoid his interference, the Pope moved the council to the Papal State, leaving those members loyal to the emperor behind. The council fell apart.

In 1549, Pope Paul died. The favourite to succeed him, commended by Paul himself, was the English Cardinal Pole, a fervent reformer, one of Valdés's humanist circle. Like Contarini, he believed in justification by faith, and he had been forced to quit Trent (allegedly on the point of nervous breakdown) when he realised his views were to be anathematised by his church. Carafa denounced him as a heretic and he missed the papacy by one vote. Instead, it went to the epicurean pederast Julius III, on the condition that he recall Trent immediately.

Calvin back in Geneva

Geneva had not fared well without Calvin. Catholics clashed with Protestants, and so did Protestants, and the result was chaos so, in 1540, they shamefacedly asked him to return and take their religion in hand. 'I would rather die a hundred times,' said Calvin, but after eighteen months of solicitation he returned, with, since the city could not face the humiliation of losing him again, a much stronger hand.

He reorganised the church on what he saw as the New Testament model, with four kinds of ministers: pastors had overall care of the flock; elders oversaw discipline; teachers taught (in church and school); and deacons dealt with charity. He wanted clergy to be appointed by clergy, but he had to spend years fighting the council for this freedom (a new round in the medieval contest between state and church, which Luther had been happy to concede to German nobility from the start). He had no use for bishops or archbishops, each pastor sharing equal authority. Churches were plain and services simple; they sang biblical psalms but not man-made hymns, and they used both liturgy and unscripted prayer. Alehouses were closed and various 'immoralities' banned, such as dancing, theatre, slashed breeches and non-biblical Christian names.

While in Strasbourg, Calvin had written a second edition of the *Institutes*, capitalising on the book's extraordinary popularity by turning it from an introduction to Reformed Christianity into a comprehensive exposition of the faith, drawing the truths that Luther, Zwingli and Bucer had excavated from scripture into a lucid, systematic structure. *Institutes* set out the church order that he now built in Geneva, and Calvin restructured the book to make his most treasured idea its foundation: the absolute control of God over everything that happens.

> If one person is struck down by the fall of a house or a tree, if another wandering through desert paths is kept safe, the unspiritual will attribute these things to luck. But those who have learned from the mouth of Christ that every hair of their head is numbered will believe that every single event is governed by the secret direction of God.

Calvin is most famous today for the 'Calvinist' doctrine of predestination, which flows naturally from this: God, not us, chooses whether we will be saved, and he made the decision before the world began. Calvin by no means invented predestination: it was as old as Augustine; Luther, Zwingli and Bucer taught it, and Luther considered it the cornerstone of the gospel, a matter of powerless humanity's utter dependence on God. Nevertheless, Calvin made it his own in several ways. For one, he unashamedly embraced the logical conclusion that if God predestines who will be saved he also predestines who will be damned, while others ducked it. (Luther accepted this 'double predestination' but kept quiet about it.) Moreover, Calvin defended predestination all the more because other reformers, including Melanchthon, were retreating from it, and his defence made them retreat all the faster.

The importance of Calvin's thinking was, as with Aquinas, not in any particular idea, but in working his predecessors' ideas and practices into a single, integrated system. Luther did his theology on the hoof; Calvin was a lawyer, with an answer for every question and a dot for every i. Luther could no more have written *Institutes* than Calvin could have inspired *Table Talk*, a collection of memorable things Luther said while eating.

Whatever Genevans thought of Calvin, his church was a magnet for immigrants and religious refugees. For fifty years, Geneva did not have a single native minister. Naturally, this intensified tensions, adding patriotism to other resentments, but it also meant that the Calvinist package rapidly became the new international version of Protestant Christianity, perfect for export.

Burnings: Geneva and England

In 1553, a Spanish doctor called Michael Servetus was burnt for heresy in Geneva, with Calvin as a prime mover in the prosecution. Servetus denied the Trinity and condemned infant baptism, considering them the source of all that was wrong in Christianity and that they made it unnecessarily offensive to Jews and Muslims. He also tried to persuade the council to sack Calvin and give him all his goods. For this killing, Calvin is widely remembered today as a bloodthirsty tyrant, which is absurdly unjust. Religious killing is a horrible thing, but the only reason it was done in Calvin's name is that Servetus came to Geneva rather than anywhere else. He was already under sentence of death in Catholic France, and Calvin got written support for the death sentence from every major Protestant centre other than Basle. He asked the Genevan council to behead Servetus for the sake of mercy, but they refused. The execution transformed Calvin's status at home and abroad: suddenly he was taken seriously as the leader of international Protestantism, and his opponents were so discredited that, for the first time, he was able to take complete control of the Genevan church.

The same year, fires were stoked for English Protestants. After six marriages, Henry VIII had died leaving a son and two daughters. Edward, who became king at the age of nine, had been taught Protestantism by men who now tried to teach it to the rest of England. Archbishop Cranmer produced an English-language liturgy based largely on Luther's services – which offended both Catholics and Reformed – and then replaced it with a more radically Reformed prayer book, omitting traditional rituals and any mention of the bread and wine being Christ's body and blood.

But in 1553, Edward died and his elder sister Mary took the throne. She was the daughter of Henry's first queen, Catherine; Mary's family and her life had been wrecked by Protestantism, and she was determined to restore English Catholicism. She burnt 300 Protestants, from a woodcutter to the archbishop of Canterbury. (Cranmer recanted to save his life, but when Mary insisted on burning him anyway, he recanted his recantation and put the hand that had signed it into the flames first.) Unfortunately, the cheerful courage of the victims made them look suspiciously like martyrs. Worse still, Mary married Charles V's son Philip, heir to the throne of Spain, which made her religion look like a foreign invasion. Worst of all, she died in 1558 without an heir. The crown went to her sister Elizabeth, the daughter of Henry's second marriage to Anne Boleyn, for which he had created the Church of England, which made her a bastard in Catholic eyes. The English ecclesiastical seesaw was about to swing back – for what was to be the last time.

Pope Paul IV

Protestantism had triumphed in Germany. After years of conflict, the emperor was defeated by Protestant princes and forced to agree to a permanent settlement. The 1555 Peace of Augsburg gave up hope of restoring religious unity to the empire, allowing every ruler to choose between Lutheranism or Catholicism (but not Calvinism) for his own territory. This left Germany something of an ecclesiastical patchwork quilt; but Protestantism had won not only the right to exist but also the majority of Germany.

The hardening of religious divisions was hardly improved by the election of Pope Paul IV, whom we met before as the inquisitor Cardinal Carafa. Under the previous pope, Julius III, the council of Trent had returned to the business of condemning Protestant understandings of the eucharist – both bread and wine turn entirely into the body and blood of Christ, so not only is Protestant theology inadequate, but their insistence on giving people both the bread and the wine is wrong – however, this was the only important decree the council passed before Julius died, and Paul IV abandoned it, wanting all reform in his own hands. He achieved little, beyond insisting that bishops live in their dioceses and that monks who had left their houses be arrested. He had greater impact through the Roman Inquisition, which purged Italy of the last remnants of Protestantism as well as attacking humanists. He tried to bring Cardinal Pole back from Mary's England for a heresy trial, but she refused to lose him. He took control of the Society of Jesus, which lost its less traditional freedoms. He made moral demands of the Roman population every bit as puritanical as Calvin's, banning travelling entertainers and dancing, and he had fig leaves painted on the naked figures on the ceiling of the Sistine Chapel. He started the *Index of Forbidden Books*, banning Catholics from reading certain writings and calling for them to be burnt. As well as the obvious Protestant offenders, the *Index* also included Petrarch and Machiavelli, Jewish and Muslim writings, the complete works of Erasmus and most Bibles in translation (other than Latin versions). The vast Bible bonfires in Italy were one of the more surreal aspects of the purification of the church.

Pope Paul's extravagant hatreds extended from Protestants and humanists to Jews and Spaniards. Against all papal interests, he fought Philip of Spain in the last papal war to date against a Catholic monarch, and he herded Roman Jews into ghettos and made them wear yellow hats on the suspicion that they were in league with Protestants. This was of course mere paranoia, though Luther had indeed hoped to win Jews to his gospel, putting their previous unbelief down to the fact that 'The papists have so demeaned themselves that a Jew would rather be a sow than a Christian.' When they largely rejected his efforts, and even tried to convert Lutherans, he was disappointed enough to recommend – unsuccessfully – that they be forced into farm labour, their synagogues and scriptures be burnt, and their prayers be banned.

When Paul IV died in 1559, the people of Rome destroyed the buildings of the Inquisition, released its prisoners, burnt its files and dismembered the Pope's statue. His successor recalled the council of Trent, which concluded its attack on Protestantism by affirming purgatory and the sacrifice of the mass. The Pope ratified the complete legislation of the council and bishops wept to see the decades of frustration finally overcome, and a robust, bold, new Catholicism was launched on the world.

The attempt to overcome Protestants by executing them, which had claimed 3,000 lives, tailed off as the two sides took more and more to war. The urge to burn was directed, for reasons that have never been sufficiently explained, increasingly at witches. A paranoid pyromania seized both Catholics and Protestants, especially the former, and intensified throughout the next 100 years, resulting in the killing of tens of thousands of men, women and children – yet one more incomprehensible and sickening stain of blood on the hands of the body of Christ.

5

Wars of Religion (1558-98)

Maria: Marry, sir, sometimes he is a kind of puritan.
Sir Andrew: O, if I thought that, I'd beat him like a dog.
Shakespeare

The religious hopes of all English Christians rested on Queen Elizabeth I, and she disappointed most of them, one way or another. On the one hand, the religion she unveiled for the Church of England in her first couple of years on the throne was emphatically Protestant: it reused most of Cranmer's English liturgy, proclaimed Reformed teachings and removed all kinds of traditional regulations and practices that her sister Mary had reintroduced. On the other hand, there remained many Roman Catholic elements that continental churches had purged – priestly robes, ornaments, kneeling, the sign of the cross, saints' days, confirmation – and there was far less preaching. Many Protestants saw it as a good start to reformation in England and eagerly awaited the next step. But though Elizabeth was happy to keep them dangling, she had already gone as far as she ever would. She had, in fact, created Anglicanism, a third way between Rome and Geneva.

It was a religion to unite the moderate (or indifferent) majority, and doubtless England would have come to accept it soon enough, were it not for an unexpected by-product of Mary's bonfires. Hundreds of English asylum-seekers had flooded Geneva and Zürich, and they now came home, fired with a new vision of what church should be. The Church of England did not match it.

And so the great struggle for the soul of England was not between Protestantism and Catholicism, but between two Protestantisms: the puritan movement and the Anglican establishment. Puritans complained that the church was 'but halfly reformed', smeared with the 'dregs of popery'; the prayer book 'an unperfect book, culled and picked out of that popish dunghill, the... mass book, full of all abominations'. The establishment argued, like Luther, that as the Bible has nothing to say about robes or ornaments in church, they do not matter one way or the other, which means that the government (not individual churches, less still individual believers) can choose to keep them or dispense with them. The puritans insisted, like Zwingli, that the Bible gives a precise blueprint for church life, so adding robes and ornaments is sacrilegiously deviating from the blueprint. To retain Catholic traditions is to prefer the commands of the Antichrist to Christ's.

The puritan movement drew in a large minority of the population, combining those who merely wanted more preaching and fewer ornaments in church with those who wanted to abolish bishops. At the heart of it was a hatred of Catholicism and everything associated with it. John Foxe's bestselling *Book of Martyrs*, the greatest ever work of propaganda in English and the most intentionally stomach-churning thing you can buy in a Christian bookshop, documented the burning of true believers by the Roman Catholic Church. This joined with news of the continental burning of Bibles to convince readers that it was not merely a church to be reformed but a murderous, Antichristian empire. Every remnant of Catholicism was to be stripped from true worship.

Nevertheless, all Protestants adored Elizabeth as a saviour from the diabolical fires of Rome, and she needed their support, because in Catholic eyes, her reign was doubly illegitimate: she was both a heretic and a bastard. Worse still, in 1559, France and Spain made the treaty of Cateau-Cambrésis, ending seventy years of war and freeing them to crusade against Protestant nations. Mary Queen of Scots declared herself the rightful queen of England, and she had powerful French backing. For as long as she could, Elizabeth kept France and Spain at bay with talk of royal marriage, but it was a precarious game. And so, for the foreseeable future, she would have to tolerate steadily increasing puritan complaints, pretending to weigh their petitions with cautious consideration.

Calvinist wars

Scotland had its own Genevan exile, who was far more successful in importing Calvinism than the English. The Scottish preacher John Knox had spent nineteen months as a galley slave for his part in a Protestant uprising; he then took refuge in King Edward's England and joined the flight to Geneva from Mary's bonfires. The Scottish monarchy had thrown its lot in with

Catholic France as a defence against repeated English invasions; but when Mary Queen of Scots married the French heir, it looked just as much like a foreign takeover bid as the English Queen Mary's Spanish marriage had. So Protestantism and Scottish independence became powerful allies, uniting lords and commoners against the throne, led by Knox.

In May 1559, Knox led another armed uprising. French troops supported the queen, but English troops supported the rebels. The result was that both foreign powers agreed to leave Scotland alone, a triumph for Knox and independence. Under Knox's guidance, parliament accepted a Calvinist creed and outlawed Catholic forms of religion from the mass to saints' holidays – laws that Mary conspicuously flouted. Knox applied the Presbyterian system of Calvin's Geneva to the entire nation, forming an egalitarian network of local elders ('presbyters') who met for decision-making in national synods. So Scotland was a Calvinist nation with a Catholic monarchy: the incongruity could not last, and it was Mary who lost. The murderous irregularities of her sex life provoked her overthrow in 1567, and she abdicated in favour of her one-year-old son, who would rule with the advice of the Protestant nobility.

The peace between the great Catholic monarchies of France and Spain after 1559 looked like bad news for Protestants everywhere, but it turned out that any crusade against heresy would come from Spain alone, as France was debilitated by religious civil war. The celebrations of Cateau-Cambrésis included a jousting tournament, in which the French king was stabbed in the eye by a lance. Although four convicts were beheaded for biological experimentation, royal physicians failed to push back the bounds of medical science fast enough to save the king's life. Mary's husband inherited the French throne but died after eighteen months. France was left in the control of the Italian Catherine de' Medici, the queen mother, the perfect opportunity for aristocrats wanting to reduce royal power to join forces with the Protestant middle classes of French towns.

There were perhaps 1,000 underground Reformed congregations in France, and now they started seizing Catholic churches and worshipping with armed guards to protect them from repossession. To avert civil war, Queen Catherine arranged a conference at Poissy in 1561 between Calvinist and Catholic theologians, which merely confirmed Catholic convictions that Calvinism was blasphemy. So in 1562, she issued a decree allowing Protestants to worship publicly outside French cities, but demanded they evacuate all seized parish churches. This settlement lasted a matter of weeks, until 1,000 Protestants were found worshipping in an urban barn. Anti-Protestant violence rapidly claimed hundreds of lives throughout France, and the country descended into thirty years of civil war, massacres, robbery, destruction and indiscriminate murder.

In the Netherlands, Protestantism (Lutherans, Calvinists and Anabaptists) got much of its following from the fact that the country was ruled by Catholic Spain. The Dutch nobleman William of Orange led a rather feeble uprising in 1566, but Spain's gratuitously savage reprisals and economic punishments ensured that next time, the nationalists would have far wider support.

In 1570, French Protestants and Catholics achieved what looked like lasting peace, granting Protestants places of worship throughout the country, plus control of four cities. France decided to celebrate its new unity by attacking Spain, sending 15,000 troops to help the Dutch. While preparations were being made, a leading Calvinist noble married the king's sister in Paris in 1572 to cement the religious union. The Calvinist outlaw Admiral de Coligny, along with thousands of Protestants, came to Paris for the wedding. He was a bitter enemy of Catherine de' Medici, and he was shot. When Coligny survived the attack, Catherine pre-empted Protestant reprisals by ordering a massacre of all Protestants in Paris on 24 August, St Bartholomew's Day. How many died is hard to say, but it was at least 3,000 in Paris and many times that number throughout France. The war was revived.

The St Bartholomew's Day massacre dashed Dutch hopes for French support against Spain, and so their war of independence dragged on for years. It ended with the Protestant north gaining independence and becoming a prosperous republic, the United Provinces, while the Catholic south remained Spanish. This is where today's Holland and Belgium eventually came from. There was now such a variety of religion in the north, though, that not even Calvinism had anything like a majority. Calvinist authorities were forced to rule by religious coalition, and the United Provinces became the most pluralistic society in Europe, a haven of toleration for dissidents.

Mary Queen of Scots, though she had abdicated in Scotland, never gave up her claim to the English throne, and in 1586, she formed a plan with English Catholics to overthrow Elizabeth. The plot was discovered and Elizabeth reluctantly executed her, but before she died, Mary named King Philip of Spain as her successor as rightful ruler of England. Philip launched the Spanish Armada, the greatest naval force the world had ever seen, against

England in 1588, bearing 19,000 soldiers and 180 monks. The Armada was utterly destroyed, partly by English naval skill and partly by unfavourable wind, which for England was perfect proof that God was on their side.

This victory secured Elizabeth's throne, freeing her to take action against the puritans. Under relatively mild pressure from the authorities, puritanism turned – for now – from a clamorous movement for church reform into a matter largely of personal spirituality.

But not all puritans could accept this. For years, they had been insisting that following the biblical blueprint was essential to being a true church. If they accepted that the Church of England was not, and was never going to be, properly reformed, then should it not be shunned as a false church? A small minority of puritans gave up on the Church of England and started their own underground churches, and so the puritans joined the ranks of radicals who were horrified to find their ideas taken to their logical conclusion by more radical followers. Elizabeth's anti-puritan crackdown gave new impetus to this defection, but it had been happening for years: there had, after all, been no further reform since the second year of her reign.

These separatists found having to take control of their own religion such a liberating experience that they decided that this was how church should be: not whole parishes dragged along to worship, following the pattern ordered by the state, but a holy minority choosing to come together, worshipping in the ways they find in the Bible, electing their own ministers. 'The Lord's people is of the willing sort.' This democracy, or 'congregationalism', was close to continental Anabaptism, except that the separatists maintained Calvinist beliefs about predestination and so on, and they continued to baptise babies – largely because they were frightened of becoming Anabaptists, who they thought were insane hooligans. In 1593, the two leaders of the London separatist church were beheaded for sedition, and the congregation were allowed to go free, so long as they emigrated to Holland.

That same year, the French wars finally came to an end, with the conversion of King Henry IV. He had come to the throne as a leading Protestant in 1589 (because the old king had been assassinated by a Catholic monk, illogically enough). This looked like wonderful news for the Protestants, until he became a Catholic. He reckoned, rightly, that this would win the support of the Catholic majority, while maintaining his existing allegiances: 'Paris is worth a mass,' he reportedly calculated. He has often been criticised for putting politics before religion, but if that religion is the kind that France had witnessed for the last thirty years, this doesn't seem so unreasonable. In 1598, the Edict of Nantes confirmed that France would be Catholic, but gave Protestants considerable freedom. Both versions of Christianity became legal in the same country at once.

The most tolerant country in Europe was the commonwealth of Poland-Lithuania, which housed not only thriving Reformed, Lutheran and Catholic churches but also the Socinians (after Fausto Sozzini), who denied the Trinity and the deity of Christ.

6

The Ends of the Earth
(1492–1600)

> **The Captain named the peak we saw Easter Mountain, and the country the Land of the True Cross.**
> *Pedro Vaz de Caminha, on the discovery of Brazil*

The age of reformation had also seen the rebirth of Catholic foreign mission, which did much to compensate for the church's cataclysmic losses at home to Protestantism. The two great trading nations of Portugal and Spain became explorers and colonists, and so, in a measure that seemed fair and sensible at the time, the Pope in 1493 drew a line down the middle of the Atlantic, granting exclusive trading rights and missionary obligations in the west to Spain, and in the east to Portugal. ('I would like to see the clause of Adam's will that excludes me from a share of the globe,' said the French king when colonialism became more competitive.) This alliance between Christianity and commerce characterised sixteenth-century European expansion, the results varying from heroic missionary self-sacrifice to lawless, murderous plunder.

As the Spanish made conquests throughout South America, Franciscan and Dominican missionaries made converts, all with surprising speed. Already by 1530, Columbus had conquered his 'West Indies', Cortes had taken Aztec Mexico and Pizarro's brisk subjugation of Inca Peru was underway. The West Indies and Mexico had bishops, and one pair of Franciscans in Mexico had baptised 200,000 people, peaking at 14,000 in one day.

On arrival, the commander would read natives a decree explaining that the Pope ruled the earth; that if they submitted immediately to his rule they would be taught and baptised into his religion; and that if they resisted 'we shall do you all the mischief we can': they would lose all their lands, possessions and families and become slaves. The precise terms were of little relevance as it was read in Spanish. Those who submitted had to settle in labour camps where they were forced to work for the Spanish in return for protection and Christian teaching. Life expectancy under such protection was about two years. Columbus demanded a quarterly quota of gold from his 'Indians'; those who failed him had their hands cut off and were left to die. Whole American populations were wiped out by a combination of war, executions, forced labour and, above all, new European diseases such as measles and smallpox. The survival rate on the Caribbean island of Hispaniola in the first fifteen years of Spanish rule was one in forty; by 1550, the population of the Americas had fallen by perhaps 95 per cent.

And yet religious mission was not merely a cynical front for mercenary acquisitiveness; the unprovoked genocide is made even more depressing by the fact that most of those responsible genuinely believed they were doing God's work, extending the rule of Christ and saving heathen souls. There were those like Pizarro, who, when reminded about his duty to provide religious teaching for his Peruvian subjects, explained, 'I have not come for any such reason; I have come to take away their gold'; but more were like Columbus, who believed, 'The Trinity has made me his messenger.' Natives kidnapped as slaves, thought Queen Isabella of Spain, 'can, being used by Christians, be converted to our faith more quickly'.

On the other hand, there were monks who had crossed the Atlantic to preach the gospel and make disciples, and who were dismayed and ashamed to discover that their job was to baptise into slavery those who had been 'converted' at the end of a sword. The Dominican Antonio de Montesinos, preaching before the western dignitaries of Hispaniola in 1511, protested,

> You are in mortal sin for your cruel oppression of these innocent people. Tell me, by what right do you keep them in such cruel and horrible servitude? Are they not human beings? Do they not have rational souls? Are you not obliged to love them as you love yourselves?… How is it that you sleep so soundly?

The answer seems to have been a resounding shrug.

Bartholomew de las Casas was a Hispaniola labour-camp manager who became a Dominican priest. Four years later, in 1514, he saw a native rebel leader burnt alive, refusing to the last to convert because he did not want to go to heaven if white men were there; Las Casas realised he had become part of a diabolical evil, released his workers and spent the rest of his life campaigning for justice in America. He described for European readers the squalor of the camps, the atrocities and massacres by the Spanish, from live burial to killing babies for bets, and the gentle goodness of the Americans. His books were banned and burnt, thanks to their Protestant propaganda value, but he persuaded Emperor Charles V to pass laws restricting the labour camps in 1542.

The restrictions had limited impact, but Las Casas continued his campaign, and in 1550, he arranged an official debate on the subject in the Spanish capital Valladolid. His opponent argued, following Aristotle, that some races are naturally inferior to others and therefore their rightful slaves. Las Casas insisted that there are no people so base that they cannot be civilised 'as long as the right and natural method is used: love, gentleness and kindness'; and that in fact the Americans already have such virtue that 'they would be the most blessed people in the world if only they worshipped the true God'. Las Casas's moral victory did little directly to help the Americans, but perhaps his greatest achievement was that out of this most despicable episode in Christian history, he brought the first great advocacy of human rights.

Africa and India

By 1550, the Portuguese controlled the Brazilian coast, so the papal dividing line was shifted 1,000 miles west to recognise their rule. On the other side of the Atlantic, they had been colonising and circumnavigating Africa. They had spent the fifteenth century edging their way down the west coast in search of gold and pepper, and trying to find a way to India that avoided the Turks. They finally got there by sailing around the cape in 1498, while Columbus was still insisting he had found the short cut. By this time, they had also sailed up the river Congo and converted King Mbanza Kongo, baptising him as John I. In return for bringing the gospel to sub-Saharan Africa, the Portuguese had taken 150,000 slaves to work their Atlantic sugar plantations and to sell to Latin America in order to make up for the depleted stock of native labour there. Unlike American slaves, these were generally bought from African traders rather than being kidnapped directly.

In Asia, unlike America and Africa, Europeans came across civilisations more sophisticated, wealthy and powerful than their own, and they were persuaded to evangelise without the benefit of abduction and torture. On reaching southern India, the Portuguese found there was already a church there, the ancient Thomas Christians who traced their own origins back to the missionary journeys of the apostle Thomas, an unproven but plausible enough legend; they had certainly been in India for well over a millennium. Their existence was less surprising to the Portuguese than it is to us: it was generally believed in Europe that there was a great, long-lost church in the Far East, and explorers were eager to reunite with them, not least in order to join forces against Islam. The Thomas Christians were not that church, however, being low in numbers (10,000 in a subcontinent of 90 million people) and in class (all converts from Hinduism lost their caste status), and the Europeans' main response to discovering them was to try to impose Roman Catholicism on them.

The first mass conversion of Hindus was from the low-caste pearl-fishers of the east coast, who were being devastated by Muslim attacks and were advised by a native Christian to ask the Portuguese for protection. To seal the deal, the whole population of 10,000 to 20,000 were baptised in 1536, at least doubling numbers of Indian Christians (depending of course on how one defines 'Christian').

In 1542, Francis Xavier, peerless missionary and a founding member of the Jesuits, arrived in India, leaving seven years later for Japan. Told that he should take a servant, it being beneath the dignity of a papal representative to do laundry, he replied, 'It is such dignity that has debased the church of Rome. The way to real dignity is washing one's own underwear.' Finding that the pearl-fishers had not been taught a single thing about Christianity since their supposed conversion, Xavier preached to the converted as well as winning thousands of new believers. He translated the creed, the Lord's prayer, the Ave Maria and the ten commandments, and he toured the villages teaching them to the people, starting with the boys. 'Give me the children until they are seven,' as he famously said, 'and anyone who likes can have them afterwards.' By his reckoning, he baptised 10,000 in one month, and he believed that many were healed by his Gospel readings.

The Thomas Christians were ruled by the archbishop of Mesopotamia, but the Portuguese resented his attempts to supply them with bishops. They repeatedly accused the bishops of heresy and sent them to Europe for trial, where they were repeatedly acquitted. Rome started appointing western bishops of Goa in 1559, and in 1599, the bishop held the Synod of Diamper to bring the natives to heel. Having packed it with 100 priests ordained for the occasion to ensure a majority, he read out a series of decrees in Portuguese, according to which the Indian church became subject to Rome and Goa, and adopted Roman Catholic practices with a few minor variations. Any resistance to the ruling, once it was understood, was of course put down ruthlessly. The church of St Thomas was subsumed into the global empire of St Peter.

Japan

Xavier came to Japan equipped with information given him by a Japanese outlaw in India, assured that they were 'very eager to learn what they do not know, about both God and the world', and that if he impressed them with his holy life and his answers to their questions, 'the king, nobles and other discriminating people would become Christians' within six months. The reality was disappointing. They were delightful people, honourable, kind, reasonable, hungry for wisdom, and Xavier had profound respect for them, but they were slow to move from curiosity to conversion. One great barrier, he found, was their 'hateful and annoying objection, that God could not be merciful and good if he had never made himself known to the Japanese before we came – especially if those who had not worshipped him aright were condemned to everlasting punishment in hell'. Another was, 'If what we taught was true, how was it that the Chinese knew nothing about it?'

Xavier saw that the local lords would need to be converted for the people to follow, and he concentrated his efforts on them, abandoning his monastic poverty when he saw it offended Japanese sensibilities. But when the total number of people baptised was only a few hundred in the first two years, all commoners, he decided the real root of the problem was their respect for the religious traditions of China, and so in 1552, he set off to convert the Chinese. He died before reaching the mainland.

Soon enough, though, the local lords of Japan started to respond to Jesuit preaching. The first was baptised in 1563, and over the next decade, all his 50,000 subjects followed his lead. The same thing happened in several regions, and by 1587, there were 200,000 Christians in Japan, in 240 churches. But in that year, the new ruler attempting to reunify Japan announced the expulsion of all foreign missionaries: 'Japan is a country of the gods and it is wicked for these priests to come here preaching a religion of devils.' It took ten years for repatriation to begin in earnest, but a serious assault on Japanese Christianity lay ahead.

7

More Wars (1600–60)

The English have sixty different religions and only one sauce.
Domenico Caracciolo

In 1603, Queen Elizabeth passed the English throne on to James, the son of
Mary Queen of Scots, who had been king of Scotland since the age of one.
He was a perfect choice, enjoying the expectant approval of Protestants and
Catholics, and, by ruling both kingdoms, finally bringing Scotland under the
English crown without a shot being fired. But like Elizabeth, he disappointed
both puritans and papists, insisting from the start that there would be no
change in the church. Catholic disillusion with James was vented in Guy
Fawkes's gunpowder plot, which provided a focus for English papaphobia in
the annual, effigy-burning festival that continues to this day. James met with
puritan leaders to hear their petitions in 1604, which went so far as replacing
the rule of bishops with the Presbyterian system of Scotland. But James had
found Presbyterianism a serious hindrance to royal power, and he told them,
'No bishop, no king' – rather prophetically, as it turned out. The one request
he granted them was for a new translation of the Bible, the Authorised Version
of 1611. He required all ministers to declare their approval of bishops and the
entire contents of the prayer book, which resulted in ninety being sacked for
dissent.

A new wave of separatists then left the Church of England, many joining
the exiles in Amsterdam, where they started disagreeing and separating from
each other. The most radical of all was the pastor John Smyth, who first fell
out with other separatists over some very obscure issues, such as his
insistence on reading the Bible in the original Greek and Hebrew in church.
Then in 1609, he renounced infant baptism. Since the separatists agreed that
church consisted not of 'all the profane of the parish' but only believers, he
argued that only believers should be baptised. Those christened as children
need proper baptism as consenting adults. Most outrageously of all, he

baptised himself, knowing no truly baptised person to do it for him, before baptising his followers. Then they cut their last ties to Calvinism by rejecting predestination: we choose whether or not to be Christians, in every sense. The first Baptist Church was born.

It was such a logical conclusion to separatist voluntary religion that it largely subsumed the parent movement. But it only took the Baptists a year to split. They had become similar enough to the Mennonite Anabaptists of Amsterdam to accept them as true Christians, and Smyth decided he had been wrong to baptise himself when they could have done it, so he asked them for a third baptism. His co-leader, Thomas Helwys, insisted this was unnecessary. Smyth ended up, along with most of the Baptists, joining the Mennonite Church. Helwys decided it was wrong to live safely in exile when all England lived in damnable ignorance, so he took a ten-person Baptist Church back home. He seems to have died in prison in about 1615.

One of the few separatist groups that survived sailed on the *Mayflower* to New England in 1620, missing their target, the new British colony of Virginia, by 500 miles. This blunder would allow them, should they survive, complete religious freedom.

Arminianism and the Thirty Years' War

Calvinism in Holland suffered a more eminent defection, in the person of the pastor and professor Jacob Arminius. He had been commissioned in 1589 to refute Dirk Coornhert, a Catholic humanist who attacked the Calvinist doctrine of predestination as repellent, unjust and unbiblical. The more Arminius studied the issue, the more he put off publishing his response, because he was increasingly convinced by Coornhert (who had already had a similar effect on two previous Calvinist pastors with the same job as Arminius).

Arminius's new understanding of predestination – about which he kept very quiet for a long time – was that, instead of arbitrarily choosing to save certain people and damn certain others, God chose in two rather fairer ways: first, he chose to save all who become Christians; and then he foresaw which individuals would and would not become Christians with his help, choosing the former and giving them the ability to believe. 'God truly wills the salvation of all men,' but he only draws them 'through sweet persuasion'. Humans have free choice as well as God.

When these ideas became public, they caused huge conflict in Holland, which continued long after Arminius's death, until a Calvinist general seized control of the country. A national synod met at Dort in 1618, packed with Calvinists from across western Europe. It condemned Arminianism, forbade its preaching and issued ninety-three 'canons' defining Calvinist religion more rigidly than Calvin ever had. Arminians fled the country, but seven years later, a new government restored the policy of toleration.

In Germany, Calvinism had gained ground in the latter decades of the sixteenth century, and several states were now Calvinist, but Calvinism was still officially illegal throughout the empire. The elector of Saxony launched vicious attacks on those Lutherans who seemed too close to Calvin, which only drove more people into Calvin's posthumous clutches. These Protestant divisions allowed a resurgence of Catholic power in the empire, and once again, Protestant and Catholic states in Germany allied themselves in defensive blocs.

Then, in 1617, the ardent Catholic Archduke Ferdinand was named heir to his uncle, who was also the Holy Roman Emperor, as king of Bohemia. He curtailed the freedoms that Bohemian Protestants had enjoyed, and they voiced their complaints by throwing two imperial representatives out of a window – the quaintly named 'defenestration of Prague'. A revolt followed, which put a Calvinist on the Bohemian throne; but Ferdinand became emperor, and with the support of Bavaria and Spain launched an attack to reclaim the Bohemian crown. The mutually assured destruction of the Thirty Years' War had begun.

Nobili and Ricci

Asian Catholicism was enjoying continued success. In the Philippines, the missionaries were virtually unopposed and converted the entire population through teaching and social work with little bloodshed either way. Jesuits in Vietnam faced considerable opposition but nevertheless made thousands of converts.

In China, after seventeen years of trying to ingratiate himself, the Jesuit Matthew Ricci gained permission to enter Beijing and pay his respects to the emperor. Dressing like a Chinese noble, he won respect by giving the emperor clocks and maintaining them, and he was allowed to build a church. He taught a most accommodating version of Catholicism, allowing converts to maintain their veneration of ancestors and of Confucius, and he used Confucian terms for Christian ideas like 'God' and 'heaven'. He died in 1610, leaving 3,000 converts and considering himself a sower rather than a reaper. His Jesuit successors continued to impress and accommodate Confucians by successfully predicting eclipses, which allowed them to calculate their lucky days.

Developments in Japan were less happy. Thirty years after the decree expelling missionaries, fifty remained in the country, and in 1617, the government started purging the religion by force. The missionaries were burnt; native believers were crucified, sometimes upside down on the beach so that they drowned when the sea came in, or boiled, or hung over cesspits. When it seemed that these heroic deaths only made Christianity more impressive, the tactic changed to torturing Christians into submission instead. The campaign continued throughout the century and – to all appearances – entirely destroyed the young Japanese church.

The Jesuit Robert Nobili brought the friendly, evangelistic approach of Ricci to India, after the arrogance of earlier missionaries had made Christianity roundly despised by respectable Indians. Dissociating himself completely from the European church, he presented himself as a Brahman, dressed as a guru, learned an impressive set of languages, took up vegetarianism, embraced the caste system and held open-air religious debates. New followers kept all Hindu practices except the inescapably idolatrous. Thanks to his undercover evangelism, high-caste Indians finally started 'converting', though whether they realised they were is debatable.

Before long, Nobili's cover was blown, and he faced the wrath of both Rome and India, Rome accusing him of compromising the gospel, India of duplicity and subterfuge. He insisted to the Indians that he was not a 'Paranga', which is what they called their European immigrants, Nobili maintaining that the term only referred to the Portuguese. To Rome, he argued that mission was not about turning Indians into Europeans but teaching them the essential elements of Christianity and letting them decide for themselves how to incorporate them into Indian life. Both sides in the end gave him the benefit of the doubt, and when he died in 1656, he had baptised 600 men, women and children of high caste. To modern, pluralistic westerners, Nobili's acceptance of native tradition seems self-evidently right; but the fact that his toleration of the caste system meant feeding communion to Christian *dalits* ('untouchables') on the end of a stick demonstrates that issues of cultural tolerance can be more complicated than they first appear.

In fact, Nobili's approach became something like official Catholic policy for a while. In 1622, the Pope established the Sacred Congregation for the Propagation of the Faith to oversee world mission. The fact that its Latin name gave English the term 'propaganda' is a quirk of language rather than a fair reflection of its methods. It aimed to spread Christianity without European culture and to appoint native priests and bishops as soon as possible.

War in Germany and England

The Thirty Years' War in Germany had started as a straightforward imperial attack to reverse the Calvinist revolution in Bohemia, but quickly achieving this, the Catholics then pressed on and took other Calvinist and then Lutheran states in the empire, restoring Catholicism. This victory encouraged the emperor to issue the Edict of Restitution in 1629, requiring the return of all churches won by Protestants in the last seventy-seven years, expelling Lutherans from Catholic lands and outlawing Calvinists throughout the empire.

But the extremity of this brought the king of Lutheran Sweden into the war, followed by France and Spain, and it became a protracted contest between them for territorial gain, in which the original religious quarrel was forgotten and Germany was absolutely devastated and brutalised after thirty years as a battle ground. The final peace treaty of 1648 more or less returned the map of the empire to its pre-war shape, except with some territorial gains for the Catholic Church, including Bohemia, in return for finally granting Calvinism the right to exist. The Pope denounced the concession but found that his influence was becoming negligible.

The war had a phenomenal impact on the European mind. You could say that it began as the last religious war and ended as the dawn of an age when for the first time, it could be said 'Religion and politics don't mix'; or in the words of Cardinal Richelieu, the French chief minister responsible both for the repression of Protestants at home and for supporting German and Swedish Protestants against the emperor, 'The interests of the state and the interests of religion are completely different things.' The war was the atrocious climax to 120 years of religious combat in Europe; in retrospect, it was the war to end religious war. As the dust of battle settled, so did a kind of religion fatigue, a realisation that religious differences were now permanent and would have to be tolerated. Religious minorities long continued to be hated and assaulted as a political and social menace, but governments became less inclined to consider religion as an end in itself. The secularisation of Europe had begun.

The British were twelve years behind in this process and still in the middle of a passionate campaign for the country's soul. It started with King Charles I's attempts to restore traditional ritual to British churches. His religion was what is today called 'Anglo-Catholic': it kept the liturgy and creed of the Elizabethan prayer book intact, and the sovereign independence of the Church of England, but reintroduced traditional ornaments, vestments and ceremonies. Charles's archbishop of Canterbury, William Laud, argued that England had never ceased to be Catholic and never split from Rome – which was news to a lot of people – but was merely the best-reformed branch of the church. Puritan preaching was banned, Arminian preaching promoted.

It was widely assumed that Charles was simply a devious Roman Catholic. He was certainly devious, but his religion was precisely what it claimed to be: he never wanted to restore the Pope. It smelt, however, like 'flat popery', in the words of the farmer MP Oliver Cromwell, and Charles's marriage to a French Catholic who refused to attend any Protestant services, including her husband's coronation, did not help. Even the most moderate Protestants were alarmed. Parliament protested, so Charles decided to rule without it. No parliament, though, meant no new taxes (the reason that kings called parliaments), so Charles had to dredge up all kinds of obsolete and disused levies, arresting those who refused payment as well as fining landowners who failed to buy knighthoods. The 'eleven years' personal rule' was so hated that Charles achieved the stupendous feat of making his bête noir of puritanism suddenly seem like good, old-time religion.

Many puritans quit England for New England in search of religious freedom. Once they found it, it proved too precious to be wasted on people who would not use it properly: Congregationalism became law, and only the converted could vote. They expelled a Baptist called Roger Williams, who then started a settlement on Rhode Island, offering religious freedom even to those who had a different religion. At the same time, Charles I leased the colony of Maryland to the Catholic Lord Baltimore, who, unable to make it officially Catholic, decreed toleration too. In England, a new Baptist group appeared, which, unlike Smyth's and Helwys's, accepted Calvinist ideas about predestination and remained on friendly terms with puritans in the

Church of England. Because of their different opinions over whether Christ died for the elect or all humankind, Baptists were called either the Particular (Calvinist) or the General (non-Calvinist) Baptists.

Charles overreached himself. James I had successfully replaced the Presbyterian system in Scotland with bishops, after buying off the nobility with church land; Charles first reclaimed this land for the church, losing his only allies outside the bishops, and then in 1637, he tried to impose a version of the English prayer book on Scotland. At its inaugural service, a woman threw a stool at the bishop and rioting broke out. The Scottish General Assembly abolished not just the prayer book but bishops, and when the king refused to recognise the assembly's authority, a vast Scottish army invaded England. Charles had no way of raising sufficient funds for the war without recalling the English parliament and giving them – at least for the moment – whatever they wanted.

The puritan parliament abolished the innovations of Charles's personal rule, but when it pressed on to deeper political and religious radicalism, it lost enough support for war to break out between king and parliament in 1642. During the war, parliament scrapped the prayer book and bishops; and in return for Scottish military support, it promised to replace them with the Scottish order of worship and Presbyterian Church government. Failing, not surprisingly, to get Archbishop Laud convicted of treason, parliament simply passed a law declaring him guilty and had him killed.

In the same year that the Thirty Years' War ended, King Charles surrendered. Thanks to Oliver Cromwell's policy of promoting soldiers of ability regardless of social rank, the army was a hotbed of political and religious radicalism, and it now demanded the king's execution. To win parliament's agreement, the army drove out every MP who disagreed, which was most of them. The remnant not only had Charles killed but abolished the monarchy and the House of Lords. They went on to outlaw such evils as swearing, maypoles, Sunday sport, the theatre, Christmas and Easter. Many alehouses were closed, and churches were stripped of their ornaments and artwork. (The army had come close to demolishing the 'pagan temple' of Stonehenge.) And they decreed religious toleration, allowing anyone to go to whichever church they fancied, or if none suited, to invent their own. This indulgence did not extend to Catholics, Anglo or otherwise, but it did to Jews.

Russia underwent a puritan campaign at the same time. Reformers imposed austere fasts, fought drunkenness and the abridging of liturgy, and they executed people for drinking tobacco. A new patriarch of Moscow, Nikon, replied with a counter-reformation that remade the Russian Orthodox church in the image of the Greek Orthodox church. Nikon became the most powerful churchman in Russian history; his opponents formed a breakaway church, the Raskolniki ('Separatists') or Old Believers. Nikon was eventually deposed, but his reforms remained.

Religious freedom in England meant an outbreak of wild new sects. The Seekers horrified the General Baptists by demonstrating that not even they had taken radical puritanism to its logical extreme. If, as the Baptists had concluded, true baptism had died out in all Catholic and Protestant churches, then people cannot simply bump-start it themselves; they have to wait for God to send a new generation of apostles. The Seekers stopped all sacraments and ordinations until further notice.

The Ranters scrapped all religious and moral rules too, with predictable results. The Muggletonians believed that anyone who knowingly rejected their teachings was damned, so they considerately told no one what they were. Miraculously, the first Christian sect to ban evangelism lasted until the 1970s.

The most successful new sect was the Quakers, who taught that all people have an inner light from God, which is all the religion one needs. They did not deny the Bible but claimed it told them nothing they did not already know. Their greatest offence was equality: as all people have the same standing before God, they refused to doff their hats to their betters, interrupted parish sermons to correct the minister and allowed women to preach. And because true religion is all about what goes on inside, they abandoned all outward rituals and ministers altogether. ('We are not of the opinion that the sprinkling water on a child's head makes him a Christian.') The Seekers had found what they were looking for and largely joined up. Various sects had rashes of prophetic stunts, such as the Quaker leader whose inner light told him he was Jesus, and so re-enacted Palm Sunday by riding into Bristol surrounded by singing women.

For most English people, this mix of religious anarchy and moral tyranny had gone far too far. Just as Charles had achieved the impossible in putting the puritans in power, the puritans now returned the favour. In 1660, his son, Charles II, reclaimed the throne, restoring the rule of bishops to the churches of England and Scotland. Cromwell was hanged and beheaded, despite having died in 1658.

The final result of the contests of the Reformation is that both sides have lost. The Protestants have failed to reform the Catholic Church; Rome has failed to stamp out the revolution. And yet the church as a whole, though irrecoverably divided, has had the spring-clean of a lifetime, and the transformation is permanent.

Latterly, though, the quieter but even greater revolution of the mind, science, has been brewing, having been given an unexpected kick-start by the Dutch spectacle-maker Hans Lipperhey, who in 1608, arranged two lenses in a tube and found he had created a new toy for the royal courts of Europe, the 'spyglass', which made distant objects look triple the size. Soon more far-reaching uses would be found for it. For better or worse, the ability of science to disprove religious claims and its power to explain and control the world are going to make religion work very hard to justify its existence.

Part 4

Globalisation

1

The Earth Moves (1609-89)

A gateway and a road are opened to a new and more excellent knowledge.
Galileo Galilei

In 1609, the professor of maths at Pisa University heard of the new Dutch invention, the 'spyglass', and he made one himself. His own was much more powerful, allowing him not merely to spy but to discover a new universe, our own. Galileo saw craters and mountains on the moon, dark patches in the sun, satellites around Jupiter and Saturn, and Venus waxing and waning like the moon: things 'never seen from the beginning of the world right up to our day', he enthused.

It is hard to appreciate or exaggerate just how scandalous and revolutionary these finds were when they became public. The ancients such as Aristotle, the scriptures, the Church Fathers, common sense and universal experience agreed: the earth was a fixed point at the centre of the universe. It was an imperfect globe at the heart of a structure of seven perfect, concentric spheres – seven crystal layers, like a glass onion. Each sphere contained a planet – the moon, Mercury, Venus, the sun, Mars, Jupiter, Saturn – and revolved around the earth; and the outermost shell of the cosmos was the unmoving realm of the stars. According to Aristotle, everything on earth was made from four elements – earth, air, fire, water – while the heavens were made entirely from a fifth, ether.

Galileo's findings, for those who accepted them, created new heavens and a new earth. Craters and sunspots meant the planets were imperfect, presumably made from the same stuff as the earth. The satellites ruined the perfect number of seven planets. Worst of all, the phases of Venus and various other discoveries proved Copernicus right: the sun, not the earth, is the centre around which all else revolves.

Many did accept Galileo's findings, including Catholic authorities as high as Pope Urban VIII, but his theories faced powerful opponents and serious objections. As well as the trauma of humanity losing its central place and finding itself so fundamentally wrong, there was the most obvious evidence: if the earth is spinning at 1,000 miles per hour and hurtling through space, then how does everything stay so serenely on the surface? Galileo could not say. A compromise theory, that the planets orbit the sun and the sun orbits the earth, seemed to fit the evidence just as well. And did the Bible not say that God 'laid the foundation of the earth, that it should never be moved', and that he once made the sun and moon stand still? Galileo was a devout Catholic, and he argued that such passages were figuratively, not literally, true, as his observations proved, but Catholic authorities were no more prepared to let scientists reinterpret the Bible for them than Calvinists.

The fundamental problem was not that of one set of ideas versus another, but of how we know anything. The Christian understanding of understanding was that God has revealed all truth through his appointed authorities. If learning from them was to be replaced by observing and calculating for oneself, who could say what certainties would be demolished next?

By a bizarre convention, Galileo and friends were allowed to write astronomy books using the sun-centred universe as a model, so long as they made it clear that it was a fiction, an absurd nonsense that just happened to help their calculations, like infinity minus one in modern maths. But Galileo broke the rule in his 1630 *Dialogue about the Two Major World Systems*, which made it clearer than he realised which system he sided with. His old friend Pope Urban could not afford to seem soft on heresy, and so in 1633, Galileo was interviewed by the Inquisition (who had already passed the book as sound but then had second thoughts).

The Galileo of legend is broken down with threats of torture and burning, until he finally recants, adding under his breath, 'But it does move.' In fact, he insisted from the start that he had never believed in the Copernican universe: 'A long time ago... I was undecided between the two opinions,' but once the church had condemned the Copernican opinion, 'my uncertainty stopped'. Still, he and his book were condemned, and he had to do public penance and stay under house arrest for the rest of his life. (People as well connected as Galileo were not generally burnt, only their books.)

Galileo was a founding father of science not just in his discoveries, but as a pioneer of experiments. He applied the principles of earthly physics to the movements of stars and planets, and he used mathematics to measure both, integrating maths, physics and astronomy for the first time. His *Dialogue* remained banned to Catholics until 1835. In condemning him, the Catholic Church not only opposed the truth about creation but became an adversary of the modern world.

Descartes

The other great mathematician of the age was a less reluctant revolutionary. While Galileo's discoveries threw him into an unwanted conflict with traditional thinking, the Frenchman René Descartes dismissed all existing philosophy and started from scratch, simply because he thought he could do better. A product of the Reformation era, he saw all authorities in hopeless conflict and concluded that you know nothing until you work it out for yourself, with mathematical certainty (perfectly possible for anyone who tries carefully enough).

Even our own senses can deceive us, so Descartes taught himself to doubt everything he had ever seen or heard. There was only one thing he could not doubt – that he was doubting, and therefore that 'he' existed. 'I think,' he thought, 'therefore I am.' Having proved himself, he put two and two together and came up with infinity: God exists too. The idea of God is perfect and infinite, so Descartes's finite, imperfect mind could not have invented it; it must have been put there by God himself. Of course, proving God was nothing new; where Descartes was burning the boats was in demanding such rigid standards of proof – standards his own proof did not really come up to. It was another body blow for the idea of authority. Galileo proved the authorities wrong; Descartes offered the infectious example of denying all authority except that of one's own mind.

The story of Descartes shutting himself in an oven while he doubted is probably the result of a mistranslation (of 'stove-heated room'), but it perfectly illustrates how he searched for truth by shutting out everything his senses tried to tell him, while Galileo found it by looking around. It was the ancient contest between Plato and Aristotle again, reason versus observation; and Descartes had not backed a winner.

Puritans, pietists and tolerance

In England, the puritan revolution was over. After 1660, the theatres and alehouses reopened, and while most people wanted a quiet church life without disturbance from puritan or Catholic, many also wanted revenge on the anarchic, killjoy commoners who had seized their country. King Charles II, however, wanted toleration: he was a closet Catholic, and he knew that if he tried to convert the Church of England, he would follow his father into the head-basket, so instead, he argued for universal free choice in religion.

This delicately balanced tension was resolved when a band of puritans captured London and killed twenty-two people in an attempt 'to replace King Charles with King Jesus'. Parliament went for the jugular. Puritans were banned from working for the state or church. There was a new, anti-puritan prayer book in 1662. Ministers who disapproved of bishops were deposed, so the Presbyterians were forced to become another alternative sect. Baptists and Quakers were outlawed again, and mobs broke up their meetings and killed them. When plague hit London in 1665, most vicars took a holiday in the country, but many sacked puritans stayed and worked in the deserted churches. Their reward from parliament was that puritan ministers were banned from coming within five miles of any city ever again.

In France, King Louis XIV sought absolute power, unifying the country in Jesuit Catholicism, without papal interference. He declared the Pope fallible and inferior to ecumenical councils, but Rome cut off Louis's supply of bishops until he compromised. He was more successful against the Protestants. Each year, new laws were passed to make sectarian life impossible. Protestant churches were wrecked, their schools and hospitals closed. They paid more and more tax, while being banned from decent jobs. They even had their children confiscated. Catholic nonconformity also suffered. Cornelius Jansen was a Dutch theologian who criticised the complacent ritualism of the Catholicism of the day and revived Augustine's attitude of helpless trust in God. The Jesuits, who had become hugely powerful, attacked Jansenism because it disparaged everything they stood for, and with the support of king and pope, they destroyed it.

A more successful revival movement arose in Germany. In the aftermath of the Thirty Years' War, Lutheran churches were entrenched in their theological positions, the vigorous spiritual life and profound relationship at the heart of Luther's faith overcome by passive devotion to rigid Lutheran orthodoxy.

That at least was how the Frankfurt pastor Philipp Jakob Spener saw it, and so in 1670, to breathe new life into Christianity, he created the first house group, a midweek meeting at which keen believers read the Bible, discussed and prayed. They encouraged each other to live holy lives, shunning dancing, cards and overeating. For these 'pietists', as they were called, Christianity was not about right doctrine but about spiritual rebirth and godly living – a shift of emphasis that was to work its way across every denomination of Protestantism.

In 1685, the French experiment in toleration officially ended, as Louis XIV revoked the 1598 Edict of Nantes, and Protestant asylum-seekers flooded into England, Holland and America.

In England, Charles II wanted toleration, but he did not have enough power over an intolerant parliament. Instead, he let William Penn, the Quaker son of an old friend, establish Pennsylvania, another American haven of religious freedom. Charles, despite prolific fathering, had failed to produce a legitimate son, which made the fact that his brother James was a Catholic rather worrying for parliament. For the first time, parliament split into two opposing parties: the 'Whigs' wanted to stop James becoming king; the 'Tories' let their royalism overcome their religion. Eventually, with the support of the church, the Tories won, and in 1685, James became the last Catholic king of England.

James II gave Catholics the top jobs, opened the country to Jesuit missionaries and declared complete toleration. Dissenters were not sure what to make of it: their lives were easier, but for how long, if James restored Roman Catholicism? In 1688, after James had seven critical bishops arrested and tried, Anglicans and Dissenters, and Whigs and Tories, united to call his son-in-law and daughter, William and Mary, from Holland to take over. James fled. In England, parliament made Dissenters (but not Catholics) legal. In Scotland, the bishops refused to accept William as king, so the country returned to Presbyterianism, with the blessing of the English government.

German pietism got its big break in 1688, when the German elector, soon to become Frederick I, the first king of Prussia, invited them to start Halle University. (The Pope objected that he had not consented to the creation of Prussia, but his consent and objections were becoming increasingly irrelevant.) From Halle, pietism thawed the churches of Germany.

2

The Age of Reason
(1689–1730)

> Know then thyself; presume not God to scan;
> The proper study of mankind is man.
> *Alexander Pope*

Newton and Locke

During the English plague of 1665, Isaac Newton retired to the country, where the most disruptive apple since Adam's dropped into his life, and he discovered gravity, publishing his conclusions twenty years later. The idea that when you drop things they go downwards was not desperately controversial; the idea that a few simple equations determine the movement of everything in creation, from planets and seas to fruit, was. Newton was a devout though unorthodox Christian (he denied the Trinity but scoured the design of Solomon's temple for clues about the second coming); and his physics grew out of his Christian belief in a rational, orderly creator. At the same time, revealing the machinery of the universe was a blow for the belief that God directly dictated every event. The mystery was draining out of the cosmos, replaced by understanding.

The English philosopher John Locke was a more literally revolutionary thinker, his 1690 *Treatises on Civil Government* justifying the recent overthrow of King James II. He argued that government was not designed and decreed by God but a contract between ruler and ruled, purely to protect life, liberty and property. When rulers destroy instead of protecting, the ruled are entitled to depose them and choose new ones. We have not only duties but rights. Locke was only talking about dire emergencies, and he considered the present monarchy ideal; but he was opening the door to something radically different.

Locke placed enormous value on reason, but he had no time for the idea that you can work out everything you need to know while shut in an oven. First, we need to gather information through our senses, then we can make sense of it; knowledge is observation interpreted by reason. Human reason discovers no truths on its own, but it has to test every claim to truth. Hence Locke argued for 'reasonable Christianity', stripped of mystery and blind faith in authority, leaving the teaching and miracles of Jesus, ethical living and life after death. Locke had no doubt that God existed (there must be an original, uncaused cause of everything, and nothing within the universe could qualify), but he had suspiciously little interest in the Trinity. He defended religious freedom not just as a political expedient but on principle: if truth is self-evident, it needs no coercion, if not it justifies none. He did not extend this to Catholics or atheists, both of whom were politically unsafe. With Locke's ideas, the Enlightenment – the quest to remake the world according to reason – was launched.

China, and elsewhere

The Jesuit mission in the imperial Chinese court so thrived that the new church now had its first Chinese bishop and liturgy, with total baptisms over the six-figure mark. The missionaries were in a precarious position, though, being inscrutable western barbarians and facing the ebb and flow of imperial politics, while fellow Catholics distrusted their policy of allowing converts to venerate Confucius and their ancestors. In 1693, a French bishop in China banned such accommodation.

The Chinese emperor himself came to the Jesuits' defence, explaining that Christians and Confucians were merely honouring heroes and loved ones of the past, an important aspect of their ancient culture. No one was being worshipped but the Lord of heaven. The Pope begged to differ, and when both Catholic parties appealed to Rome he forbade any such veneration and the Christian use of Confucian terminology. The emperor, outraged to discover Christian allegiance to an emperor over the seas, expelled every bishop and missionary who followed these orders, and the church crumbled.

In contrast, Catholicism was coming to dominate South America, thanks largely to the policy of organising converts into villages where they were safe and well provided for, had religious teaching and strict discipline, and were in complete dependence on the missionaries.

After 200 years of Catholic mission, the Protestants and Orthodox finally joined in. Anglicans started forming organisations such as the Society for the Propagation of Christian Knowledge (SPCK) in 1698 to spread their faith in North America and Asia. The Danish king sent pietists trained at Halle to his little colony in India. They were very successful there, but when they wanted to expand, the king declined to finance the saving of souls outside his own territories. However, the SPCK was glad to provide the money, and so the first interdenominational mission blossomed.

Russia, generally considered the most backward state in Europe, was being reformed by Czar Peter the Great. This included colonising the vast expanse to the north and east and converting its pagans. Russian Orthodox missionaries also established a church in Beijing, which maintained a steady native membership of about ten people. As in France, Peter's autocracy meant curtailing the independence of the church, which was rather easier in his case: when the patriarch of Moscow died in 1700, Peter simply never replaced him, and twenty-one years later, he appointed a synod to oversee the church – a system that remained until the Russian Revolution. Eventually, half the monasteries were closed too.

The decline of the Trinity

The coinciding of two such unprecedented religious campaigns as the Reformation and the missionary movement suggests a tremendous surge of self-confidence in European Christianity. In fact, it provoked a crisis of confidence. Explorers, expecting to find savages to convert and forgotten churches to reunite with, discovered magnificent cultures founded on noble, ancient, but quite alien faiths – Confucianism, Hinduism, Buddhism – while at home, the true faith turned into a riot of competing creeds. The certainty that Christianity was God's one single message to humankind was being eroded. And now the ideas of Newton and Locke were starting to make people feel more rational and scientific even when they weren't, raising the question: just how rational is traditional Christianity?

The deist movement among the British upper classes held that reason and true religion are the same thing, so anything beyond common sense in religion is worthless. All religions come from the same root but have branched off into superstition; deism was a return to the original. Deists argued that God created humanity with enough sense to know right from wrong, to know he exists and to worship him, and then he left us to it. The idea of subsequent revelation and miracles seemed unnecessary and rather vulgar: if God created nature perfectly, why would he need to fiddle with it? Deism was perhaps the most radical demolition of Christianity in the name of Christianity ever. Gone were Bible stories from the bloodier Old Testament miracles to the resurrection ('It has the whole witness of nature against it'); doctrines from the atonement to the Trinity, from the inspiration of scripture to the damnation of the heathen; and most religious ceremonies. It was hugely controversial of course, but this being the age of reason, deists tended to be fined for their heresy rather than burnt. Though never a mass movement, they had a large readership: 'The common people... are now grown as much ashamed [of the gospel] as their betters,' judged Jonathan Swift.

In fact, the vast majority continued to see the Bible as God's infallible revelation, but they rationalised their faith in other ways. For one, they increasingly dismissed the authority of the church, so that the Bible alone was their religion, ignoring the Church Fathers who had been so important to the reformers. Thinking Christians were increasingly uncomfortable with the concept of the Trinity: not only was the maths deeply questionable, but there seemed to be very little basis for it in the Bible. The only explicit mention was 1 John 5:7–8, which in 1715, a Cambridge theologian proved to be an insertion missing from all Greek manuscripts before 1500, so it had to be cut.

It was among British Dissenting ministers, who had less respect than Anglicans for tradition, that unitarianism – belief in the holy unity rather than the holy Trinity – broke out. So Presbyterians, Congregationalists and Baptists met in London in 1717. Some wanted to make a joint statement on the Trinity and sack those who would not sign it; others objected that if the word of God was their only authority, they could not depose ministers for disagreeing with a human declaration. The Congregationalists, Particular Baptists and some Presbyterians removed their unitarians; most Presbyterians and General Baptists accepted them. Many of the dismissed pastors joined the Church of England, finding little point in being Dissenters if they could not dissent. The Unitarian denomination was not started until 1773.

Deist ideas spread through Germany thanks to Christian Wolff (a name for traditionalists to conjure with), the professor of mathematics at the pietist University of Halle. Following Descartes, he argued that no dogma is true unless proven with mathematical logic. He rejected the idea of supernatural salvation from sin, reasoning that we progress towards perfection through natural good sense. The king did not share Wolff's optimism, and in 1723, for the good of the flock, he gave him forty-eight hours to leave the university or be hanged.

Revival

Even the orthodox majority of European Protestants hated anything disruptive or excessive: miracles and revelations they accepted unreservedly so long as they happened 2,000 years ago. To claim 'extraordinary revelations and gifts of the Holy Ghost', said the bishop of Bristol, 'is a horrid thing, a very horrid thing'. French Catholicism, like Russian Orthodoxy, was held in the vice of royal absolutism, which tolerated nothing unsettling to the monolithic state. The Pope, who seemed to be losing his religious as well as his political authority, was reluctantly forced by Louis XIV to condemn the French mystic Madame de Guyon, and he more willingly repeated denunciations of the Jansenists. Catholic mission outside South America was collapsing. While the puritan lands of North America had grown and prospered, the spiritual ideals of their founders had declined.

The one major stream going against the tide of reactionary, passionless religion was German pietism, now invigorated by an influx of refugees from Moravia and Bohemia. These were followers of Jan Hus who had become a distinct branch of Protestantism, and since the Thirty Years' War had re-established Catholicism in their homelands, they had been under serious attack. In 1722, a group sought asylum on the Saxon lands of Count Nikolaus von Zinzendorf, an enthusiastic pietist educated at Halle. As the 'Moravian Brethren' grew under Zinzendorf's leadership, drawing in German pietists as well as foreign fugitives, the settlement became an almost monastic commune, under the name of Herrnhut ('the watch of the Lord'), devoted to daily worship and strict discipline, though without vows or celibacy. It was controversial enough to get Zinzendorf expelled from Saxony for ten years, but eventually, Moravianism was officially accepted as part of the state church – a triumph for Zinzendorf, as pietism was all about the renewal of Lutheranism, though many Moravians preferred being a separate church. (Other pietists could cause equal offence: the preaching of miners and women got the entire 25,000-strong Protestant population of Salzburg expelled).

The Moravians became eagerly committed to mission, and not just to the heathen but to the unsaved closer at hand. They went first to Greenland and the West Indies, then into Germany, England and North America to convert the Christians. Their missions to slaves ignored racial distinctions and triumphed where the dry, segregated, paternalistic religion of Anglican missionaries had failed.

3

Born Again (1734-69)

Stop, Gabriel! Stop! And carry with you the news of yet one more sinner converted to God.
George Whitefield

Deism was declining in England when the Parisian exile François Arouet visited. He loved this common-sense religion, with God as absentee landlord, and the freedom of English society: 'An Englishman, as one to whom liberty is natural, may go to heaven his own way,' he reported. Under the pen-name of Voltaire, he published *Letters on the English* in 1734 in England, praising English reasonableness, from pluralism to Locke and Newton, from fair tax to inoculation; the French translation was outlawed and burnt. Back home, he became the most celebrated writer of the age, excelling in everything from satirical plays to history and championing the Enlightenment values of reason, free speech and progress against corruption, dictatorship and superstition. He incessantly ridiculed irrational Catholicism for venerating relics of the navel and foreskin of Christ; for hating the Jews while adoring their scriptures; for making virginity a virtue; for having a God who needs worship and punishes doubters; for its rich bishops and ragged priests; and above all, for 'hating your neighbour for his opinions'.

Voltaire had no great interest in weaning the ignorant multitude 'who are not worthy of enlightenment' from their faith. Traditional Christianity promoted obedience and order, and so proved a very useful pack of lies: 'If God did not exist, it would be necessary to invent him,' he often said. British deism had been one more shade in a panoramic spectrum of religious opinion; in France, it was the only real opposition to monolithic Catholicism, polarising debate and drawing all dissent into rationalistic radicalism. For all Voltaire's devotion to coexistence, a life-and-death struggle was in the offing.

The evangelical revival

With rather warmer feelings for the deity, in 1734, Jonathan Edwards, a Congregationalist pastor in Massachusetts, felt dissatisfied with the passive, soulless religion of his flock and launched into a series of sermons about justification by faith, insisting that his parish stop merely calling themselves Christians, turn from their sins and get saved. It was the right message at the right time, and a blaze of religious passion swept the region until, within a year, Edwards was satisfied that virtually the whole town and its neighbours were converted. Similar revivals broke out elsewhere in British America.

It seems there was something in the air. In Wales, the teacher Howell Harris and the curate Daniel Rowland independently experienced the same kinds of conversions, as did the 19-year-old George Whitefield in England on the same day as Harris. All became touring preachers – Harris outdoors and in homes as he was not ordained – and before long, they were drawing crowds of thousands.

Meanwhile, shiploads of pietist missionaries and refugees were heading for Georgia, in North America, and they made a powerful impression on two of their fellow passengers, the Anglican missionary brothers John and Charles Wesley. A dangerous storm struck during a German service. 'A terrible screaming began among the English,' recounted John. 'The Germans calmly sung on.' 'Was you not afraid?' he asked them. 'No,' they explained; 'our women and children are not afraid to die.' For the sake of his soul, Wesley ate nothing but rice and biscuits, slept on the floor and followed a thirteen-hour daily timetable of devotions and study, and yet he utterly lacked the spiritual assurance of the pietists.

On landing, he met the Moravian leader Spangenberg and asked for advice about his conduct. Spangenberg changed the subject:

'Do you know Jesus Christ?'

'I know he is the Saviour of the world.'

'True; but do you know he has saved you?'

'I hope he has died to save me.'

'Do you know yourself?'

'I do,' Wesley said. But he knew he did not.

The Wesleys' mission, unlike Spangenberg's, was a disaster. They left Georgia followed by scandal, John fleeing the law at night across swampland.

Home in London, and miserable as sin, they met another Moravian, Peter Böhler, who convinced them they had intellectual belief but no faith: 'My brother, my brother, that philosophy of yours must be purged away.' True faith comes from God in an instant, bringing rebirth and an utter certainty of salvation. Believing him, John wanted to stop preaching, but Böhler told him, 'Preach faith till you have it; and then, because you have it, you will preach faith'; and so he did.

The Wesleys' friend, George Whitefield, meanwhile, had become such a celebrity preacher that he had to go to church by coach 'to avoid the hosannas of the multitude'. The message that most Anglicans were not true Christians was utterly scandalous, as was the idea of miraculous change in people's lives. When churches started closing their doors to Whitefield – or just getting too full – he multiplied the scandal by preaching in fields and market squares, like Harris. Whitefield was a flamboyant preacher whose first sermon was said to have driven thirteen people mad, and he rarely failed to draw tears; 'I'd give 100 guineas', said the actor David Garrick, 'if I could say, "Oh!" like Mr Whitefield.'

Whitefield was somewhat put out when John Wesley started to provoke even greater scandal. Wesley was soon preaching the born-again gospel in the fields too, but when he did it, pandemonium broke loose. 'You might see them, dropping on all sides as thunderstruck,' he reported. Listeners were thrown into convulsions, screamed, groaned, fainted, beat the ground or laughed uncontrollably. They claimed healings, exorcisms and visions.

The evangelical revival had burst upon the English-speaking world. The preachers and their converts were soon covering most of the British Isles with their never-ending tours, preaching in all weathers several times a day to crowds of up to (by Wesley's estimate) 32,000. They were constantly beaten by mobs and bombarded by stones, fire, bricks, fruit, mud and water; often rioters were rounded up by clergy and local officials. Whitefield extended the circuit to North America, which he visited thirteen times, travelling from Georgia to New England. Everywhere, crowds of thousands heard the devastating indictment of their sin and the liberating offer of certain salvation through faith alone. Whole communities were changed, as drunkenness, violence and sport were replaced with Bible-study and hymn-singing.

Charles Wesley added to their impact by writing between 4,000 and 10,000 hymns. Hymns had had little role in English religion until now, the

Church of England, true to its Calvinist roots preferring to sing psalms. The Dissenters had gone first with Isaac Watts's first hymn book in 1707, when they were tolerated enough to make a noise, though Charles Wesley owed more (as in much else) to the example of the pietists.

Less than a month after John Wesley had taken to the fields, the evangelicals had started falling out over predestination, which the Wesleys, like most Anglicans, denied ('It represents the most holy God as worse than the devil,' cried John), but which the other evangelical leaders accepted and treasured. So there were soon two streams of the movement. (Wesley also violently quarrelled with the Moravians.) It is Wesley's following that proved the most enduring, because while Whitefield was content to preach, Wesley organised his hearers into groups to meet weekly, hear sermons, pray, sing and keep tabs on each other. The Wesleyans also taught perfection: with God's help, Christians can and must live lives completely free from sin – eccentric, but extremely influential.

No one intended for a moment to become another denomination of Dissenters; their meetings were simply extracurricular classes for keen Anglicans. Wesley wanted only ordained clergy to preach, but most of them wanted nothing to do with him, so he let lay men and even women do it. Still, he refused to let his followers give up on their parish churches, however degenerate. Many Dissenters disdained the revival, but in America, they joined it from the start. Whitefield preached alongside Congregationalists and Baptists and sent converts to their churches. Scottish evangelicals quit their Presbyterian state church as they were not allowed to choose their own parish ministers and founded the Scottish Free Church.

Attack of common sense

Frederick the Great of Prussia had been brutally abused by his father for writing poems, playing the flute and philosophising. By the time he became king in 1740, he had embraced deism. He immediately reinstalled the deist Christian Wolff at Halle University, and the reign of pietism was finished. He brought Voltaire to Prussia as his Chamberlain and tried to match his ideal of the 'enlightened despot'. He restricted torture and execution, gave new freedoms to the press and new rights to peasants, and he granted complete religious freedom even to Jesuit missionaries – but not to Jews, whom Voltaire said deserved punishment for uniting 'the most sordid greed with the most detestable superstition and the most invincible hatred for all who tolerate and enrich them'. Such religious freedom was also established by Catherine the Great in Russia; Emperor Joseph II in the Holy Roman Empire even extended it to Jews.

In the rising generation of rationalist radicals, many were moving on from deism to full-blooded atheism. Denis Diderot published the first modern encyclopedia between 1751 and 1772, in which Voltaire and friends publicised modern discoveries and ideas, and attacked Christianity. It was banned and burnt.

The Scottish philosopher David Hume examined long-treasured proofs of God's existence and blew them to bits (though less ruthlessly, he left publication until after his death). It was said that the universe must have been caused, so there must be a God; but a finite, imperfect universe can hardly prove an infinite or perfect maker. Why not a committee? Moreover, if God can exist without a cause, why cannot the universe itself? Hume also demolished the idea that biblical miracles prove Christianity. For one thing, all religions claim miracles, so all are equally proved and disproved by them. More importantly, no rational person believes in miracles. A miracle is by definition not simply something extremely unusual but a breaking of the law of nature, an event that universal experience tells us simply does not happen. So whenever someone reports a miracle, which is more incredible: that the impossible happened or that the report is unreliable?

The most iconic incident of the age was the earthquake that hit Lisbon on All Saints' Day in 1755. The city was destroyed, and Portugal's days as a world power were over. It was a Sunday, and instead of working in the fields, everybody was in church, and so 30,000 people died. Voltaire's poem on the tragedy took the opportunity to fulminate against the idea that God is in control of everything that happens.

In Hamburg University, Hermann Reimarus wrote a critique of the Bible (also unpublished in his lifetime). Moving beyond deist lampoons of its tall stories, he tried to establish the real history of the New Testament. Jesus, he argued, was merely a political freedom fighter and preacher of Judaism. When he died in failure, his followers were reluctant to return to fishing, now they knew they could make a living from preaching; so they stole his body, pretended he had been resurrected and told everyone that he was coming back imminently. Christianity is therefore not merely an ancient legend but the basest fraud.

On a larger canvas, Edward Gibbon wrote *The Decline and Fall of the Roman Empire*, charting the tragedy of Rome's descent into Christianity, 'the triumph of barbarism and religion'.

The new romantics

If the evangelicals' ecstatic orthodoxy was a reaction to the arid rationalism of the Enlightenment, then the 'romantic' philosophy of Jean-Jacques Rousseau, a Genevan watchmaker's son living in France, offered a rather different one. Like Wesley, Rousseau insisted that the emphasis on reason and intellect had left the emotional, spiritual side of human nature out in the cold and been morally harmful. The cure is not to be born again, however, but to rediscover nature. Like the deists, Rousseau had a fanciful history of the human race to support his ideas: before civilisation, we were good, happy, free and in tune with nature; we are corrupted and restricted by society. He preached social equality, individual freedom, common ownership and government by the will of the people. He preferred the simple faith of the Gospels to the arrogant dissections of the Enlightenment, and yet he had no time for religious rules and doctrines, preferring to venerate nature and the spirit behind it. His writings were banned and burnt.

In the British Isles and America, the thirty-year-old evangelical revival was going from strength to strength. Wesley's groups alone had 30,000 members, with 100 travelling preachers, and counting. Evangelical groups provided welfare, work and schooling as well as orphanages for the poor. Evangelical Anglicans and Baptists as well as Moravians won the first great response to the gospel from American slaves and established the first black-led churches. Wesley himself, in his sixties, rode 3,000 miles a year to preach 800 sermons, and while earning up to £1,400 annually from his popular writings, he lived as ever on £30, a worker's wage.

The Particular Baptists and Congregationalists did well from converts of the revival. The General Baptists and Presbyterians had largely become unitarian and suffered decline, but now many of the Baptists were getting evangelically revived and formed a breakaway group. Even the Church of England was being changed. Anglican evangelicals, such as John Newton of 'Amazing Grace' fame, often distanced themselves from field-preaching and such scandals but broadcast the born-again gospel from their own pulpits.

In 1769, after years of hearing about Whitefield's phenomenal success throughout British America, Wesley gave in and sent his own missionaries. The following year, Whitefield made his thirteenth two-month-long ocean crossing and died in New Hampshire, having finally preached himself into the ground.

4

Revolutions (1769–1831)

> The tree of liberty must be refreshed from time to time with the blood of
> patriots and tyrants. It is natural manure.
> *Thomas Jefferson*

We have not heard much from the Pope over the last 100 years: there has not
been much to hear. Other Catholic powers followed France's lead, making
bishops answerable to the crown rather than to Rome, especially where
Enlightenment ideals had taken hold, and the Pope's role in international
affairs had been to choose between bootless blustering and rubber-stamping.

The Jesuits had become hated throughout Europe for their devotion to
enormous worldly power and wealth. One country after another outlawed the
society throughout the 1760s, and put huge pressure on Rome to abolish it.
As a compromise, the Pope offered radical reforms, but when France
threatened to take its church away from Rome altogether, he capitulated, and
in 1773, he dissolved the order. Ironically, the only countries where Jesuits
survived were Protestant Prussia and Orthodox Russia, thanks to their
policies of toleration.

Revolutions American and philosophical

British America was alive with the disparate spirits of Whitefield and
Rousseau, and when disputes arose about Britain's need to tax the colonies,
without realistically being able to offer them representation in parliament,
American protests reverberated with Rousseau's ideas of rights, equality and
the conditional contract between governed and government; and after war
broke out, so did the 1776 Declaration of Independence, drafted by the deist
Thomas Jefferson. As the French had just lost Canada to Britain, they were
more than happy to help Britain lose America.

George Liele, a slave freed by his loyalist owner in the war, was not only the first black Baptist minister in Georgia but also the first American overseas missionary, going as a servant to Jamaica in 1780. The British authorities censored his sermons and prayers, but his church of 350 included a few white members.

In 1781, the Prussian professor Immanuel Kant established himself as one of history's greatest thinkers with his self-styled 'Copernican revolution in philosophy', which at last settled the ancient debate between defenders of reason and observation as the source of knowledge: both are wrong. You only know what you experience. Reason tells you about theory and ideas but nothing about the world outside your head; observation only tells you how things appear to you and is always shaped by your unproven preconceptions (for example, the principle of cause and effect, the regularity of nature). But while you cannot truly know the world beyond yourself, you can have a good working relationship with it, once you accept on faith the preconceptions that make sense of it.

This has major implications for religion. We cannot know whether God is real – or the soul, morality, rights or free will – but we experience a moral impulse, an inner voice that says, 'Thou shalt...' If we accept this voice, on faith, as authoritative, being from God, then life makes sense: there is a God, and right and wrong; we have moral responsibilities and free will; we have insufficient time in this life to become what God tells us to be, therefore our souls are immortal. 'I deny knowledge to make room for faith,' said Kant, and he did indeed lead a rallying of faith from the onslaught of reason; but still, the faith Kant was left with was largely one of ethics, with little room for the rest of religion.

While John Wesley was helping the working classes to help themselves, Anglican evangelicals were campaigning in parliament for reform of prisons and schools, and, most of all, slavery. Europe and its colonies were full of African slaves. One hundred thousand a year crossed the Atlantic, crammed in ships with decks sometimes two feet apart. In 1784, the MP William Wilberforce was converted and devoted his life to fighting slavery, which is just as well, because that is precisely what it took. Wesley scandalised the world one last time (and even his brother this time) by ordaining ministers for America and rewriting the Book of Common Prayer for them.

The USA having won its independence, Anglicans there no longer wanted to be called 'the Church of England', so they declared their own independence and became Episcopalians. In 1787, the Congress finally agreed a brief constitution for the new nation, securing it halfway between the dangerous extremes of monarchy and democracy. What religion were they going to be? No church had a majority. Quakers, Baptists, deists and many revivalists, for different reasons, thought every person should make up their own mind. So all the Constitution said was that no one could be kept out of office for religious reasons. In 1791, the Bill of Rights banned the government from interfering in anyone's religion.

The evangelical revival seemed to take time out for the revolution, but now, with the country exploding with immigrants, revival started again. Camp meetings in Kentucky attracted ten times the population of its largest city, and earthy emotional preaching was greeted with convulsions and conversions – though in the older states, leaders were at pains to win souls without that kind of behaviour.

The French Revolution

French soldiers, having helped Americans establish freedom, equality and human rights, came home to a land with book-burning, torture and the death penalty for making your own salt. Its parliament seemed designed to let the lords and clergy unite to outvote commoners, and even that had not met for 200 years. It was also in financial crisis, which is why in 1789, Louis XVI had to call the parliament, but the commoners, with the help of hungry parish priests and streets full of armed mobs, took it over. Jefferson visited from America to advise them. They declared *The Rights of Man*, embodying the ideas of Locke and Rousseau about freedom, human rights and equality. They abolished tithes, confiscated all church land (which, being 20 per cent of France, did the national pocket no harm) and closed all monasteries. Bishops and priests would be elected by the people – of whatever faith – and Rome would have no say. The Pope forbade Catholics to accept this, so the French church was split between supporters of the revolution and of the Pope.

During this crisis for Catholicism, Protestants were starting to take over the traditionally Catholic field of foreign mission. William Carey was an English Particular Baptist pastor and cobbler who wanted to launch evangelical mission, but the Baptists had overdosed on Calvinism, insisting that God has predestined who will be saved and that no one should insult God by trying to do his job for him. Nevertheless, Carey founded the Baptist

Missionary Society and went to India, which was coming ever more under British domination. He set up a church and spent five years translating the Bible into Bengali. Unfortunately, it was an entirely literal translation: the words were Bengali, the sentences were not. He went back to Genesis and started again, printing eight revised versions, as well as Bibles in numerous other languages.

The French Revolution was getting more radical. After Louis XVI tried to let in a foreign invasion, rioting peasants got themselves another new parliament, the most democratic one anywhere yet with votes for absolutely everyone (except women). It abolished slavery. It abolished monarchy in general and Louis in particular, sending him and his family to the guillotine. In a wave of panic, tens of thousands of suspected traitors went the same way. The parliament abolished Christianity and designed a replacement faith, with no God but reason, and a rational, religion-free calendar of ten-day weeks, saints' days being replaced with fruit, vegetable and flower days. They also introduced metric measurements, which have lasted rather better. Many churches were closed, and signs appeared in cemeteries explaining that 'Death is Extinction'. France declared war on most of western Europe and invaded Belgium and Holland, introducing them to the benefits of democratic republicanism and the grocery calendar.

The regime then produced another new religion, the Cult of the Supreme Being, which involved burning effigies of atheism and survived for six weeks. Led by the celebrated general Napoleon Bonaparte, the French army conquered Italy, and in 1798 it took Rome, capturing the Papal State and the Pope himself. In 1799, Napoleon took home leave and overthrew the parliament, making himself 'first consul' and later hereditary emperor. The people, finally discovering that what they wanted was not democracy but a hero, were ecstatic.

Freidrich Schleiermacher

Like Kant, Friedrich Schleiermacher was brought up by a powerful pietist father after his mother's early death. From the age of ten he was troubled by his failure to share the spiritual experiences of those around him, and by intellectual doubts about doctrines such as the atonement and the incarnation. He implored the help of his father and teachers, but they refused to discuss threatening questions and disowned him. Nevertheless, he became a Reformed chaplain in Berlin (and in time, a resistance leader against Napoleon's occupation).

He got on well with Berlin's poets and philosophers, but their passion for freedom and the spirit of nature had no time for Christianity, with its far-fetched doctrines and restrictive rules – and vice versa. So for them, in 1799, he published *Religion: Speeches to its Cultured Despisers*, marrying romanticism and religion. 'True religion', he insisted, 'is a sense and taste for the infinite,' a feel for transcendence. God does not scold or interfere, he is simply the ever-present infinite ground of our being. Miracles are in the eye of the beholder: to really spiritual people 'all is miracle'. Sin and salvation are red herrings: God made us imperfect, to strive after perfection by getting tuned into him; to show us the way, he made Jesus the first perfectly tuned-in person. The Enlightenment was right to reject outmoded doctrines, but it left the universe dry and spiritless. Religion breathes life into it. And so it came to pass that liberal Christianity was born.

The Irish were almost entirely Catholic but controlled by Britain and Protestant landlords. They had their own parliament, but since only Protestants could vote, it was little use to them. Realising, thanks to America and France, that things can change, they revolted, and so Britain closed down their parliament and absorbed it into theirs, and in 1801, Britain and Ireland became the United Kingdom. Catholics could now vote in elections, but, as in Britain, not for Catholics.

American ideas of freedom also influenced those black Americans who were owned by their libertarian compatriots, as did the Bible story of Exodus. In 1800, Gabriel Prosser led a large slave revolt in Virginia. It failed due to betrayal and terrible weather; its leaders were executed and new laws clipped the slaves' freedom of speech, movement and association. New Jersey, however, became the last northern state to abolish slavery in 1804.

Napoleon

The church had come through one of the most threatening centuries of its history, submerged in a tide of rationalism at home, and mission churches largely collapsing abroad, though the evangelical revival and Schleiermacher's liberalism offered two rather different kinds of hope. The papacy still seemed to be in terminal decline, though not for the first time, and it came upon the most unlikely saviour.

Napoleon worshipped no God but himself, but he wanted to revive the French church: the revolutionary assault had done little to destroy popular Catholicism, and it was a friend to social order. So Napoleon offered Pope Pius VII a deal. He would restore the church if the Pope approved his regime, but bishops would be chosen by and swear allegiance to Napoleon, and Jews and Protestants would still be tolerated. Pius agreed, but he became increasingly annoyed by Napoleon's manipulation of the church. In 1804, Napoleon induced him to come and crown him emperor in Notre Dame, replaying the favour Pope Leo had paid Charlemagne 1,000 years before, but in a pointed twist of the tale, Napoleon whipped the crown out of the Pope's hands at the last minute and crowned himself. (The same year, the Holy Roman Emperor was persuaded to take the more realistic title of 'emperor of Austria'.) Finally, when Napoleon annexed the Papal State to France, Pius excommunicated him, so Napoleon arrested the Pope.

In Britain, Wilberforce saw the slave trade abolished throughout the empire in 1807. As the majority of slaves did not survive being traded, this was a major victory; but as the law still allowed slavery, and considered the condition hereditary, there was a long way to go. And now the mills of the industrial revolution were throwing up huge new towns, so Wilberforce and friends had to work for a fairer deal for factory workers and chimney sweeps too.

Twenty years after John Wesley's death, one British person in twenty belonged to his Methodist societies. (Originally, all evangelicals were called Methodists, but the nickname became the Wesleyans' own.) They ordained ministers, had sacraments and became a denomination, as large as all other Dissenters put together. They were especially successful in the growing industrial towns, where they were most needed and where the Anglican parishes could not cope. Just when they were starting to become respectable, a convert called Hugh Bourne started preaching in Cheshire, to mining crowds too large to fit indoors, despite the fact that, being a little shy, he spent whole sermons with his hands over his eyes. Inspired by stories of American camp meetings, he took to the fields, and thousands came. Methodist leaders were appalled at this reminder of their recent roots, and when Bourne persisted they expelled him. They even refused to let his converts into their churches, so in 1811, he created the Primitive Methodists.

In 1813, the General and Particular Baptists pre-empted the ecumenical movement by a century and became the Baptist Union.

When Napoleon was finally defeated by the rest of western Europe, the victors returned his conquests, releasing the Pope and giving him back the Papal State. He celebrated by recreating the Jesuits. Napoleon had raised the prestige of the papacy higher than it had been in 200 years. The next Pope capitalised by cancelling all reforms made in the Papal State, restoring feudalism, replacing civil rights with secret police and putting Jews back in the ghettos.

But not all clocks were turned back. While Spain and Portugal were being conquered by Napoleon, South Americans had taken the chance, inspired by the North American and French revolutions, to win independence, and over fifteen years, the colonists lost all control of South America. It had been the one really successful foreign mission though, and the continent remained Catholic.

Mormons

In the USA, as revivals rolled on, the number of what the English called Dissenters exploded. Methodist membership was already 200 times what it had been at the turn of the century. The number of denominations themselves was also rocketing, thanks to pioneer individualism, every kind of theological dispute, and sheer space in which to split up. The first major black denomination was founded in 1816, thanks to less-than-positive experiences in white churches. The African Methodist Episcopal Church became the major forum for black protest and social welfare.

Inspired by US camp meetings, Joseph Smith was told by God not to join any existing church but wait for something better. In 1823, he discovered that the native Americans were the lost tribes of Israel who came to America in 600 BC, when one of them, Moroni, returned from the dead in New York to tell him. Moroni told Smith that he had written their history in a mysterious, ancient script on gold plates before their faith died out, that it was the third testament of the Bible and where it was buried. Smith dug them up, and four years later, he was allowed to take them out of the box, whereupon Moroni gave him a pair of magic glasses allowing him to understand the hieroglyphics. Then the Moronial visitations, for want of a better adjective, stopped, and Smith got down to the job of translation and organising his disciples in the Mormon Church.

If the USA was taking over as the world's greatest sect machine, the UK was still churning them out. One new alternative was the Plymouth Brethren, who despite their name first arose in Dublin. They tried to reject all organisation and traditions, and they employed no minister, allowing all members (apart from women) to preach and administer sacraments. They aimed to live in close-knit communities united against the godless modern world, but they soon split into various factions over questions of how to go about it. More influentially, they were excited by biblical prophecy, insisting on taking it absolutely literally, which meant most of it was still to be fulfilled – imminently, of course. Everything would get worse and worse until Christ suddenly returned, believers floating up into the air to meet him ('the rapture'), and he would rule the earth from Israel for 1,000 years.

Irish Catholics were not satisfied voting for Protestants to represent them in England and managed to elect their leader, Daniel O'Connell, as MP. British law banned him from taking his seat, but fearing violence, Britain finally allowed Catholics and Dissenters to take public office.

America's successful experiment in religious freedom was an inspiration and reproach that the old world could not ignore. But religious freedom is not the only kind, and there were now 2 million slaves in the USA, increasing rapidly. The Baptist visionary Nat Turner led a slave revolt that killed sixty whites. White churches increasingly organised plantation missions, but the black Methodist David Walker vehemently condemned them for preaching servitude, and called slaves to revolt in the name of the heavenly master with whose gospel Europeans 'mingle blood and oppression'. In 1829, the Oblate Sisters of Providence became the first black monastic order, facing mob violence for their presumption and an archbishop who wanted them to give up and become servants.

Genesis

On 27 December 1831, the Feast of St John the Divine, author of Revelation, Captain Robert Fitzroy went to investigate the islands and shores of South America in *HMS Beagle*. He already had one naturalist onboard, but wanting aristocratic company, he took a second – despite the fact that he was an unqualified 22-year-old who was supposed to be going into the church, and Fitzroy was worried about his disreputable-looking nose.

And so it was that Charles Darwin left home to do some bird-watching in the Galapagos Islands – a major voyage of discovery for the man, one of unparalleled self-discovery for humankind. He kept quiet about it for a long time. When the news broke, Captain Fitzroy wished to God he had followed his nose.

5

Planet of the Apes (1831-70)

Whereas Christ turned water into wine, the church has managed
something more difficult: it has turned wine into water.
Søren Kierkegaard

Charles Finney was perhaps the first professional evangelist, quitting his New York law practice not to be a pastor but purely to preach to the unconverted. Employed by the Presbyterian Church, he channelled his courtroom skills into the gospel. More unprecedented, he dismissed the notion that those who want a revival have to pray, preach and leave the rest to God. Instead, he pioneered the 'new measures', a recipe for revival. Meetings were late at night or early in the morning, his preaching colourful and down-to-earth, his prayers like chats. He publicly prayed for and preached at individuals by name; and, for those sinners who felt the call of God, he reserved an 'anxious bench' at the front where, as one observer said, they 'could hardly avoid being affected by a tide of emotions'.

Finney pioneered his evangelistic strategy in the frontier lands from 1831, and indeed, he created a massive new wave of revival. To add to his unorthodox behaviour, he let women speak, taught Wesley's perfectionism, declined to get local-church approval for his missions, and shovelled his converts immediately into church membership. It was all heartily disapproved of, especially in the east, but when it converted thousands, it turned into a template for copycat evangelists throughout the country.

The new generation of US evangelicals campaigned fervently against slavery, alcohol and restrictions on women. Temperance organisations were extremely successful, and Maine became the first state to ban alcohol. Finney refused communion to slave-owners, though he did not let black Christians into leadership. The American Anti-Slavery Society was formed in 1833, declaring, 'All those laws which are now in force, admitting the right of slavery, are, before God, utterly null and void.' Many southerners considered abolitionists to be telling 'John Brown to come down here and cut our throats in the name of Christ'. The same year, slavery was abolished throughout the British empire. Wilberforce, after a half a century's struggle, had died the previous month in sure and certain hope of the abolition.

The Oxford Movement and German liberals

Following their new political freedoms, Irish Catholics were delighted when parliament decided to reduce the disproportionate number of Anglican bishops there. The most vocal opponents of these changes included the Oxford academic John Keble, who in an 1833 sermon accused Britain of throwing off episcopal rule and thereby becoming an ex-Christian nation. He and friends including John Henry Newman launched the 'Oxford Movement', campaigning for a revival of the Church of England rather different from Wesley's, with church hierarchy dominating the state, recognition of the full apostolic authority of bishops and restoration of the ancient doctrines of Christ's flesh and blood being present in the eucharist, offered as a sacrifice to God. If it sounds a little Catholic, many Anglicans held similar beliefs; where the Oxford Movement shocked them was in their increasing distaste for Protestantism: 'The Reformation was a limb badly set; it must be broken again to be righted.' They argued that the Church of England was neither Protestant nor Roman Catholic, but the best reformed branch of Catholicism, stripped of the excesses of medieval Rome.

They broadcast this message in a series of tracts culminating in 1841 with Newman's *Tract 90*, which rather fantastically reinterpreted the Calvinist Thirty-Nine Articles of the Church of England, arguing that they were entirely in agreement with the Roman Catholic council of Trent. In the uproar that followed – one reader said he would no longer trust Newman with his silver – the bishop of Oxford banned any further tracts.

Newman had a disillusioned rethink. His problem with Roman Catholicism had been the way it added new ideas like purgatory and transubstantiation to ancient Christianity. But then, is it not right for a living faith to grow and develop? Roman Catholicism was the tree that the sapling church of the New Testament grew into; the Church of England was just a branch that cut itself off. And so, in 1845, Newman, followed by several hundred others, joined the Church of Rome, and the movement that started as a protest against giving ground to Catholicism culminated in its leaders becoming Roman Catholics – although others stayed as an Anglo-Catholic party within the Church of England. The other irony is that Rome, claiming to have been a full-grown tree forever as it were, did not much care for Newman's theology either.

In Germany, the liberal Protestantism that Newman despised as heresy was gaining ground. In 1835, D.F. Strauss published *The Life of Jesus*. A number of such biographies was around, largely by old-school Enlightenment rationalists, who explained, for instance, Jesus walking the water as an optical illusion. Strauss ridiculed this kind of detective game, while also dismissing orthodox faith in the Gospel stories and Reimarus's accusation that they are simply lies. For Strauss, the Gospel miracles were 'myth': fictions that encapsulate the true meaning of Jesus, more important than any historical fact. The Gospel-writers took Old Testament miracle stories and wove them into the life of Jesus to show how he fulfilled the Jewish hope in God.

Strauss's teacher at Tübingen University, F.C. Baur, was more interested in the true story behind the New Testament. He noticed that dissension over circumcising Gentiles had dominated the early church, and observing Paul's argument with Peter, he concluded that these two led the opposing factions. Since only four of Paul's letters mention the conflict, the others must be later forgeries. Books that speak well of Peter and the law (Matthew, Revelation) were written by Peter's side. Those that support both sides (Mark, Acts) are much later attempts at reunion. Those that show no interest in the dispute (most of the New Testament) were written after it was forgotten, up to 170 years after Jesus' death. The weaknesses of Baur's theory are obvious, and no one accepts it today; but he started an investigation into the creation of the New Testament that has absorbed scholars for 170 years, shedding invaluable light on the first churches but without anything like a resolution in sight.

Albrecht Ritschl was the most influential German theologian of the time, and he maintained that the New Testament gave a reasonably reliable record of Jesus, the perfect human. In him and in the life of the church, God reveals himself. But that is all we know of God – what we learn from his activity in our lives, not what he is in himself – so all the metaphysical speculation about the Trinity and the composition of Christ, from the Church Fathers on, has been a blind alley, corrupting the biblical faith with Greek philosophy.

Then in Denmark we have Søren Kierkegaard, an unhappy man, particularly unhappy with liberalism, which seemed to have abolished sin and salvation, merely wanting to make a good humankind better. 'Take away the distressed conscience, and you might as well turn the churches into dance halls,' he protested. Kierkegaard saw an infinite chasm between us and God. The only way it can be bridged is in the old-fashioned idea that God became a human being. How is that possible? It isn't. Truth is not rational, it is paradoxical; whatever makes complete sense is not worth knowing. 'The thing is to find a truth which is true for me, to find the idea for which I can live and die. What would it matter if I found "objective truth"... and it made no difference to my life?' Kierkegaard passionately attacked the complacency of state-church Lutheranism; and in setting himself against the prevailing philosophy devoted to finding logical order in the world, he eventually fathered existentialism. But he died, as he lived, lonely, largely unheard and generally assumed to be mad.

Mormons, and opium

Offering a little relief from this theologising, in 1840, Joseph Smith took the Mormons out west to found Nauvoo, Illinois. Troubled by the issue of those who get converted after they die by evangelists in the spirit world but still cannot enter heaven because they were never baptised, they started proxy baptism, immersing live believers on behalf of dead ones. After a while, they found they lost track of who had and had not been reclaimed, and so they had to start again, keeping records this time. The Mormon Church is now a world centre of genealogy.

Twenty-six years after its discovery, the *Book of Mormon* was superseded by Smith's revelation that monogamy was finished, and Mormon marital limits were lifted. This was as well for Smith, who apparently already had over a dozen wives here and there and allegedly managed to squeeze in twice as many again throughout the following year, before he was killed by a monogamous lynch mob.

China was finally opened in 1842 when British traders bombed down its doors to the only import in which it was not already self-sufficient, opium. This combined with flooding and political turmoil to throw the most consistently illustrious civilisation in history into a collapse from which it is only now really recovering. European missionaries stormed in, but few were eager to hear them.

Potato blight hit Ireland in 1845, and over 1 million people died in the following years. Many more emigrated, to England and America, both countries' largest Catholic influx ever. While the British government provided relief, it also kept exporting food from Ireland, fostering indelible resentment.

Mills, factories and railways were creating a new world, starting in Britain, with vast wealth for the middle class, and exploitation, squalor and brutality for the workers who created their prosperity. While evangelicals fought to outlaw the worst abuses, the German philosopher Karl Marx preached working-class revolution to seize control of industry. He described religion as a fiction that makes life bearable for the suffering but becomes the enemy of freedom when workers prefer it to revolution: 'Religion is the sigh of the oppressed creature, the heart of a heartless world and the soul of soulless conditions. It is the opium of the people.' The year his *Communist Manifesto* came out, there were, coincidentally, liberal revolutions all over Europe. Pope Pius IX fled Rome dressed as a woman, but within a year, most of the revolutions were overturned.

Back in power at Rome, Pius IX became the longest-serving Pope ever. In 1854, he issued the papal bull declaring that the Blessed Virgin Mary was, alone of the human race (with one obvious exception), conceived without original sin. The masses loved it, but some more liberal Catholics asked whether – as there was no hint of this teaching in the Bible, it was not mentioned for over a millennium, and it was then denied by such notables as Anselm and (technically) Aquinas – they were supposed to accept it purely because the Pope said so. The answer seemed to be, yes.

With China successfully penetrated by Europeans, Japan alone withstood western assaults. When America finally overcame its reserve with gunboats in 1859, missionaries charged in and made an astonishing discovery. Two centuries after the church was destroyed, in which time, Japan had been hermetically sealed, missionaries found over 200,000 Christians in underground churches dating back to Francis Xavier's mission. The French missionaries congratulated them on surviving eight generations of persecution alone and gave them a list of everything they had to change, splitting the church between those who bowed to French demands and those who told them to go and find someone else to liberate. The Christians were also rediscovered by the Japanese and 40,000, refusing to yield to renewed attack, were taken off and died in exile. At the same time, David Livingstone was 'opening' Africa, walking thousands of miles with wife and child in tow, mapping it and firing up his many fans to bring Christianity and commerce to the natives.

Descent

In the surprisingly quiet decades since Darwin's Galapagos journey, the main scientific controversy had concerned fossils, Charles Lyell arguing that the variations throughout layers of rock mean that they must have formed over millions of years, rather than six mornings and six evenings. Philip Gosse, a Plymouth Brethren zoologist, offered an alternative: God could have put the fossils there on day two to test the faith of geologists. He had been a highly respected scientist up to that point.

Finally, in 1859, Darwin let the sabre-toothed tiger out of the bag. *The Origin of Species* reported how the finches on the various islands he visited were closely related, but physically adapted to their different environments. Considering how few from each generation survive and breed, in every species, and how each individual is slightly different from its parents and siblings, clearly the ones that live are the ones that happen to be best equipped to survive; and they pass this better equipment to their offspring. So species we see now were not all at the same time lovingly crafted by God; they gradually mutated, over ages, from the same ancestors, by a process of natural selection, a constant, brutal, random culling. Darwin made virtually no comment on where humans fitted in, but the implication was obvious, and he eventually unpacked it in *The Descent of Man*: we evolved.

In his own way, Darwin hit the church as hard as Muhammad. Who needed a creator now? Humanity, to those who believed, seemed to have been relegated from God's greatest masterpiece to bald apes with the same family tree as their pets. Life itself had turned into a careless, callous accident, the world God's gladiatorial arena. Who could trust the Bible? Adam and Eve had joined the rank of Hansel and Gretel, and doctrines like creation and the fall were broken. Humankind was once again evicted from the garden.

In fact, many Christians embraced the discovery with alacrity, as 'fresh matter for adoring the power and wisdom of God'. Genesis became a myth depicting the hand of God at work in creation, not a scientific treatise on his methods. More, however, vehemently rejected Darwin. Bishop Samuel Wilberforce took on leading Darwinists (except the timorous Darwin) in public debate. According to popular myth, T.H. Huxley's wit and brilliance triumphed over the bishop's cheap jibes; in fact, Darwin considered Wilberforce's scientific counter-arguments 'uncommonly clever'.

The fall and rise of the Roman pontiff

Italian soldiers were fighting for independence from Austria to unify their loose bundle of states into the nation of Italy, supported by Napoleon III of France. The Pope, who ruled a large part of Italy, was not expecting an invitation to be king, and he fought against them. Catholics from across Europe joined his army in 1860, but they lost. The united Italy stripped Pius of the whole Papal State except Rome itself. Jews were finally freed from his ghettos. Napoleon III suggested that losing political influence would increase his spiritual influence, but Pius was not consoled. In 1864, he published *The Syllabus of Errors*, denouncing 'progress, liberalism and modern civilisation'. He crushed Catholic movements for political freedom, toleration and human rights, and he banned Italian Catholics from voting.

In 1865, the American Civil War ended with slavery being abolished throughout the USA. Over a third of the southern population had been slaves, and freedom meant unemployment, poverty and relentless, brutal harassment. A great resurgence of the supernatural followed the war. American Methodists, reviving the teaching of Wesley and Finney, taught that Christians could become perfectly sinless, in an instant, miraculous transformation. Thousands got this 'second blessing' (the first being salvation) at camp meetings and the 'holiness movement' spread across the country. Their charismatic package also included 'faith missions', which refused funding because they relied directly on God for money.

Pius IX had not left Rome in a decade, calling himself a prisoner of the Italians – who would have seized Rome had not Napoleon III's forces become his protectors. So it was in the Vatican palace in 1869 that Pius chaired the first ecumenical council in 300 years, the council to end all councils. The vast agenda included marriage, morals and magnetism; education, Asian ceremonies and duelling; and extensive condemnations of modernity. Almost the first subject to be debated was one that arose at the last minute: papal infallibility. The proposal stated that the Pope cannot err when speaking 'in the exercise of his office as pastor and teacher of all Christians' about 'a doctrine concerning faith and morals to be held by the whole church'. A considerable minority opposed it, but all but two of them contrived to be absent for the final vote. There were enough dissidents to form a breakaway church, the Old Catholics, but on the whole, the bishops cast down their crowns. Pius announced the new dogma amid a stunning display of

Hollywood-style thunder, lightning and breaking glass, taken by many as an unmistakeable divine interjection, though in whose favour was not so clear. Napoleon III had been right after all.

But this was as far as the council got. Otto von Bismarck, the prime minister of Prussia, was uniting Germany under his rule, which led to war with France in 1870. Napoleon had to withdraw his army from Rome, so immediately, the Italians captured it. They gave the inhabitants a referendum on joining Italy or staying papal, and they voted 100 to one for Italy. After a millennium, the Pope's kingdom was ended.

6

World War and World Church (1870–1933)

I grew up in a world where Protestants who had just proved that
Catholics do not believe the Bible were excitedly discovering that they did
not believe it themselves.
G.K. Chesterton

As chancellor of a united Germany, Bismarck took the somewhat old-
fashioned line of persecuting the minority religion, in this case Catholicism.
He expelled Jesuits and other orders, and he took control of Catholic schools,
marriage and church appointments. Catholics resisted until every bishop left
in Prussia was in prison. Bismarck admitted defeat and left them alone.

In Britain, the government was forced to respect Nonconformist churches
for their sheer numbers, and it finally allowed non-Anglicans to go to
university, as long as they did not study theology. Evangelicals had yet
another transatlantic revival, thanks to Dwight Moody and to Ira Sankey, who
accompanied him with effusive Victorian hymns; the Moody and Sankey
hymn book was the century's bestseller. In London, the Methodist minister
William Booth started the Salvation Army to bring the opium of the masses
to the urban underworld. It demanded military-style discipline from
members and banned alcohol altogether, identifying it as their greatest and
most easily remediable source of misery. Like the Methodists, the Salvation
Army became a denomination by accident, but it never had sacraments,
partly because it was not supposed to be a church and partly because of the
wine. Moody and Booth both followed the holiness movement, urging
hearers to get filled with the Holy Spirit to empower their 'walk with the Lord'
and their evangelism.

Industrialisation and political reform brought such things as drains, jam
and a more comfortable life even to the working class. The middle class got

fruit, vaccines and political power too. The idea of 'progress' – social, political, technological, even moral – made many Victorians feel that they were getting further without God's help than they ever had with it.

Things were also better than ever for Jews in Christian Europe. That is saying very little, but the more inhuman laws and most ghettos were gone. One in five Jews, however, lived in Russia, a land largely untouched by modernisation, in economic and political turmoil. The year the czar was assassinated, 1881, they suffered over 300 pogroms, which were enthusiastically supported by the Orthodox Church and often organised by the police. The government shut them up and heaped on them every abuse it could scrape up. One million Jews fled west into Europe, where they were just in time to bear the blame for new economic problems and inspire a new wave of anti-Semitism.

The German philosopher Friedrich Nietzsche launched a devastating attack on the whole Judeo-Christian tradition. Ancient Judaism had been an admirable, life-affirming faith of conquest and vigour, he said, but when Israel was conquered, instead of accepting natural de-selection, they turned Judaism on its head, deciding that God was on the side of the weak, suffering and desperate, 'the God of the sick'. In truth, the essence of life is the will to power, and the order of nature rewards the strong; Christianity hates both, preferring submission, self-denial, forgiveness and compassion. It is 'the anti-natural castration of a god into a god of the merely good'. The development through the survival of the fittest that Darwin had described as a fact of life became almost a manifesto for Nietzsche. His psychoanalysis of Christianity was undeniably brilliant, but when he talked darkly of exterminating 'the bungled and the botched', it is questionable how preferable his alternative was. For the last eleven years of his life, he was insane, writing, for example, to summon the heads of Europe to meet him in Rome, signing himself 'The Crucified'.

After 800 years of Turkish rule, there were still 2 million Armenian Christians. With Turkish power waning, and with European backing, they pressed for reform. In response, Turkey killed perhaps 300,000 and forcibly converted more to Islam.

As the holiness movement grew, it was increasingly opposed in US churches. Holiness radicals started telling their followers to leave their old, dead churches, and the churches were inclined to agree. The parting of the ways came in 1894, and America found itself with twenty-five new denominations.

The twentieth century

As the twentieth century dawns, the churches are in troubled times. A smaller proportion of the population go to church than at any time since the dark ages. The working class is being lost to the cities, and the educated class to science and progress. There is a greater crisis of confidence than ever before in the Bible and traditional beliefs; and while liberals can focus on Christian morals instead, even those morals are being disparaged. Looking to Asia and Africa, though, more missionaries are abroad than ever before, and thanks to their enormous sacrifice, the gospel is reaching something like a worldwide audience for the first time.

Liberals are becoming more prominent in Protestant churches, even gaining ground in the USA. They throw themselves into social work, Christianity being 'not a matter of getting individuals into heaven,' as the American Walther Rauschenbusch says, 'but of transforming life on earth into the harmony of heaven'. The disadvantage of this is that liberal foreign missions become devoted to importing superior western culture to the dark lands.

With notable exceptions, evangelicals' response to this is tragic. They retreat into rigid formulations of traditional beliefs and other-worldly spirituality. Enthusiastic debates about when the world will end are not a good sign. After a century and a half as the powerhouse of social transformation, they are starting to look down their noses at such unspiritual concerns.

Pope Leo XIII calls off Catholicism's war with the modern world. He supports workers' rights, calls for social justice and tells priests to organise welfare. He even talks vaguely about democracy. He encourages Catholics to do science and write unbiased history, and he opens the Vatican archives. He allows Catholics to take part in Bible scholarship, within limits. He also makes friendly noises to Protestants and Orthodox, conceding that Anglican orders are valid. He tries to get the Papal State back, but as he still does not allow Italian Catholics to take any part in politics, it is a losing battle.

Feeling the time might be right to attempt Catholic liberal theology, Alfred Loisy enters the ring against German Protestants. To fight them on their own ground, Loisy accepts their scepticism about the Bible and orthodox theology. Leo condemns his work wholesale and excommunicates him.

The Pentecostal explosion

Charles Parham, one of the holiness movement who had quit the Methodists, was telling his students at a Holiness Bible College in Kansas about being filled with the Holy Spirit, when it occurred to him that in the book of Acts, those filled with the Spirit at Pentecost all spoke in foreign languages. So he told them this was the sign of being genuinely filled, equipping them for overseas mission, and he encouraged them to ask God for the gift. On the first day of the new century, Agnes Ozman started 'speaking in tongues', and others soon joined in. Parham took his discovery on a nationwide revival tour, sending his students to find out what language they had been given and to evangelise the appropriate place. Unfortunately, their 'tongues' bore no relation to any languages on earth, so they concluded that it was the language of heaven, given them for worship rather than mission. This was the third blessing, to cap salvation and sanctification: baptism in the Holy Spirit. Pentecostalism, the fastest-growing form of Christianity ever, exploded into being.

In 1904, the last of the great evangelical revivals struck Wales. For two years, people skipped work to ensure a place in the daily prayer meetings, and rugby matches were cancelled because they could not find twenty-two men willing to stop singing 'Bread of Heaven' for long enough. On the basis of 'Anything they can do...' the Pentecostal pastor William Seymour started prayer meetings for revival at his mixed-race chapel in Azusa Street, Los Angeles. Revival erupted, and thousands came, mainly from Holiness churches, taking the third blessing home to share around. Many Holiness leaders, having been rejected by the Methodists as unhinged extremists, passed the same verdict on Pentecostals; other Holiness churches were converted wholesale, or split both ways. Traditional Christians explained their embarrassing babbling as demon-possession; for Pentecostals of course, the fact that other churches could not tell the devil from the Holy Spirit confirmed that they were dead.

A number of Europeans, especially Scandinavians, came over and took the blessing home, where it created the same conflicts and new churches. Meanwhile, Pentecostal missionaries crossed the world in their hundreds. Their confidence that the power of the Spirit would make such worldly measures as training and inoculation unnecessary meant a high failure rate, but an even higher success rate. In 1910, the Tennessee Pentecostal George

Hensley, preaching on the text 'They shall take up snakes,' ended by grabbing a rattlesnake and commanding his flock to do the same or be 'doomed to eternal hell'. They obeyed. He kept at the snake handling until 1955, when he died of a snake bite. Today, he has 2,500 followers.

A group of rich American businessmen, dismayed by how many of their ministers had become liberals, printed a twelve-part book, *The Fundamentals*, and sent out 3 million copies, one to every church employee and theology student in the USA. It outlined the fundamental doctrines of Christianity, insisting that those who call themselves Christians believe and preach them: Jesus was God, born of a Virgin; he died in our place, rose from the dead and is returning soon for his 1,000-year reign; the Bible is infallible and hell is forever. *The Fundamentals* helped evangelicals see themselves as fundamentally anti-liberal, and it gave us the word that dominates twenty-first-century talk of religion, 'fundamentalist', which originally meant 'conservative Protestant' and now, if anything, means 'someone more religious than I approve of'.

The First World War

At nineteen, the German Albert Schweitzer decided to devote himself to scholarship until he was thirty, and then to 'serving humanity'. He made major contributions to medicine, music and theology, demolishing the nineteenth-century liberal biographies of Christ, which portrayed him as essentially preaching good will, good deeds and good sense – as a nineteenth-century liberal, in fact. Schweitzer argued that Jesus' central teaching was that the world was about to end and be replaced with the heavenly kingdom. He was an apocalyptic extremist with whom today's reasonable Christians shared little common ground. (Schweitzer had little experience of the fundamentalists.) At thirty, he went to Africa as a missionary doctor, though his employers forbade him to preach.

Between them, the empires of Europe, the USA and Japan encompassed more than half of humanity. This included almost all of Africa, where after many decades of missionary struggle, Christianity started taking off; and despite exploitation and repression, Europeans were revered for bringing peace and education. The church grew healthily in Asia too, while in both continents, Islamic resentment intensified. A powerful Islamic revival movement, led from Egypt, demanded the purge of western values such as

secularism (though embracing western science), better religious education
and a return to the scriptures. Islam began a new century of resurgence.

Missionaries were increasingly troubled by the embarrassing number of
denominations they represented, finding it hard enough to convince the
heathen without confusing them with old European conflicts. So 1,200 met
at the World Missionary Conference in 1910 and declared their new mission:
'to plant in every non-Christian nation an undivided church of Christ'. Three
major organisations arose from the conference. The International Missionary
Council set up local councils in Asia to encourage the churches to cooperate
with each other and hand over authority to locals; an increasingly large
number of members were nationals from the new churches. The Life and
Work Movement campaigned for denominations to ignore their differences
and work together for social justice. The Faith and Order Movement
campaigned for denominations to remember their differences, discuss them,
and reunite. They considered returning to the Nicene creed as the basis for
unity, just like so many centuries ago, but then that would exclude many
liberals. They did find much to agree on, though, and more importantly, a will
for unity. It started to look as if the churches might finally find peace and
goodwill among themselves.

In 1914, Europe was thrown into the First World War, and within months,
one and a half million people were dead. While the western armies endured
four soul-destroying years of futile, deadlocked carnage, the war spread out
from eastern Europe through Asia and eventually included the USA. Fearing
wartime conspiracy from its 2 million Armenian Christians, Turkey decreed
their wholesale deportation. About half were killed.

The suffering and instability of Russia sparked off the communist
revolution, and it became the first permanently atheist state. Initially, Lenin
decreed religious toleration, but knowing the faith would become a focus for
the opposition of millions of starving peasants, he set about destroying it. He
banned church schools, Sunday schools and pastoral visiting. Monasteries
were converted to barracks. The patriarch excommunicated Bolshevik
leaders, but when he realised they had won, he called on all Russians to
accept them.

The war left the west reeling and shattered. The nineteenth-century
bubble of liberal optimism was burst. The celebrated technological
revolutions in communication, transport and arms had turned war from a
glorified rugger match into the slaughter of a whole generation. The very idea

of moral progress was hanging from the barbed wire in a French field. Such a nightmare might seem as promising for religious resurgence as the Black Death, but none came. The war confirmed doubt and disbelief more than anything. The church had lost its nerve. It still failed to reach the ever-growing mass of urban workers; thanks to Lenin, it was increasingly wary of social action, and governments were taking over welfare anyway. When the victors' economies quickly picked up, many people had more comfortable and entertaining lives than ever; for those who did not, politics increasingly looked a better answer than religion. Churchgoing took a long, long downturn.

Karl Barth

The young Reformed pastor of a Swiss mining village, Karl Barth had trained under the great German liberals, but he found that their gospel of human progress had little to say to his flock. In 1914, ninety-three German academics, including almost all of Barth's teachers, had signed a manifesto proclaiming their support for the aggression that started the war: 'The salvation of European culture depends on the victory which German "militarism"... will achieve.' Barth's greatest hero ghost-wrote the Kaiser's declaration of war. Was this all their theology was good for, to fabricate God's approval of the morality of the day?

In 1922, Barth published a commentary on the book of Romans. 'It fell like a bomb on the playground of the theologians,' said one Tübingen professor. Barth condemned liberal religion as the science of finding God, when real Christianity is about God finding us. Religion begins and ends with God, 'the Yes to our No, and the No to our Yes'. Like Kierkegaard said, there is an infinite gulf between us and God, so theology built on human ideas will fall into it and smash – and good riddance. But God speaks to us. Not in words on a page to be picked at with academic tweezers – we hear him in Jesus Christ, God's first and last word. The Bible records that word, and Christian preaching broadcasts it, and when we read and hear, God's word comes to us anew. Enough religious humanism: let God be God.

The Irish campaign for independence from Britain culminated in a wartime uprising at Easter 1916. The British put it down harshly enough to get the republican party Sinn Fein most of the Irish seats in the 1918 election. But Sinn Fein boycotted Westminster, set up their own parliament and declared independence. After more fighting, Britain offered to split Ireland into an independent Catholic south, and the north, where the Protestant majority wanted to stay in the UK. After a civil war over whether to accept the offer, the acceptors won.

Now that women were getting the vote for the first time in the UK and US, pressure was on the church to allow women ministers. In fact, Baptists, Congregationalists and Pentecostals had been ordaining them for years. Maud Royden, a prominent lay leader, campaigned for the same in the Church of England. Canon Lacey spoke for many when he said, 'The scheme of the ladies who desire ordination has for a long time been known to me; I have never had occasion to do anything but laugh at it.' Royden was dismissed, and she became a Congregationalist minister.

Prohibition and monkeys

The evangelical war on alcohol in the USA was intensifying. Many states had been on the wagon for half a century, and in 1919, the Eighteenth Amendment to the Constitution banned alcohol throughout the nation. Since Americans had been spared many of the horrors of the First World War, the nineteenth-century idea of progress was not dead yet, just ailing. Come prohibition, it got completely hammered.

The Soviet regime's war on the drug of religion was also hitting its stride. In the famine of 1922, the government confiscated church treasures for famine relief. They gaoled the patriarch of Moscow and replaced him with the 'Living Church', a committee of collaborators who cleansed the clergy of anti-Leninists. The government also opened up cases of holy relics and were delighted to find that far from getting struck by lightning, they sometimes just found waxwork fakes. In 1925, the Godless League was formed; originally devoted to ecclesiastical vandalism, it was entrusted with atheist evangelism, including plane rides for peasants to prove there was no spirit in the sky.

In 1925, the state of Tennessee arrested the science teacher John Scopes for telling his class about evolution. The three-time presidential candidate W.J. Bryan had persuaded fifteen states to draft anti-Darwin legislation; Scopes was persuaded by a local Methodist to get himself convicted so that they could overturn the law as unconstitutional on appeal. The 'Monkey Trial' was the first to be broadcast live on radio, and it attracted such crowds that it was held on the lawn. Stalls sold Bibles or monkeys depending on one's persuasion. 'Civilisation is on trial,' declared the defence, and the papers talked of an era-defining contest between religion and scepticism, science and fundamentalism. The judge, opening in prayer every day, banned the defence from presenting any scientific evidence for evolution, so they called W.J. Bryan himself and made an ass out of his literal faith in Genesis. Scopes was convicted, but the verdict was overturned on a technicality, so the law was never challenged. The humiliated Bryan died within days of the trial, the law against evolution was quietly forgotten and US evangelicalism became considerably quieter.

The ecumenical movement was producing concrete results. The UK Methodist factions reunited; Canadian Methodists, Presbyterians and Congregationalists merged into the United Church; Indian Methodists reunited with Anglicans; and the Church of England agreed to share communion with Old Catholics. Rome, however, was solidly opposed. Pope Pius XI promoted reunion with Orthodox and Protestants, but only by their accepting all Catholic dogma, and in 1928, he banned Catholics from religious conferences with other Christians: 'This charity tends to injure faith.' In 1929, Pius finally agreed a deal with Italy. He renounced his claim to rule the Papal State and even Rome, but he became sole ruler of the Vatican State, a nation of 700 people, and he received 750 million lire from Mussolini.

Prohibition was not going very well. Smuggling flourished, creating a huge criminal refreshments industry. Production of sacramental wine, excluded from the ban, increased by 800,000 gallons a year; Boston had four times as many bars as all Massachusetts had in 1925. In 1933, President Roosevelt declared, 'I think this would be a good time for a beer,' and repealed a constitutional amendment for the first time.

7

Totalitarians (1933-58)

We have seen truth crucified and goodness buried, but we have kept going with the conviction that truth crushed to earth will rise again.
Martin Luther King

Germany had got an £11 billion bill for damages after the First World War. Its exchange rate with the pound multiplied a billion times in five years, and it went through eighteen governments in fifteen years. It took a miracle to save Germany; unfortunately, the miracle was Adolf Hitler. Hitler's religion was inspired by Nietzsche – a faith in the destiny of Germany to lead the superior 'Aryan' race, purging weaker elements and crushing feebler races. He quickly banned Jews and other unwanted nationalities from holding state office or teaching, and he boycotted Jewish shops.

The 1933 Protestant Church elections were a landslide for the religious Fascists called 'German Christians'. They denied the baptism of Jews, sacked anyone married to a Jew and renounced Jewish practices like saying 'amen' and 'hallelujah'. The Lutheran Martin Niemöller gathered opponents into an alternative called the Confessing Church.

One of its leaders was Karl Barth, who attacked Fascist Christian theology. The 'German Christians' argued that the Bible tells us about religion and personal morality, but in politics we see God's will in the way nature works, that might is right. Barth insisted that Christ, known through the Bible, is God's only word ever, and any revelation we think we find in nature is not worth the mud it's written on.

Barth saw himself championing the truths of the Reformation, but even those closest to him felt it was unprecedented extremism. His friend Emil Brunner (equally opposed to Fascism) tried to restore balance, arguing that God's voice is heard through his creation – very faintly, but enough to open a door for the gospel. Barth hit the roof, insisting there is no truth outside Jesus. Their rupture illustrates something of Barth's style: Brunner's book was called *Nature and Grace*, Barth's reply was called *No!* As if oblivious to this doctrinal contest, Hitler passed the Nuremberg laws in 1935, stopping anyone with a Jewish grandparent from marrying an Aryan or being a German citizen. 'No one should be prohibited from safeguarding the purity of their race,' affirmed the archbishop of Freiburg. Barth was sacked from Bonn University for refusing to salute Hitler. Vast numbers of Christians were arrested for preaching Jewish or anti-Nazi ideas, or on fictional charges in the campaign to dissolve the monasteries.

In Stalin's Russia, an anti-religious campaign was breaking the church. Throughout the 1930s, the vast majority of churches were closed, Orthodoxy surviving only as an underground sect, its priests vagrant outlaws, many of whom died in prison camps. Whole museums and university departments were dedicated to atheism. In Spain, communist soldiers killed 8,000 Catholic clergy; Mexican communists killed 300.

Throughout Africa and Asia, meanwhile, Christianity continued to take root. In many places, numbers had doubled in fifteen years, largely because locals were taking control of their own churches, finally making Christianity an established native religion. After two centuries, Pius XI at last appointed more native bishops in China, and the first in Japan, Ceylon, Korea and Uganda. The Chinese ruler Chiang Kai Chek was baptised, and his cabinet became increasingly Christian.

Japan, after its success in the First World War, was in a conquering mood. Christians were conspicuously dubious about this, which made the rest of Japan dubious about them. The government imposed involuntary ecumenism on them, uniting all Protestants into the emasculated 'Church of Christ' and demanding Shinto rituals and emperor veneration. The Anglican and Holiness churches that resisted were outlawed and their leaders arrested. The Japanese imposed the same policy in Korea, which had the opposite effect of making Christian dissidents there the most respected patriots.

The Second World War

Hitler, despite a pact with the Vatican, was systematically dismembering German Christianity in favour of Nazi neo-paganism. Pius XI declared that Nazism was the enemy and made Catholic bishops preach against it: 'Spiritually we are all Semites.' In the early hours of Martin Luther's birthday in 1938, the Nazis destroyed and looted Jewish shops, homes, schools and synagogues. Jews were banned from driving, owning businesses and going to school or the cinema, and they each had to wear a yellow star. Pius left an anti-racist bull unfinished when he died in 1939. He was succeeded by Pius XII, who was hopelessly committed to achieving peace and reconciliation between the two sides of the Second World War.

When Hitler grafted Poland onto Germany, its popular Catholic Church was the backbone of Polish resistance, so hundreds of priests were shot and 2,647 died in camps. In all territories, Germans resurrected the Christian tradition of cramming Jews into ghettos, and they started deporting them in their tens of thousands to death camps. Few German church leaders opposed Hitler, except when he briefly tried to practise euthanasia on Aryans.

Probably the only person who had any chance of hampering him was the Pope, who had the ear of 40 million German Catholics, but he barely said a word. When German forces occupied Rome, he opened his sanctuaries to give refuge to many thousands of non-Aryans, but he was committed to neutrality in his search for peace and feared provoking Hitler, so he opened not his mouth.

As their armies liberated the death camps of eastern Europe, the allies realised what a good cause they had been fighting in. But the fact that 6 million Jews had been systematically killed left the church with some terrible questions. Where had God been? Can the omnipotent watch the most unthinkable atrocities in the history of inhumanity without lifting a finger? Then again, where had the church been? For all that some individual Christians did, the church as a whole did disgracefully little to stop the Holocaust. In fact, was it not positively responsible? Christians started to realise, with prompting from Jewish critics, that this was the culmination of a trail of Jewish blood stretching back for the worse part of 2,000 years, and Christian hands were in it all the way. Admittedly, Nazism and its nineteenth-century antecedents were aggressively anti-Christian; nevertheless, the Holocaust finally shocked Christians into realising that it was time for anti-Semitism to be buried forever.

After the United Nations failed to secure a partition of Palestine between its Arab inhabitants and Jewish immigrants, the State of Israel was established in 1948. In western eyes, the least Jews deserved was a homeland, but Muslims saw it as another European invasion of Islam, and they unsuccessfully attacked Israel. A new, bloody chapter in the history of the children of Abraham was begun.

As history slid from world war into cold war, the church fell to communists in eastern Europe, Vietnam and Korea. But in Russia, the Soviet assault on Christianity relented. Stalin had reduced the bishops to four, who oversaw a few hundred churches, with no monasteries or colleges; but he had not overcome the religious cravings of the masses, so come the war, he called a truce for the sake of national unity. There were soon 20,000 churches.

The long, slow recession of the western church also stopped. In Europe, the revival of churchgoing was only a blip, but in the USA, figures mounted steadily. The dismantling of Europe's empires sped up the conversion of overseas missions into indigenous churches.

The ecumenical movement united Faith and Order with Life and Work to form the World Council of Churches (WCC), which met in Amsterdam in 1948. One hundred and forty-seven denominations were represented, from all over the world. They agreed a kind of minimalistic creed, which declared that they 'accept our Lord Jesus Christ as God and Saviour'. The WCC campaigned for local churches to work and worship together, and it organised prayer for unity. Various evangelical churches shunned it because of its liberalism; Pius XII finally accepted it, without joining, and he lifted the ban on discussion with non-Catholics. The Church of England and the Methodists started reunion talks.

Black and white

While Fascism was destroyed in Europe, the National Party came to power in South Africa in 1948 and introduced apartheid, to keep whites from being contaminated by blacks, and both from being contaminated by 'coloureds', and to give whites absolute power. It banned sex and marriage between races, breaking up homes where necessary. Millions of blacks were expelled from white regions. The bigger and better part of every kind of public service, from schools to park benches, was reserved for the master race. The Dutch Reformed state church thoroughly supported apartheid and not only preached it but practised it in church; the other churches criticised apartheid from the start. Throughout Africa as a whole, Christianity was mushrooming. A third of all nuns worldwide was African. More than one in four Ugandans and one in three black South Africans were Christians.

Communist China became the next great atheist regime in 1949. Foreign missionaries were expelled as imperialists who had imposed

European domination with a halo, while many Chinese Christians looked forward hopefully to creating a truly non-western Christianity. They vehemently dissociated themselves from the European church and some even handed remaining westerners over to the police. But hundreds of Chinese priests were arrested, all Christian schools and hospitals were commandeered, and the churches were controlled by the state, driving many into secret house churches; there was no attempt to destroy Christianity however.

The growth of the South Korean church seemed unstoppable; even the war against the communist north just made Christianity more popular. Sixty-five per cent of the army were Christians, and the combination of American mission and communist threat fuelled the growth.

After a devastating hurricane hit Jamaica in 1951, Britain started recruiting Jamaican immigrants to replace the workforce killed in the war. Two hundred and fifty thousand answered the call throughout the decade, as well as many from Africa and India. Most of the Jamaicans were Christians and came as missionaries to a spiritual wilderness; but shocked by how lifeless and racist churches were, the majority started separate black churches, often Pentecostal.

The USA hosted the second WCC conference in Illinois in 1954, which focussed on evangelism. The council agreed that evangelism is a positive thing, that it is about introducing people to Jesus and his church and also about creating a better world. For the first time, Pentecostal churches attended, after their leader David du Plessis helped mend fifty years of antagonism towards the old churches by prophesying that the Holy Spirit was ready to revisit them. In return, the WCC affirmed that Pentecostals are bona fide Christians too.

In 1955 in Montgomery, Alabama, a white person got on a bus. He demanded the seat of a black woman, who was legally obliged to go to the back. But Rosa Parks had decided not to be treated like a dog that day and stayed put. She was arrested, and Dr King, a local Baptist pastor with a good way with words, led a bus boycott. The second person in our story named Martin Luther, King had studied Gandhi's peaceful sermon-on-the-mount-inspired protest and believed the same power could bring freedom to black America. His house was bombed, and he was sentenced to 386 days' hard labour. After scarcely one black person in Montgomery had taken the bus in a year, the Supreme Court banned bus segregation. Next, King moved on to tackling the vote, which black people in southern states had but were not allowed to use. 'It is still one of the tragedies of human history', he said, 'that the "children of darkness" are frequently more determined and zealous than the "children of the light".' And who having read this far could disagree? But not this time.

8

The New Catholicism
(1958–78)

> Christ summons the Church, as she goes her pilgrim way, to that
> continual reformation of which she is always in need.
> *Vatican II*

In Germany, the Jesuit lecturer Karl Rahner was trying to modernise Catholic theology. He accepted traditional teaching that no one could be saved outside the one Catholic Church, but he turned it inside out. God is actively present everywhere, through Christ; those who respond to him – however unconsciously – and do what their conscience directs, are following Christ and are members of his church, 'anonymous Christians', whether Hindus, atheists or Calvinists. Another Catholic, Hans Küng, studied Barth's theology and argued that in the great controversy over justification by faith, there is no real difference between the Calvinism of Barth and the council of Trent; moreover, both Barth and Rome agreed with him. Then in 1958, an Italian peasant became Pope John XXIII. At seventy-seven, he was expected to keep things ticking over for a couple of years. Instead, God told him to summon a second Vatican council to rewrite the Catholic religion.

In the meantime, Krushchev came to power in the USSR. He announced a policy of coexistence with the west but not with the church. He imprisoned all kinds of professional Christians on fictional charges, shut down half of all churches and monasteries, and he banned children from going to church. Children were taken from Christian families and re-educated.

US Pentecostals, becoming more respectable and realising they had joined rather than replaced the array of Christian denominations, were now, led by du Plessis, trying to interest traditional churches in Holy Spirit baptism. When mainstream ministers started speaking in tongues and healing, their Pentecostal friends were happy for them to stay in their old, dead churches and bring them back to life. The charismatic movement was started. As tradition dictates, its leaders were denounced and expelled from their churches.

The third meeting of the WCC left the west for New Delhi in 1961. Orthodox and Pentecostal churches enrolled, and membership rules became a little stricter, requiring churches to accept not just Jesus Christ as God and Saviour but 'one God, Father, Son and Holy Spirit'.

For ten years, South Africa had become an increasingly oppressive police state. Non-whites lost the vote. After a police massacre of unarmed protesters in Sharpville, non-violent resisters decided to rethink their non-violence. Finally, a shocked leader in the Dutch Reformed Church, Beyers Naudé, broke ranks and started the interracial Christian Institute. He was forced out of the church.

Meanwhile, Martin Luther King's civil rights campaign was gaining momentum. In 1963, when peaceful protesters, including children, were assaulted by armed police in Birmingham, Alabama, a nationwide reaction culminated in 250,000 marching to Washington, where King told them about his dreams. The next year, segregation was outlawed in the USA, along with racial discrimination in employment and education. After further vicious police assaults on marchers, African-Americans got the right to use their vote, though King's non-violence became increasingly questioned by activists.

The second Vatican council met in 1962 to deliver the greatest revolution in Roman Catholicism since Luther, but its thunder was stolen by the prospect of nuclear apocalypse. The Pope played a significant role in calming the Cuban missile crisis, and the survival of civilisation allowed Vatican II to continue. Rather than impose any programme, Pope John gathered 2,500 participants to talk about what the church should be, to update and renew, with Rahner and Küng as theological advisers. By the time John died in 1963, little had been decided, but the reformers, to their own surprise, were in the majority, and Pope Paul VI continued the council.

The results were extraordinary. The mass was edited and translated from Latin into local languages; the priest had to face the congregation and laypeople were allowed both bread and wine. Catholics were allowed, even encouraged, to read the Bible in translation, including Protestant versions, and to cooperate in making more. The council scrapped the *Index of Forbidden Books* and overturned Pius IX's *Syllabus of Errors*, affirming freedom of conscience and rejecting religious coercion. Protestants and Orthodox became 'separated brothers', division a tragedy and a sin that must be ended; their churches are defective, but still part of God's plan of salvation. Even Muslims and Jews became siblings on their way to heaven. The Jews were finally absolved of guilt for the crucifixion, against the wishes of 250 delegates out of 1,000. Paul became the first pope ever to leave Europe, going to Jerusalem to share holy communion with the patriarch of Constantinople.

Charismatics and prophylactics

Every major denomination in North America and Europe had some charismatic churches. This caused violent divisions, but it also undermined denominational barriers: charismatics from different churches found that they had more in common with each other than with their unblessed pew-partners, and they got together for worship/teaching weeks. But even they were taken aback by the Spirit's ecumenism. In 1965, a Catholic lecturer in Duquesne University read the Pentecostal blockbuster *The Cross and the Switchblade*, was baptised in the Holy Spirit and passed it onto his students. Soon Catholic charismatics were having huge gatherings too.

In China, Mao Tse-Tung started the three-year cultural revolution in 1966, an attempt to keep communism fresh, which meant a fresh assault on religion: the few officially tolerated churches were closed and underground Christians arrested and killed. Estimates of practising Christians dropped to one-thirtieth of their pre-Mao level.

In 1967, Israel defeated Egyptian, Syrian and Jordanian invaders in the Six-Day War, seizing the West Bank and all Jerusalem. Humiliated Muslims increasingly followed radical teachers who demanded a return to Islam 'in its original form' – what some would call Islamic fundamentalism – to appease God's anger and regain ascendancy over the west.

Two pressing concerns that Vatican II had not mentioned were marriage with non-Catholics and contraception, and Catholics wanted a ruling (or, in most cases, the go-ahead) on both. The first, Paul VI did not much like but allowed with restrictions. Contraception he absolutely banned, despite the recommendations of the commission he set up; the 'rhythm method' was his only concession. 'It is now quite lawful for a Catholic woman to avoid pregnancy by a resort to mathematics,' announced the journalist H.L. Mencken, 'though she is still forbidden to resort to physics and chemistry.' Rome had spoken, the case was closed, but Paul was shocked by how badly

Catholics took it. Nevertheless, he also put an end to any question of priests being anything other than single men.

The swinging sixties

The British church shifted from declining to collapsing in the 1960s. New technology and wealth offered a better life than ever, while Vietnam and the bomb turned groovy kids off the morality of older generations, and pills, whether family-planning or mind-expanding, turned them on. Church membership halved throughout the decade. The same trends, though less drastic, pervaded the rest of the west. Seven out of ten Americans were churchgoers in the 1960s, but that has so far proved to be a peak. Throughout the west, though more slowly in Catholic countries, divorce became easier and homosexuality and abortion became legal. Britain also led Europe in becoming a multicultural society. Newcomers not only kept their old faiths but sometimes passed them on. In the more adventurous sections of society, eastern religions became as cool as Christianity wasn't.

Elsewhere, the tidings were much gladder. Pentecostal growth in Africa and South America was high and escalating. There were 6 million Pentecostals in Zaire; in Brazil, numbers grew by 75 per cent throughout the 1960s, and double that rate in the 1970s. Baptism in the Spirit was the one thing necessary, so everyone was a missionary; everyone had something to contribute, so down-trodden workers were the mouths and hands of God; and anyone could be a minister, so new churches appeared everywhere. In South Korea, from the 1960s to the 1980s, Catholicism increased threefold, Protestantism tenfold.

The WCC fiercely debated its own mission policy in Sweden, in 1968. Many saw mission purely as working towards a fairer society, while the more conservative insisted that saving souls was central. The agreed statement was a compromise, saying that souls and society cannot be separated and the church should challenge them both. People have to turn to Jesus to get saved, but 'turning to Jesus', since Karl Rahner, had become suitably ambiguous.

After twenty-five years of negotiations, Anglicans and UK Methodists drafted a scheme for reunion, which meant Methodists largely becoming Anglicans (again). It was put to a referendum, and rejected by Anglicans. In 1972, English Congregationalists and Presbyterians more successfully merged into the United Reformed Church, after forty years of talks.

Martin Luther King broadened his focus from segregation to the deeper-rooted problem of poverty throughout the USA. In April 1968, he addressed striking sanitation workers in Memphis, telling them, 'I may not get there with you, but I want you to know tonight, that we, as a people, will get to the promised land.' The following day, as he stood on his hotel balcony, he was shot and killed.

The victory for civil rights in America made the growing Catholic minority in Northern Ireland more interested in their own. In 1969, demonstrations, fuelled by ancient hatreds, exploded into riots, bombing and gunfights. In one last place in the world, the Reformation was still claiming lives.

Liberation and prosperity

While European Christianity declined, the African church had grown twentyfold since 1900. The Kenyan pastor John Mbiti studied traditional African religions in an attempt to help a truly African Christianity develop, instead of the version transplanted by Europeans contemptuous of African culture.

South American Catholics were developing liberation theology. They condemned the assumption that theology is something you work out and then act out. First comes action, fighting for the freedom of the oppressed; only then do you have the right to start theologising about it. They preferred Marx to the rich so-called Christians who oppressed the poor. The heart of the gospel is fighting for freedom and social justice like Moses did. If the church is not saving from oppression, it is not Christian. 'The Catholic who is not a revolutionary', insisted Camillo Torres, 'is living in mortal sin.'

Many evangelicals were unhappy about the liberalism of the WCC, and they had their own world council in Lausanne, Switzerland, in 1974, doing for evangelicalism what Vatican II did for Catholicism. They insisted on the importance of proper evangelism and the authority of the Bible, but they also rediscovered social change. And rather than just issuing statements, they made promises: to do mission, without cultural exports, and to fight poverty, keeping less and giving more.

If evangelicalism was recovering its nerve and social conscience, certain branches had a lot more of one than the other. Evangelicals made up 20 per cent of the US population and rising. They now emerged from their multiplying, money-spinning, multimedia subculture, spending their money on TV networks, religious theme parks and presidents. Jim and Tammy Faye Bakker set up the Praise the Lord (PTL) cable network. The glossy emotionalism of their Pentecostal kitsch inspired Tammy Faye to patent her own waterproof mascara. They preached 'prosperity doctrine' – that serving the Lord makes you rich – and in that department at least, they practised what they preached: PTL brought in up to $150 million a year. *The Late Great Planet Earth* by Hal Lindsey decoded biblical prophecy revealing that the Soviets, Arabs and a ten-nation European Union led by the Antichrist would attack Israel in the battle of Armageddon, triggering the return of Christ to rule from Jerusalem, 'within forty years or so of 1948'. It was America's bestselling 'non-fiction' book of the decade and has shifted 30 million copies. Surveys in the 1980s and 1990s suggested 40 per cent of Americans accepted the scenario, including Ronald Reagan, who declared, 'Everything is in place for the battle of Armageddon and the second coming of Christ.'

In 1975, the Episcopal Church of Canada started to ordain female ministers, and US Anglicans followed. The English synod voted in favour of the principle but against the practice.

Thousands of black South African children demonstrated in Soweto about school conditions, in 1976. When the police shot a 13-year-old, protests flared up nationwide, and in attempts to crush them, 600 people were killed, many of them children. Black leaders were imprisoned and killed. Church leaders such as Beyers Naudé and the Anglican Archbishop Desmond Tutu became leading non-violent opposition figures in the mould of Martin Luther King, while other political activists left the country and trained for guerilla war.

9

John Paul II (1978-2000)

Some people were saying 'Women priests in the church! I'm going to leave the church.' And I think most of us were saying, 'Goodbye.'
Eddie Izzard

In 1978, the new Pope promised to combine the strengths of the last two, progressive and conservative, and therefore called himself John Paul. In fact, he called himself John Paul I, rather limiting his successor's choice of names. From a working-class family, he had already ruffled feathers by calling on priests to sell holy ornaments and give the money to the poor. On becoming pope, he even refused to be crowned. A month later, he was dead.

The second John Paul was Polish, the first non-Italian Pope since the Reformation. He promised not to roll back Vatican II and argued for human rights and religious freedom – areas where the church was now as much sinned against as sinning. In every other way he was conservative, refusing to rethink divorce, celibacy or women priests, and opposing liberal theology. The theologian Hans Küng had been arguing against papal infallibility, saying that leading the church meant serving, not ruling. On John Paul II's succession, Küng lost his licence to teach. Rome insisted his university remove him from his post, which it did and then gave him another one.

In South America, liberation theology overtook the church hierarchy. Oscar Romero became archbishop of San Salvador and preached for three years against the murder and torture of political dissidents, until, in 1980, he was shot while taking a funeral in a hospital. The Pope himself was shot in the stomach on the feast of Our Lady of Fatima by a Turkish hit man nine feet away, while waving from the pope mobile in St Peter's Square. Eventually recovering, he read the top-secret prophecy given to three children in Fatima, Portugal, in 1917, and was convinced it foretold the shooting. (Published in 2000, it describes a frail pope being killed by arrows and bullets from a crowd of soldiers.) One year on, he visited Fatima and made an offering of the bullet to the Virgin. He also visited his assailant to forgive him in person.

A horrific new disease among gay men in New York and California caused panic in the USA in 1981 and infected 4,000 people in two years. At first called GRID (Gay-Related Immune Deficiency), AIDS was greeted by right-wing evangelicals, such as Revd Jerry Falwell of the Moral Majority campaign, as 'God's judgment because of the homosexual promiscuity of this land'. The fact that it now kills half a million African children each year suggests that as an instrument of divine justice it was misguided. Because transmission could be prevented by condoms, Rome faced considerable pressure to change its teaching on contraception, which it has successfully resisted for twenty-four years, in which time, AIDS has killed 20 million people.

The coming of a Polish pope committed to social justice coincided with a peak of economic crisis and party corruption in Poland. John Paul visited repeatedly from the start, to a reaction somewhere between Beatlemania and the second coming. The Solidarity union led strikes in which strikers held mass and waved pictures of the Pope, demanding freedom, money and mass on television. Prime Minister General Jaraselski imposed martial law, outlawed Solidarity and 'disappeared' its leaders.

Foreign investors were putting pressure on South Africa to change, but in the era of Reagan and Thatcher, western governments were not interested. So in 1986, Prime Minister Botha declared a state of emergency, restricting the media and giving police special power to crush the anti-apartheid movement. Campaigners such as Archbishop Tutu defied him, urging all Christians to boycott the next elections. 'I thank God I am black,' said Tutu. 'White people will have a lot to answer for at the last judgment.'

China, leaving the Cultural Revolution behind, announced a new openness towards the west. While this did not make life much easier for Chinese Christians, it revealed a staggering fact. One Chinese person in 100 had been a Christian when the communists came to power; now after Mao's annihilation programme was thought to have finished them off, it turned out they were heading towards something like one in twenty.

Mikhail Gorbachev became the Soviet leader in 1985, promising *perestroika* and *glasnost*, restructuring and openness. The laws that had been trying to destroy the Russian Orthodox church, among others, for seventy years, were eventually scrapped. In 1989, Gorbachev visited the Pope and publicly misquoted the Bible. He told the Eastern Bloc that Big Brother was not watching them any more, and within months, European communism was finished.

Jim Bakker seemed to be finished too. The rival tele-evangelist Jimmy Swaggart uncovered his liaison with a prostitute, whom Bakker had paid handsomely for silence. In 1989, he was charged with swindling his followers to the tune of $158 million. He denounced the court proceedings as satanic, but the allegations were not looked into and he was gaoled. On release, he wrote a long book about his life and teaching, suitably summarised under the title *I Was Wrong*. Swaggart's moral crusade declined after he himself was caught with a couple of prostitutes. A new kind of blackmail was brought to light by Revd Oral Roberts, who climbed up his glass spire and announced that God would kill him if his flock did not give $4.5 million. They did.

Eastern European voters brought down communism and the Berlin Wall. The Catholic opposition came to power in Poland. Anti-communist demonstrators at a Romanian cathedral, backing a deposed pastor, were massacred by police (to the applause of the Orthodox patriarch), and a bloody revolution began. Everywhere, the church was given freedom, legality and bishops, and where possible its former property.

In 1992, the Church of England synod agreed, after seventeen years of debate and by two votes, to ordain women priests. There was serious rebellion from Anglo-Catholics, and there were defections to Rome, where the reform was seen as a major setback to ecumenical discussion, but the anticipated breakaway church never materialised. Still, half of all male ministers refused to take communion from women.

The ecumenical movement had rather run out of steam. There was little prospect of further reunions, and new churches were christened weekly. But at least in the post-Christian west, a kind of grassroots spiritual ecumenism had survived institutional ecumenism. Younger generations practically ignored denominations. That denominations, failing to integrate, might simply be allowed to disintegrate, looked like the best hope for the future of unity.

Reconciliation and ethnic cleansing

The Church of England had announced that the 1990s would be the decade of evangelism. After media outrage, bishops quickly assured a panicked world that the evangelism would only be aimed at Anglicans. In 1993, the curate of

Holy Trinity Brompton, a charismatic church frequented by well-heeled Londoners, took over its 'Alpha course' for new converts, and remarketed it for inquisitive non-Christians.

Four years of negotiations between Nelson Mandela and President De Klerk ended in agreement, and South Africa had multiracial elections in 1994. In a surprisingly peaceful transition, considering the violence running up to it, apartheid was over, although the scars ran deep. The same year, Unionists and Nationalists in Northern Ireland agreed a ceasefire while they tried to talk about a settlement. A series of peace agreements between Israel and Palestine was rejected by Islamic radicals who responded with the suicide bombing of civilians, drawing equally indiscriminate reprisals.

The century of atrocities in Europe concluded with the conflict between ethnic groups in the former Yugoslavia, where thousands of Muslims were killed by Serb nationalists, a reminder to the west that ancient tensions with Islam, though perhaps forgotten, were not gone. In Rwanda, the systematic massacre by Hutus of 800,000 Tutsis and moderate Hutus, with both sides largely Catholic, led to accusations that priests and nuns were seriously involved, though few have been convicted. Rome seems to take the line that the church itself is not implicated in the activities of its priesthood.

Charismatics who had been predicting revival for decades were finally rewarded with the Toronto blessing. The Toronto Airport Christian Fellowship introduced the world to the spirituality of falling down, shaking, laughing and doing animal impressions (most popularly dogs, lions, chickens and cockerels). More specialised manifestations included running, pogoing, calling 'Cooee!' and simulating childbirth, as well as yawning and coughing (the latter both long known in church life but rarely recognised as the work of the Spirit). Proclaimed by jet-setting enthusiasts as a revival, it was later rebranded as 'a time of refreshing' when it turned out that, for whatever reason, it was failing to convert people. There were now reported to be four times as many ex-charismatics in Britain as charismatics.

The Alpha course and Toronto blessing promoted each other. Taken on by churches across the world from Catholic to Pentecostal, Alpha presently has 28,700 courses happening in seventy-seven countries, though when many churches expect their whole membership to complete the course at least once, it is hard to measure the amount of successful evangelism.

In 1996, led by Desmond Tutu, the Truth and Reconciliation Commission began its task of touring South Africa and hearing stories of violation, torture and killing during apartheid from victims and perpetrators. The policy of Mandela's government was to forego the right to retribution, in favour of bringing the truth to light and reconciling the country, and so amnesty was promised to all who confessed. Supporters of apartheid ridiculed it as 'the Crying and Lying Commission' and Tutu as getting over-emotional about blowtorches and death farms. Others criticised him as too Christian in his emphasis on forgiveness. When the commission wound up in 1998, the Dutch Reformed Church finally found its prophetic voice and vehemently condemned apartheid as fundamentally wrong and sinful, four years after its abolition.

In February 1998, the Saudi Muslim leader Osama bin Laden declared a defensive jihad against the USA to liberate the Jerusalem mosque and drive American armies out of Islamic lands. 'We, with God's help, call on every Muslim who believes in God and wishes to be rewarded, to comply with God's order to kill the Americans and plunder their money wherever and whenever they find it.' That August, his al-Qaeda network attacked US embassies in Kenya and Tanzania, killing 224 people.

In March 1998, Pope John Paul II issued *We Remember*, an apology to the Jewish people for 2,000 years of abuse from Christians which admitted no responsibility on the part of the church. Nevertheless, his prayer at the Wailing Wall in Jerusalem was widely welcomed as an act of reconciliation. The British government finally started direct negotiations with Sinn Fein, and all sides in Northern Ireland agreed a deal seventeen hours after the deadline, on Good Friday. Success would depend upon concessions and cooperation being accepted by zealots, Protestant and Catholic. Today, a final settlement seems almost as far off as ever, yet the reality of peace and prosperity in Northern Ireland would seem hard to forfeit.

The 1990s completed a century of collapse for British churches. Attendance dropped by a quarter throughout the decade of evangelism, the collapse not only continuing but accelerating. 'In some sections of the western church, we are bleeding to death,' declared the archbishop of Canterbury. And yet censuses and surveys seem to show that three-quarters of British people share Christian beliefs. In Britain, Christianity no longer has much to do with the church, apparently.

In 1999, Catholics and Lutherans finally agreed to agree about justification, making an official joint doctrinal statement. The Toronto Airport

Christian Fellowship again launched the latest charismatic blessing, supernatural gold fillings. Several hundred of the flock received the gift, followed by other gold-related anointings, which they passed on down the usual channels. Scoffers were directed to Psalm 81:10, 'Open wide your mouth and I will fill it.'

10

The Third Millennium

After the fall of so many gods in this century, this person, broken at the hands of his opponents and constantly betrayed through the ages by his adherents, is obviously still for innumerable people the most moving figure in the long history of mankind.
Hans Küng

The opening years of the twenty-first century have been dominated by one event, the destruction of the World Trade Centre in New York on 11 September 2001 by passenger jets hijacked by al-Qaeda, which killed 3,000 people. Smaller attacks followed in Bali, Casablanca, Istanbul and Madrid. A shocked, enraged and humiliated America attacked Afghanistan, which housed fifty-five al-Qaeda training camps, and Iraq, which had no link to al-Qaeda.

The consensus of western leaders and media was that genuine Muslims are people of peace and goodwill towards the west, while the terrorist fringe 'pervert the peaceful teachings of Islam' in George Bush's words. And yet when images of the atrocity, broadcast across the world, were followed by scenes of jubilation in Muslim communities from the east end of London to the West Bank, the reality was clearly more complicated. In truth, Islam is no more monolithic than Christianity. It has its moderates, its traditionalists, its militants, its nominal adherents; its motley history, its mixed messages. Muslims in general tend to see the west as Christian, yet appallingly secularised and decadent; the great division is between those who want coexistence and those who want victory. The Islamic world bears bitter grievances, especially over the treatment of Palestinians and the presence of US troops in Arab lands, grievances which the 'war on terror' has hardly eased, even before the sexual abuse and torture of Iraqi prisoners at the Abu Ghraib gaol came to light. As a campaign to weaken Islamic terrorism, the most generous thing that can be said about the war is that Bush's Palestinian peace plan is more likely to help. Meanwhile, the politics of the USA, the pioneer of secular society, are increasingly dominated by evangelical religion. The historic conflict between Islam and the Christian west has, after four quiet centuries, returned to the prominence it maintained for a millennium. There are 6 billion people in the world, and 2 billion of them are Christians, compared with 1.3 billion Muslims; but Islam's share of humankind has increased by 83 per cent since 1900.

Other momentous changes are happening to the shape of global Christianity. In 1900, 80 per cent of Christians lived in Europe and North America; now it is less than half that amount. As recently as 1960, 14 per cent of Christians were in Africa and Asia; now it is 32 per cent. Then, nearly half of all Christians were European; now it is about a quarter. There are six times as many Anglican churchgoers in Nigeria as in England, and almost as many Pentecostals as in the whole of Europe. Just as for its first millennium, the church was predominantly Middle-Eastern, and in its second millennium European, the church is moving again, its centre of gravity shifting south, into sub-Saharan Africa and South America. If the church in Britain recovers it will probably be thanks to missionaries from South America and Africa and on their terms.

While half of all Christians are still Catholic, Pentecostalism has come from nowhere in the last century to claim (if you include charismatics) between one in six and one in four Christians, according to different calculations. Even those figures veil the achievement of Pentecostalism, when you consider that Catholic membership is largely a count of baptised babies, while Pentecostal and charismatic churches tend to count only active members.

Also increasing rapidly are the Christians (currently numbering 60 million) in 20,000 indigenous church groups not linked to any international denominations, especially in African churches drawing on Pentecostal and native spirituality. What new Christianities Africa will give the world, we wait to see. Including these indigenous churches, there are 34,000 Christian denominations worldwide.

If the predominance of the developing world makes Christianity largely a religion of the poor again, it is also making it overwhelmingly conservative, a religion of miracles and ancient beliefs. The story of the secularisation and the theological and social liberalisation of the church in the west is starting to look like an aberration, the west increasingly out of touch with the church.

What this will mean for the western church is graphically illustrated by the Church of England's inability to stand by the appointment of the celibate but unrepentant homosexual Jeffrey John as bishop of Reading in the face of African condemnation.

As in recent centuries, Christians have successfully fought slavery, industrial exploitation and then racial segregation, so significant numbers of Christians in the west now are mobilising against the greatest institutional evil of today, world poverty. The fact that poverty kills 30,000 children a day means that the problem is overwhelming, but also that the smallest change will affect huge numbers of people.

Forty million people now suffer from AIDS, 'the worst catastrophe ever to hit the world', according to Unicef. Pope John Paul insisted, 'Humanity cannot close its eyes in the face of so appalling a tragedy!' and yet resolutely refused to allow Catholics the basic precaution of condoms – the archbishop of Nairobi actually blaming them for the spread of AIDS, and the president of Rome's Pontifical Council for the Family teaching that the virus 'can easily pass through'. While this indefensible disinformation continues, the 'tragedy' claims 14,000 new victims a day. Meanwhile, the Catholic Church is said to provide care for a quarter of them.

When Pope Benedict XVI succeeded John Paul II in April 2005, in one of the quickest papal elections ever, it was clear that Rome was opting for more of the same. This is unusual: proverbially, 'a fat Pope always follows a thin one'. But as a major architect of John Paul's policy, Benedict is meant to keep the ship sailing in the same direction. He was chosen as a defender of the church from modern western values where they are deficient and immoral, pledging to oppose 'all attempts of adaptation or of watering down'. During twenty-four years of leading the Congregation of the Doctrine of the Faith (the modern successor to the Inquisition), he earned the nickname Cardinal Rottweiler, though it remains to be seen whether he will bring the same approach to the papacy.

There was much talk before his appointment of the possibility of seeing the first pope from the developing world. It has not happened, but it will. And, as one of Benedict's qualifications was the fact that he was seventy-eight and therefore a rather less permanent prospect than John Paul II, the opportunity is likely to come around again soon.

And so the varied mission of the church across the world continues into its third millenium, as does its mixed record in getting God's will done on earth as it is in heaven. The church of Jesus has been an affair of genocide and jumble sales; of heroic self-sacrifice and self-defeating hysteria; of holy mysteries; of philosophers and philanthropists; of crusading geese, charismatic animal impressionists and high-rise, maggot-eaten monks; of charity and chastity; and, above all, of men and women – good, bad, indifferent, extremely different, wise, wonderful and simply incomprehensible. And, it is alleged, the house of God. Mysterious ways indeed.

Glossary

allegorising   reading the Bible for its hidden message rather than the literal meaning.

Anabaptists   radical Protestants who baptise only adults and reject the state church.

Anglo-Catholics   Anglicans who retain Catholic ideas and ritual, without the papacy.

Apollinarianism   the belief, following Apollinaris, that Christ inhabited a human body with no human soul.

apostasy   abandoning one's religion.

Arianism   the belief, following Arius, that the Son is not God in the same way as the Father.

Arminianism   branch of Protestantism that, following Arminius, rejects predestination.

asceticism   the life of self-denial for the sake of the soul.

atonement   what Jesus achieved for humankind on the cross; theories vary.

Bogomils   eastern movement rejecting the material world as evil.

bull   papal decree.

Calvinists   followers of Calvin, believing in predestination and denying any change in the bread and wine.

canon   the group of books officially accepted as holy scripture.

cardinals   senior papal officials; either clergy in Rome or major bishops elsewhere.

Cathars   western movement rejecting the material world as evil.

Chalcedonians   those who accept the council of Chalcedon; Orthodox as opposed to Monophysites and so on.

Congregationalism   denomination where every congregation is self-governing.

Conventuals   Franciscans who accept the owning of possessions.

deism   belief in a creator who does not interfere with his creation.

Dissenters   the non-Anglican Protestant denominations of the eighteenth century.

docetism   the belief that Jesus was an immaterial spirit and did not suffer.

Donatists   church, following Donatus, that took a hard line against apostates.

Ebionites   Jewish Christians who kept the Law of Moses.

ecumenical   lit. 'worldwide': (a) (of councils) representing and recognised by all true churches; (b) attempting to reunite separated churches.

Enlightenment   the campaign to replace tradition and authority with reason.

evangelicalism   stream of Protestantism insisting on personal conversion.

excommunicate   bar a person or group from communion and thereby expel them from church *filioque*: lit. 'and from the Son': word added by Rome to the Nicene creed, saying that the Spirit proceeds from both Father and Son.

General Baptists   non-Calvinist Baptist denomination.

gnosticism   pan-religious movement with elaborate mythology considering the material world evil.

Holiness churches   denominations that believe in sinless perfection.

homoiousios: 'of similar substance'. A compromise between *homoousios* and Origen's divine hierarchy.

homoousios: 'of the same substance', from the Nicene creed. Homoousians believe Father and Son to be of one substance.

humanism   movement to revitalise medieval Catholicism with classical culture and early Christian ways.

Hussites   followers of Jan Hus rejecting the papacy and Catholic traditions.

hyper-Arianism   belief that the Son is essentially unlike the Father.

icon   picture of Christ or saints used in worship

iconoclasm   the rejection or destruction of icons.

indulgence   the absolution of sin without penance, gained by good works or money.

liberalism   modernising movement that rejects traditional doctrines.

Macedonianism   the belief that the Father and the Son are of one substance, but not the Holy Spirit.

Manicheeism   gnostic religion following Mani.

Mennonite   Anabaptist group following Menno Simons.

Messiah   Jewish holy king and deliverer foretold by prophets.

Methodists   evangelical denomination following Wesley.

Modalism   the belief that Father, Son and Spirit are three roles played by one God.

Monophysites   those who believe that Christ's humanity and divinity merge into 'one nature'.

Montanists   followers of the prophet Montanus.

Moravians   pietist followers of Zinzendorf.

Neoplatonism   late version of Platonism built around 'the One'.

Nestorians   followers of Nestorius, believing the divine and human natures of Christ to be separate.

Nicenes   supporters of the 325 council of Nicea, believing Father and Son to be of the same substance.

Nonconformists   the non-Anglican Protestant denominations after the eighteenth century.

Novatians   church, following Novatian, that took a hard line against apostates.

Particular Baptists   Calvinist Baptist denomination.

patriarch   one of several leading bishops in the east.

Paulicians   eastern movement rejecting the material world as evil.

Pelagianism   belief, following Pelagius, in free will and justification by works.

pietism   movement to revive Protestantism through personal spirituality.

Platonism   Plato's philosophy, in which the changeless spiritual realm is more real than the physical.

predestinarianism   the belief that God chose who would be saved before the world began.

Presbyterianism   system where churches are governed by equal elders.

Pure   what the Novatians called themselves.

puritanism   movement to purify the Church of England from Catholic practices.

Reformed   non-Lutheran Protestant churches with fewer traditional forms, denying any change in the bread and wine during the eucharist.

relics   the remains of martyrs' bodies, thought to have miraculous power through their connection to heaven.

sacrament   a ritual that guarantees a spiritual blessing.

separatism   movement denying the state church.

simony   the sin of paying for a bishopric.

Socinians   followers of Sozzini, denying the deity of Christ.

Spirituals   Franciscans who reject the owning of possessions.

transubstantiation   the change of bread and wine into the body and blood of Christ.

unitarians   those who deny the Trinity.

Waldensians   followers of Valdes, rejecting unbiblical Catholic traditions.

Index

A

Abelard, Peter 110–11, 112
Aetius 51
African Methodist Episcopal Church 206
AIDS 239, 246
Alberic 92
Alfred 89
Alpha Course 240–1
al-Qaeda 244
Ambrose 56–7, 59
Anabaptists 142–3, 148–9, 150, 152, 163, 164, 173, 249
Anglicanism 144, 157–8, 160–4, 172, 177–80, 185–6, 190, 194–6, 201, 205, 210–1, 217, 219, 224–5, 227, 229, 235, 237, 240, 245–6
Anglo-Catholics 177–8, 210–1, 240
Anselm 104–5, 111, 124, 213
Antony 42, 55
apartheid 229, 239, 241–2
Apollinaris 52–3, 66, 249
Apostles' Creed 83, 129
Aquinas, Thomas 119–21, 153, 156, 213
Aristotle 34, 119–20, 168, 182, 185
Arius, Arianism 48–53, 56, 61, 65, 66–7, 68, 81, 150, 249
Arminius, Jacob; Ariminianism 173–4, 177, 249
asceticism 35, 36–7, 42, 54–6, 132
Athanasius 42, 48–50, 51, 53, 55
atheism 25, 27, 34, 188, 197, 203, 222, 224, 227, 229–30, 232
atonement 57, 105, 111, 190, 203, 249
Augsburg (Diet and Confession) 147, (Peace of) 158
Augustine (theologian) 58–63, 68, 85, 112, 120, 137, 156, 185
Augustine (missionary) 70, 76
Avignon papacy 123, 125–7

B

Jim and Tammy Faye Bakker 237, 240
baptism 18, 27, 36, 42, 49, 62, 81–2, 95, 113, 142–3, 148–9, 157, 164, 166–7, 172–3, 179, 212, 226, 245;
    rebaptism 41, 47
Baptists 172–3, 177–8, 185, 190, 196, 198, 200–1, 202–3, 205, 207, 224, 230
Barnabas 18–9, 31
Karl Barth 223, 226–7, 232
Basil of Caesarea 52, 55, 68

F C Baur 211
Benedict, Benedictines 68, 70–1, 83–4, 91, 119
Berengar 105–6
Bernard of Clairvaux 111–2
Beuckels, Jan 149
Bible 21, 35, 45, 57, 58, 68, 110, 131–3, 145, 158–9, 186, 223, 237;
    allegorising 25, 29–30, 36–7, 59;
    authority 113, 125, 138–40, 141–3, 151, 154, 160–1, 179, 183, 190, 197, 221, 226, 236;
    canon 29–31, 139, 206, 219;
    translation 61, 75, 88, 125, 131–2, 139–40, 144, 172, 203, 233
bin Laden, Osama 242
Bismarck, Otto von 216–7
black churches 192, 198, 200–1, 204, 206–7, 230
Blandina 27
Bogomils 112, 249
Boniface (missionary) 79
Boris 87
Booth, William 217
Bourne, Hugh 205
Brunner, Emil 226–7
Bryan, W J 224–5
Bucer, Martin 145–6, 147, 150, 152, 153, 155–6
Bush, George 244–5

C

John Calvin 146, 149–50, 155–7, 158
Calvinism 149–50, 155–7, 158, 161–5, 173–4, 176, 177–8, 202, 210, 232, 249
Cappodocian Fathers 52, 51–54, 55–56, 68, 94
Carafa, Giovanni (see Pope, Paul IV)
Carey, William 202–3
Cateau-Cambrésis 161–2
Cathars 112–3, 117–8, 249
Catherine of Aragon 144, 157
Catherine the Great 196–7
Celtic church 75–7
Chalcedon, Definition of 66–9
charismatics 233 241–2
Charlemagne 83–5, 92, 205
Charles Martel 79–80
Charles I of Britain 177–9
Charles II of Britain 179, 185–6
Chrysostom, John 57
Church of Christ, Japan 227
circumcision 16–19, 28, 29, 44, 75, 211

Clement of Alexandria   36–7, 46
Clovis and Clotilda   68
Cluny   91–3, 96
Columba   77
Columbus   166–8
Confucianism   174–5, 188, 189
Congregationalism   168, 177, 190, 194, 196, 198, 224, 225, 235, 249
Contarini, Gasparo   152–3, 155
contraception   234–5, 239, 246
Coornhert, Dirk   173
Copernicus, Nicolaus   153, 182
Coptic Church   68
Councils   69, 80–1, 101, 126–27, 138–9, 147, 152;
   Jerusalem (48)   18–19;
   Nicea (325)   49–51, 53, 55, 61;
   Constantinople (381)   53–4
   Ephesus (431)   65, 80;
   Ephesus (449)   66;
   Chalcedon (451)   66–9,
   Constantinople (730)   78;
   Nicea II (787)   80, 85;
   Lateran III (1184),   113;
   Lateran IV (1215)   118;
   Lyons II (1274)   121;
   Pisa (1409)   126;
   Constance (1414)   126–7, 138;
   Pavia (1423)   127;
   Basle (1431)   127;
   Ferrara/Florence (1438)   127–28;
   Trent (1545)   153–5, 158–9; 210, 232
   Vatican I (1869)   215–6;
   Vatican II (1962)   232–5
Cranmer, Thomas   157
creeds:
   Apostles' 83, 129
   Nicene   37, 49–53; 61–2, 67;
   Nicene/Constantinopolitan 53, 67, 85, 88, 95, 98, 121, 127, 169, 249; 222;
Cromwell, Oliver   177–80
crusades   103–9, 111–2, 113–4, 117, 118, 121, 126, 128, 130
Cyprian   40–2, 44, 47, 62
Cyril of Alexandria   65–7, 70
Cyril, missionary   86–88

D

Darwin, Charles   207–8, 214, 218, 224
deists   189–91, 193, 196, 197, 198, 200, 202, 249
Descartes, René   184, 188, 190
Diamper, Synod of   169–70
Diderot, Denis   197
Docetism   27–8, 249
Dominic, Dominicans   117–8, 119–20, 136, 166–7

Donation of Constantine   80, 129
Donatus, Donatists   46–7, 59, 67 249
Dort, Synod of   174
Dunstan   92
du Plessis, David   230, 232
Dutch Reformed   229, 233, 242

E

Ebionites   29–31, 75, 249
ecumenism   205, 222, 225, 227, 229, 230, 233, 235, 240, 242, 249
Edict of Restitution   176
Edward VI of England   157, 161
Edwards, Jonathan   194
Elizabeth I of England   157–8, 160–1, 163–4, 172
Emperor:
   Roman: Nero 21–2; Trajan 26; Septimius Severus 33; Marcus Aurelius 34; Alexander Severus 39; Philip the Arab 39; Decius 39–40; Valerian 41; Diocletian 43–44; Galerius 43–44; Constantine 45–51, 54, 57, 61, 68, 100 (see also Donation of Constantine); Constantius 51; Julian 51; Theodosius 53, 56, 62; Pulcheria and Marcian 66; Zeno 67
   Byzantine: Justinian 68–70, 79–80, 116; Leo III 78; Irene 80, 85; Theodora 86–7; Leo the Wise 90–1; Alexius 116
   Western: Charlemagne 83–5 92; Henry the Fowler 92; Otto I 92–4; Otto III 94; Henry III 97, 99; Henry IV 99, 101–03; Conrad 111–2; Frederick Barbarossa 114–5; Otto IV 115; Charles V 138–140, 144–7, 153–4, 157, 168; Ferdinand II ; Joseph II 197
   Chinese: 174–5
Episcopalians   201, 237
Erasmus   129, 131–2, 139, 142, 158
eucharist   24, 27, 82, 95, 98, 113, 118, 123, 137, 138, 140, 141–2, 145–6, 149–150, 153, 157, 158–9, 162, 175, 209, 217, 233, 239 (see also transubstantiation)
Eusebius of Caesarea (historian)   23, 43, 45, 47–9
Eusebius of Nicomedia   48–50, 52
Eutyches   65–7
evangelicals   194–6, 198–9, 201–2, 204–5, 209, 217, 220, 221, 224–5, 229, 236–7, 239 249
evolution   207–8, 214, 218, 224

F

Faith and Order   222, 229
Falwell, Jerry   239
Farrel, William   150
Felicitas   33
Ferdinand and Isabella   131, 167
filioque   85, 88, 95, 98, 121, 127, 249
Finney, Charles   209, 215
Flavian   65–6

Foxe, John   160
Francis, Franciscans   117, 118, 119, 121–3
Frederick the Wise, Elector of Saxony   137, 139
Frederick I of Prussia   186
Frederick the Great of Prussia   196
fundamentalism   221, 225, 234

G

Galilei, Galileo   182–4
Edward Gibbon   197
gnosticism   28–32, 36, 58, 250
Gorbachev, Mikhail   239
Gosse, Philip   214
Grebel, Conrad   142–3
Gregory of Nazianzus   51–54, 56, 94
Gregory of Nyssa   52
Guiscard, Robert   100, 102–3

H

Halle University   186, 189, 190–1, 196
Harris, Howell   194–5
Heloise   110–1
Helwys, Thomas   173, 177
Henry VIII of England   144, 152–3, 157
Henry IV of France   164
Hilary of Poitiers   57
Hinduism   169, 175, 235
Hitler, Adolf   226–8
holiness movement   196, 209, 215, 217, 218–9,
   220, 250
Holy Spirit   13–4, 18, 34, 37, 47–8, 52, 53, 61–2,
   96, 217, 230;
   baptism in   95, 220, 232, 234 (see also
   filioque)
homoousios   49, 51–2, 250
homoiousios   51–2, 250
humanism   124, 129, 131–3, 142, 149, 151–3,
   155, 158–9, 173, 250
Humbert   98–100
Hume, David   197
Hus, Jan   126–7, 138–9, 140, 191
Hutter, Jakob   148
Huxley, T H   214
hyper-Arianism   51, 250

I

icons, iconoclasm   69, 78–9, 80–1, 82, 85, 86,
   124, 250
Ignatius, bishop of Antioch   27–8, 31
Ignatius, patriarch of Constantinople   87, 90–1
Index of Forbidden Books   158, 233
indulgences   131
Inquisition   118, 129, 131, 151, 153, 158–9, 183
International Missionary Council   222

Irenaeus   26, 28–32, 34
Islam (see Muslims)

J

James, apostle   13, 16
James, brother of Jesus   16–21, 31, 139
James I of England, VI of Scotland   172, 178
James II of Britain   186, 187
Jansen, Cornelius; Jansenism   185, 191
Jefferson, Thomas   200, 202
Jerome   33, 54, 57, 60, 61, 129, 132
Jesuits   151–2, 169–70, 174–5, 185, 188, 196,
   200, 206, 217, 232
Jews
   Jewish Christianity   12–25, 28–31, 42
   treatment by Christians   23, 29, 42, 56–7, 65,
   69, 82, 98, 106–9, 111, 118, 131, 157, 158–9,
   178, 193, 196–7, 205–6, 215, 218, 226–9, 234
John, apostle   13, 16, 18, 31, 94
John of Damascus   78
John of England   115
justification by faith, or otherwise   17–20, 137–40,
   147, 151, 153, 154, 155, 194, 232, 242
Justin Martyr   30, 34, 36, 46

K

Kant, Immanuel   201, 203
Keble, John   210
Kierkegaard, Søren   211–2
King, Martin Luther   230–1, 233, 236
Knox, John   161–2
Küng, Hans   232–3, 238
Krushchev, Nikita   232–3

L

Lanfranc   06
Las Casas, Bartholomew de   167–8
Laud, William   177–8
Lausanne Congress   236
Law of Moses   13–21, 23, 25, 29–30, 211
Lenin   222–3
liberalism   204, 211, 213, 215, 219–20, 221, 222,
   223, 225, 236, 238, 245–6, 250
liberation theology   236, 238
Liele, George   200–1
Life and Work   222, 229
Lindsey, Hal   237
Livingstone, David   213
Locke, John   187–8, 189, 193, 202
Lombard, Peter   112
Louis VII of France   111–2
Louis XIV of France   185–6 191
Louis XVI of France   202–3
Loyola, Ignatius   151–2

Luther, Martin 136–48, 151, 152–3, 155–6, 157, 159, 161, 185, 227
Lutheranism 140, 145, 147, 158, 163, 165, 174, 176, 186, 211–2, 226, 242
Lyell, Charles 214

M

Macedonians 52–3
Manichees 58–9, 60, 86, 112
Mantz, Felix 143
Mao Tse-Tung 234, 239
Marburg colloquy 145
Marcion 29–31, 87
Marozia 92
Marx, Karl 213, 236
Mary, mother of Jesus 64–5, 81, 104, 213
Mary I of England 157–8, 161
Mary Queen of Scots 161–3
Matthijs, Jan 148–9
Mbanza Kongo 168
Mbiti, John 236
Medici, Catherine de' 162–3
Melanchthon, Philip 147, 152–3, 156
Mennonites 149, 173
Methodists 194–6, 198–9, 201–2, 205–7, 215, 217, 224–5, 235–6
Methodius 87–88
Michael Cerularius 98–9,
modalism 34, 47–48,
monasticism 42–3, 54–6, 68, 70–1, 76–7, 82, 83–4, 91, 104, 117–9, 123, 130–1, 138 140, 144, 151–2, 158, 189, 202, 207, 222, 227, 229, 232
Monophysites 67, 68, 81
Montanus, Montanism 35–36, 67
Montesinos, Antonio de 167
Moody, Dwight 217
Moravian Brethren 191–92, 194–6, 198
Mormons 206, 212
Muhammad 74–76, 214
Muslims 74–76, 78–9, 86–9, 91, 95, 101, 103–9, 111–2, 113–4, 116, 118, 119, 128, 130, 131, 157, 158, 169, 228, 234, 237 241, 242, 244–5

N

Nantes, Edict of 165,186
Napoleon I 203–6
Napoleon III 215–7
Naudé, Beyers 233, 237
Nestorius, Nestorianism 64–7, 69, 75, 81, 119, 123
Neoplatonism 43, 59
Newman, John Henry 210–1
Newton, Isaac 188, 189, 193
Niemöller, Martin 226

Nietzsche, Friedrich 218, 226
Nikon, Patriarch of Moscow 179
Nobili, Robert 175–6
Novatian, Novatians 41, 65, 67
Novatus 41

O

O'Connell, Daniel 207
Old Catholics 215, 225
Origen 33, 37–40, 48–9, 61
Oswy 77
Ozman, Agnes 220
Oxford Movement 210–211

P

Pachomius 55, 68
Papacy 32, 41, 61, 66, 71, 80, 84–5, 93, 95, 97–103, 115–6, 121, 122–3, 125–7, 131–3, 138–40, 144, 151, 167, 176, 185–6, 188, 191, 200, 202, 205–6, 213, 215–6, 238
Papal State 80, 84, 93, 115, 138, 155, 203, 205, 206, 215–6, 219, 225
Parham, Charles 220
Patrick 67–8
Paul, apostle 13, 15–20, 22, 24, 28–32, 44, 48, 59, 60, 87, 137, 143, 211
Paulicians 86–87, 112
peasants war 143
Pelagius 60
penance 40–2, 56, 71, 97, 118, 131, 132, 133, 136–8, 151, 183
Pentecostalism 220–1, 224, 230, 232–4, 235, 237, 241, 245
Pepin the Short 80, 83
perfection 196, 209, 215, 217, 218–9
Perpetua 33
Peter, apostle 13, 16, 18–19, 22, 30–2, 41, 42, 61, 66, 77, 84, 96, 98, 116–7, 132, 133, 211
Peter the Hermit, crusader 106–7
Peter the Great 189
Petrarch, Francesco 124, 158
Philagathos, John 94
Philip II of France 114
Philip IV of France 122–3
Philip II of Spain 157, 1519, 163
Philip of Hesse 144–5, 152
Photius 87–8, 90–1
pietism 186, 189–92, 194–6, 203
Pizarro 166–7
Plato, Platonism 28, 36–7, 42–3, 59, 69, 119, 124, 184
Plotinus 43
Plymouth Brethren 206–7, 214
Poissy, Colloquy of 162
Pole, Reginald 155, 158

Polycarp   27, 64
Pope (see also papacy)
   Stephen I   41–2;
   Leo I   66, 71;
   Gregory   I 69–71;
   Stephen II   80;
   Leo III   84–5, 205;
   Formosus   90;
   Stephen VI   90;
   Sergius III   90–2;
   John X   92;
   John XI   92;
   John XII   92–3;
   Benedict IX   96–7;
   Leo IX   97–99;
   Nicholas II   100;
   Gregory VII/ Hildebrand   101–4;
   Urban II   106, 109;
   Innocent III   115–8
   Peter Morone   122;
   Boniface VIII   122;
   Clement V   123;
   John XXII   123;
   Nicholas V   129;
   Innocent VIII   131;
   Alexander VI   131–2;
   Julius II   132–3, 138;
   Leo X   137;
   Paul III   151–3, 155;
   Julius III   155, 158;
   Paul IV (Carafa)   152–3, 158–9;
   Urban VIII   183;
   Pius VII   205–6;
   Pius IX   213–6;
   Leo XIII   219–20;
   Pius XI   225, 227–8;
   Pius XII   228;
   John XXIII   232–3;
   Paul VI   233–5;
   John Paul I   238;
   John Paul II   238–40, 242, 246;
   Benedict XV   246
predestination   60–1, 143, 156, 164, 173–4, 196, 202
Presbyterianism   155, 162, 172, 178, 185, 186, 190, 196, 198, 209, 225, 235–6
prohibition   209, 217, 224–5
Prosser, Gabriel   204
purgatory   71, 123, 131, 136–7, 147, 159, 210
puritans   160–1, 164, 172–3, 177–80, 185, 194

Q
Quakers   179, 185, 186, 202

R
Rahner, Karl   232, 233, 235
Ranters   179
Rauschenbusch, Walther   219
Reformed churches   145–6, 147–8, 149–50, 155–8, 160–5, 173–4, 176, 177–8, 203, 210, 223
(see also Presbyterian, Dutch Reformed, etc.)
Regensburg colloquy   153
Reimarus, Hermann   197, 211
relics   27, 41, 64, 96, 108, 113, 116, 122, 132, 137, 148, 149, 193, 224
revival   60, 91–3, 96, 152, 191–2, 194–6, 198–200, 202, 204, 206, 210, 217, 220, 241
revolution   213;
   American   200–2;
   Chinese   229–30
   English   177–180, 185;
   French   143, 202–6;
   Russian   189, 222, 224;
   South American   206;
Reuchlin, Johannes 1 32
Ricci, Matthew   174–5
Richard I of England   114
Ritschl, Albrecht   211
Roberts, Oral   240
Romero, Oscar   238
Rousseau, Jean-Jacques,   198, 200, 202
Rowland, Daniel   194
Royden, Maud   224

S
sacraments   47, 81, 133, 138, 142, 144, 154, 179, 205, 207, 217 (see also Eucharist, baptism)
Sacred Congregation for the Propagation of the Faith   176
St Bartholomew's Day massacre   163
Saladin   113–4
Salvation Army   217
Sankey, Ira   217
Sattler, Michael   148
Savanarola   132
Schleiermacher, Friedrich   203–4
Schmalkaldic League   147, 153
Schweitzer, Albert   221
Scopes, John   224–5
Scottish Free Church   196
Seekers   179
separatists   164, 173–40
Servetus, Michael   157
Seymour, William   220
Simeon Stylites   56
Simeon the New Theologian   94–5
Simons, Menno   149

simony 96–7, 100
Sirmium, Declaration of 51
slavery 25, 27, 46, 57, 67, 70, 75, 86, 88, 131,
    161, 167–8, 192, 198, 200–1, 203, 205, 207,
    209–10, 215, 246
Smith, Joseph 206, 212
Smyth, John 172–3, 177
Socinians, Fausto Sozzini 165
Spangenberg, August von 194
Spener, Philipp Jakob 186
Speyer, Diet of 144–5
Stalin 227, 229
D F Strauss 211
Swaggart, Jimmy 240
Syllabus of Errors 215, 233

T
Tertullian 29, 33–4, 35–6, 41, 52
Theodora of Rome 90, 92
Theophylact 90–1
Thirty Years' War 174 176–7, 185, 191
Thomas, apostle 31, 169–70
Thomas Christians 169–70
Toronto blessing 241
Torquemada, Tomás de 131
Torres, Camillo 236
transubstantiation 104–5, 118, 125, 152, 158,
    210
Trinity 34, 37, 47–50, 52, 53, 61–2 85, 88, 98,
    121, 127, 221
Truth and Reconciliation Commission 241–2
Turner, Nat 207
Tutu, Desmond 237, 239, 241–2

U
Unitarians 190, 198
United Reformed Church 235

V
Valdés, Juan de 151–2, 155
Valdès 113
Valla, Lorenzo 129
Vladimir I 93–4
Voltaire 193, 196

W
Waldensians 113, 117
Walker, David 207
Whitefield, George 195–6, 198–9, 200
Whitby, Synod of 76–7
Wesley, John and Charles 194–6, 198, 201, 205,
    209, 210, 215
Wilberforce, Samuel 214
Wilberforce, William 201, 205,
William of Aquitaine 91

Williams, Roger 177
witches 159
Wolff, Christian 190–1, 196
World Council of Churches 229, 230, 233, 235,
    236
World Missionary Conference 222
Worms, Diet of 138–9
Wyclif, John 125–7, 131

X
Xavier, Francis 169–70, 213

Y
Yazid, Caliph of Syria 78

Z
Zinzendorf, Count Nikolaus von 191